GOD THE CREATED

GOD THE CREATED

Pragmatic Constructive Realism
in Philosophy and Theology

BENJAMIN J. CHICKA

Published by State University of New York Press, Albany

© 2022 State University of New York Press

All rights reserved

Printed in the United States of America

No part of this book may be used or reproduced in any manner whatsoever without written permission. No part of this book may be stored in a retrieval system or transmitted in any form or by any means including electronic, electrostatic, magnetic tape, mechanical, photocopying, recording, or otherwise without the prior permission in writing of the publisher.

For information, contact State University of New York Press, Albany, NY
www.sunypress.edu

Library of Congress Cataloging-in-Publication Data
Names: Chicka, Benjamin J., author.
Title: God the created : pragmatic constructive realism in philosophy and theology / Benjamin J. Chicka.
Description: Albany : State University of New York Press, [2022] | Includes bibliographical references and index.
Identifiers: LCCN 2021041307 (print) | LCCN 2021041308 (ebook) | ISBN 9781438487199 (hardcover) | ISBN 9781438487212 (ebook) } ISBN 9781438487205 (paperback)
Subjects: LCSH: God (Christianity)—History of doctrines—21st century. | Process theology. | Philosophical theology—History—21st century.
Classification: LCC BT103 .C45 2022 (print) | LCC BT103 (ebook) | DDC 231—dc23
LC record available at https://lccn.loc.gov/2021041307
LC ebook record available at https://lccn.loc.gov/2021041308

10 9 8 7 6 5 4 3 2 1

To
Robert C. Neville
My unofficial Doktorvater

CONTENTS

Preface   ix
    PRAGMATIC CONSTRUCTIVE REALISM   xii

Acknowledgments   xv

Introduction   1
    A SKETCH OF THE ARGUMENT   2

1 | Realism, Constructivism, and Their Discontents   11
    REALISM VERSUS CONSTRUCTIVISM IN PHILOSOPHY AND SCIENCE   12
    PHILOSOPHICAL IMPLICATIONS FOR RELIGION   20
    REALISM VERSUS CONSTRUCTIVISM IN THEOLOGY   26
    BEYOND THE IMPASSE?   29

2 | Beyond the Impasse: Charles S. Peirce and American Pragmatism   33
    "PAPER" DOUBT AND GROUNDLESS GROUNDS   34
    TRIADS IN HUMAN INQUIRY AND THE NATURAL WORLD   38
    PEIRCE'S MUSINGS ON GOD   47

3 | Pragmatic Constructive Realism   53
    PEIRCE AND NEOPRAGMATISTS   54
    PEIRCE AND CLASSICAL PRAGMATISTS   57
    PEIRCE WITHOUT PANPSYCHISM   64
    PEIRCE WITHOUT EVOLUTIONARY LOVE   67
    FROM CONSTRUCTIVISM OR REALISM TO
        PRAGMATIC CONSTRUCTIVE REALISM   71

4 | Emerging Philosophically and Theologically   75
    TWO GIANTS OF MODERN THEOLOGY   76
    TILLICH'S REALISM AND BARTH'S CONSTRUCTIVISM
        IN THEOLOGY   78
    TRANSCENDING WHITEHEAD   86

5 | John Cobb's Creative Transformation 91
- JOHN COBB'S PEIRCEAN HABIT 91
- CHALLENGES FROM AND CHALLENGES TO SCIENCE 93
- PROCESS PHILOSOPHY AND A LOVING GOD 95
- GOD'S REVEALING IN GOD'S CONCEALING 98
- GOD THE CONTAINER OF POSSIBILITIES 102
- CREATIVE TRANSFORMATION 106

6 | Robert Neville's God the Creator 111
- ROBERT NEVILLE'S PEIRCEAN HABIT 111
- THE INDETERMINATE ONE AND THE DETERMINATE MANY 113
- DIVINE WILDNESS OVER GOODNESS 116
- TRANSCENDENCE *AND* IMMANENCE? 118
- TRUE ENGAGEMENT, BROKEN SYMBOLS 120
- CHALLENGES FROM AND CHALLENGES TO SCIENCE 125
- STEPS TOWARD A MORE COMPLETE MODEL OF GOD THE CREATOR 129

7 | Reinvigorating the Cobb-Neville Dialogue 133
- CRITICISMS AND DEFENSES OF GOD THE CONTAINER 134
- CRITICISMS AND DEFENSES OF GOD THE CREATOR 140
- AN EXPLANATION OF DIFFERENT PEIRCEAN HABITS 144
- DIFFERENT NAMES FOR THE SAME CONCERN 147
- TWO VALID GUESSES AT THE RIDDLE 149

8 | A Pragmatic Constructive Realist Model of God 155
- PRAGMATIC CONSTRUCTIVE REALISM: A NEW NAME FOR A NEW WAY OF THINKING 156
- THE UNNECESSARY NATURE OF GOD THE CONTAINER 159
- CONCRETE DETERMINATIONS OF GOD THE CREATOR 165
- EMERGENCE AND GROWTH IN GOD THE CREATED 171

9 | Pragmatic Pluralism and Theological Progress 183
- THE PARADOX OF PLURALISM 190

Conclusion 193
- THE COURAGE TO CONTINUE CREATING GOD 195

Notes 199

Bibliography 219

Index 233

PREFACE

This book is an homage to my first serious theological mentor. Back when I was applying to master's degree programs in theology, I received mixed responses to my applications. I was born in Texas and raised in the United Methodist Church. I no longer remember exactly how I made the connection, but I stumbled upon Robert Neville's work due to his role in that church. I had read a limited selection of his books that were available in libraries near me before applying to Boston University, though the degree of comprehension at the time was highly suspect, and doing so primed me for an embrace of classical American pragmatist philosophy upon starting my studies in Boston. However, I grew up believing in a God who was something like a personal being, with specific intentions for myself and for others, and was confident that belief entailed being suspicious about scientific work and an outright rejection of other religious traditions. These are not the sorts of things that will be found in a book written by Neville. I am happy to report that before I was halfway through my undergraduate degree at Texas Tech University, I had rejected each of these beliefs for their inverse; all except for God, perhaps. Before I studied under Neville, I was unsure of what to make of affirming God while now giving up on the notion of specific divine intentions, accepting evolution, and encountering and respecting adherents of different religious traditions. Someone in such a position could not ask for a better teacher than Neville. I learned how accepting God as an indeterminate reality, rather than as a determinate being, leads to these concerns falling aside. I am not sure that the United Methodist community in which I initially discovered my serious interest in religion would agree, but my "conversion" was not a conversion at all. I just followed my interests through to the end. It did not hurt than I was shepherded along by a fellow United Methodist misfit.

This book is an homage to my first serious theological mentor, but it is not just that. The title on the cover should grab the attention of anyone familiar with Neville's work. His first book, *God the Creator,* published in 1968, set the groundwork for his theological architectonic, and the argument for an indeterminate God contained within has remained consistent throughout his career. Neville has made some refinements, elaborations, and clarifications through the years, in addition to now summarizing its hundreds of pages of argumentation in a few sentences in the opening pages of his three-part systematic *Philosophical Theology,* but *God the Creator* laid the groundwork for his subsequent systematic work. My twist on the title of Neville's first book indicates that while I am incredibly indebted to him, I learned too much from process theologians during my doctoral studies in Claremont to agree with him completely. Save for perhaps an extended exchange with David Griffin, it is John Cobb that Neville has debated with most directly through the years. It is therefore Cobb's theology in relation to Neville that I focus on in this book. While Cobb was retired when I moved to Claremont, he was readily available, as was Philip Clayton. Through conversations with both Cobb and Clayton, I learned how similar the concerns motivating inquiry are for process and pragmatic thinkers. I became convinced they are so similar that I could not simply reject my philosophical kin in process thinkers, as Neville had done by publishing *Creativity and God.*

I now view process and ground-of-being theology as resulting from different motivating concerns, and the differences between Cobb and Neville as equally valid motivations for inquiry. In fact, such different theological motivations are to be expected and accepted, not rejected just because they differ. Even though I knew inquiry needs to start with an accepted body of beliefs before doubt can arise, thanks to Neville teaching me Charles Sanders Peirce's philosophy at Boston University, it took me a while to arrive at this conclusion about equally valid concerns. The original prospectus for my dissertation presented ground-of-being and process theologians as engaged in a battle to the death, with Neville and his indeterminate God in the leading role for the winning side. Clayton was sympathetic to my project, but viewed it as giving up too easily on arguments for divine transcendence *and* immanence. I had "learned" from Neville that a God who creates the world from nothing cannot have the divine nature impacted or determined by that world. Conversely, while studying process theology in Claremont, I "learned" that a theory of *creatio ex nihilio* as radical as Neville's provides a God incapable of relating to and being impacted by the world and is therefore a theological nonstarter. I remember very clearly sitting in Clayton's office one day and having a conversation in which all that learning changed. We did not discuss our theological work, but the various influences of Peirce on that work. Rather than placing theologies influenced by such methodological similarities in a zero-sum game, Clayton and I concluded that there is more value in challenging our positions to help one another creatively develop than there is in defending one argument as absolutely true and rejecting a supposed opponent. I realized my deepest loyalty was to neither side of the debate between Cobb and Neville, but to fallible pragmatic inquiry. Supposed opponents with which one disagrees can actually be resources for furthering such inquiry. To pragmatic forms of inquiry, binary opposition is almost always suspect. As Peirce was fond of writing, "Do not block the way of inquiry."[1] Once the roadblock of supposedly having to choose either the unknowable, impersonal, and indeterminate God or the personal, loving, but not ontologically ultimate process God is removed, the way of inquiry into a synthetic model of God is opened. What theological claims are about God are most probable given the world in which we live, if pragmatic methodological commitments are the key to overcoming the impasse?

The pragmatic theological answer will need to move beyond the impasse of realism and constructivism in philosophy and science. Attempts to obtain firm foundations for truth can bring calamities as new knowledge of the world emerges. Naïve scientific realism would seemingly be undercut when what was taken to be "real" is shown to be incorrect, or at least a limited understanding of what is actually the case. Dogmatic realism in theology can similarly isolate believers from meaningful truths emerging from empirical investigation, or make believers outwardly hostile toward other, possibly more accurate, ways of describing reality. However, retreats from realism go against the heart of all these endeavors. Science investigates the real world, philosophy delivers truth, and theology seeks to know a real God about which true claims are asserted. Theological retreat from other disciplines to defend the rationality of given propositions seems to go against the heart of religions that claim a relevance for their doctrines that should continually impact the world. Abandoning reference to reality in favor of merely describing practices is equally unsatisfying, quickly leading to a relativism in which all those practices are arbitrary and on the verge of being pointless. However, the argument I am presenting is that a hypothetical, pragmatic, and open-ended way of thinking in philosophy, science, and theology provides a promising future. Such a position is developed through an epistemology adequate to today's best knowledge from various disciplines. The ontology implied by that epistemology can then be employed as a tool for weighing positive and negative moves in theological work. Metaphysical systems offered as proofs have a miserable record, but as fallible hypotheses about the world they can be employed as a lens to evaluate the veracity of proposed theological interpretations of reality.

Pragmatic Constructive Realism

After examining the promises and problems in realist and constructivist/idealistic approaches to truth in philosophy and science, what I label "pragmatic constructive realism" (hereafter PCR) is pointed to as the most promising way of overcoming the problems in these approaches while synthesizing their insights. My conception of PCR grows out of the work of the classical American pragmatists, especially Charles Sanders Peirce, with some necessary modifications. In order to hold together both constructivism and realism, PCR will need to emphasize the fact of human constructions displayed through theory change while indicating only extramental manifestations *of reality* could demand such theory changes. Experience plays the role of filter, and it does so through surprises *external* to and uncreated by the mind. It is necessary to be a constructivist and a realist, and the pragmatic theory of inquiry is an excellent way to hold these poles together.

I then use PCR to analyze the relationship between process theology and ground-of-being theology, more specifically between Cobb and Neville, my mentors that led me to this point. Neville published *Creativity and God* and challenged Alfred North Whitehead's separation of God and creativity. The result was a rejection of the personal, relational, and responsive God of process theologians in favor of his indeterminate creator God about which nothing can literally be said. Charles Hartshorne, John Cobb, and Lewis Ford responded in kind, arguing Neville's God may be ontologically more ultimate than their various process models, just as creativity is related to the Category of the Ultimate for Whitehead, but the ability of a nonomnipotent God disassociated from creativity to persuade entities with independent power is far more impressive than creating everything from nothing. Years later David Griffin and Neville had a separate exchange initiated by Griffin's book *Whitehead's Radically Different Postmodern Philosophy*, and the same binary oppositions were stated. However, this debate took place almost exclusively in terms of shared commitments to the philosophy of Whitehead, and where those commitments diverged. Cobb construes God alongside the world, both fluctuating between indeterminate and determinate states in a process of mutual creative transformation. Neville argues that God is the indeterminate ground of being that is asymmetrically related to the determinate world. Despite sharing agreement with most of Whitehead's philosophy, their models of God are radically opposed. Even though Neville is known as a pragmatic theologian, Peirce and the other pragmatists hardly appeared in the debate, and it was worse off for that omission. Peirce is featured heavily in Neville's own work, but not in debates with Cobb and other process theologians. However, this dialogue can be reinvigorated by analyzing sometimes explicit, and frequently implicit, commitments to PCR in Cobb and Neville. While they reach different understandings of God, analyzing their work with PCR instead of Whitehead can lead to a new third way that synthesizes some of their major insights.

ACKNOWLEDGMENTS

This is the first book I have written. I used to think the thanks and praise heaped upon friends and loved ones in acknowledgments sections was nothing more than an expected social nicety, and then I worked on this project. The completion of this work truly would not have been possible without a number of people.

First, I want to thank my wife, Jessica. Besides encouraging me when I was unsure of the direction my argument was taking, she was a logistical superhero during crucial moments. During my most intense periods of writing, she took care of everything from the most mundane to important details of our daily lives so that I could devote myself to this project. She also has a PhD in theological ethics from Boston University and provided what was effectively the first reader report for this book when she agreed to review the first full draft. I thank her for her love and daily doing the work of two people so that I could work on writing. I also thank William Cordts, Greylyn Hydinger, and Lawrence Whitney for reading the next draft of this project that I created after taking Jessica's initial comments into consideration. Besides helping me catch many typos, we all share having studied at Boston University for some portion of our graduate school careers. Due to this fact, they were all able to offer especially constructive comments on my interpretation of Neville's work, for which I thank them.

Special words of thanks are due to John Cobb and Robert Neville. Both graciously agreed to read a full draft of this book when it was close to its current form, and both returned detailed comments. The pleasure of having two major theological figures take an argument, in which they are deservingly praised but seriously criticized, in the spirit it was intended is hard to describe. The two of them are also responsible for what remains the highlight of my academic life up to this point. I disobeyed all sensible advice and focused my doctoral dissertation on two living figures. Then I doubled down on questionable choices by inviting both those figures to my dissertation defense. Cobb and Neville both accepted my invitation, to my great joy and to the shock and horror of friends and family members concerned about me making it through the day. I saw nothing to be worried about. I recall reading Cobb's work for the first time in a systematic theology course taught by Neville, who introduced Cobb as the person who should be the first to be canonized as a saint if the Methodists ever decide to adopt that practice. I had also discerned a clear pattern of foot tapping from all my classes with Neville that reveals whether or not he is excited by what is being said. The kind presence of a living saint and confirmation of my performance in the form of tapping feet is just what I needed to get through my committee's examination. I also thank my doctoral advisor, Philip Clayton, and the Center for Process Studies for realizing that bringing Cobb and Neville together like this was a momentous occasion. Clayton made sure to schedule an hour of conversation about my work between Cobb, Neville, and myself. More importantly, he had the wisdom to schedule this hour immediately *after* my defense was over and all pressure relieved. Later that day, the Center for Process Studies hosted what was advertised as a public debate between Cobb and Neville, one that Clayton and I moderated.[2] While differences were discussed and remain, it really became a chance for two brilliant yet humble Methodists to discuss shared core concerns for the first time in a long time. That day will always remain a highlight of my life.

This book is dedicated to Robert Neville as my unofficial doctor father because he has been the longest standing and most influential figure in my academic life. He was my advisor while I pursued a master of theological studies degree at Boston University, and guided my thesis on pragmatism as an underutilized method for the religion and science dialogue. I also took more courses with him than any other faculty member. Despite the fact that he taught mostly doctoral seminars and I was only in the master's program, he gladly granted me permission to take his courses every time I asked. While I did not end up in the doctoral program at Boston University, that did not stop him from making the unilateral decision that he was still my teacher. Jessica and I moved back to Boston for her own doctoral studies when I finished my coursework in Claremont, and this let Neville more easily continue to guide his adopted student. No further proof is needed of the unflinching commitment Neville has to his students, official or not, than the fact that he flew from Boston to Los Angeles to attend a dissertation defense to which he had no official connection. I will never forget driving through Southern California traffic on the way to Claremont while Neville tried to calm my nerves. Bob, you may not have officially been my doctoral advisor, but that just makes me even more grateful that you have stuck with me since we first met. I am honored not just to have such a lifelong teacher and loyal supporter, but to have such good friends as you and Beth.

INTRODUCTION

Negotiating the faults and merits of two excellent theologians could not be more in line with the heart of American pragmatism. The pragmatists understood their philosophy as a means for cutting off the chaff in order to ensure energy is spent discussing what truly matters. Focusing on Cobb and Neville amounts to cutting off classical substance theism as chaff. This point will be elaborated upon, but Cobb and Neville agree regarding its death. However, the ground-of-being tradition being creatively reconfigured by Neville is very much alive, as is Whitehead's process philosophy, championed theologically by Cobb. While certainly applying to Neville and Cobb, any ground-of-being or process theologian motivated by the pragmatists or Whitehead should be able to accept the following features of good philosophy and theology without trouble. Consistency with science is valued, often as an alternative to analytic philosophies of religion that comparatively downplay the role of experience and narrative forms of theology that deny the importance of dialogue with other disciplines. Beyond dialogue with other disciplines like science, dialogue with other religious traditions is not only valued by Cobb and Neville, but actually engaging in such dialogue should also lead to a positive embrace of religious pluralism. Such interdisciplinary and interreligious work is a crucial test of theological claims. Both Whitehead and the pragmatists provide broad definitions of experience in which sense impressions are derivative of more basic feelings and possibilities. Both philosophical ways of thinking defend metaphysics, thereby resisting a full linguistic turn in both philosophy and theology while simultaneously acknowledging a place for symbolic constructions of language. Finally, in order to defend engaging in metaphysics and avoid falling into reductive, hierarchical, and exclusive pitfalls of modern metaphysical schemes, Whitehead and the pragmatists argue that metaphysical work must be hypothetical, fallible, and open to correction.

Peirce understood human inquiry as propelled by existing commitments. He was extremely critical of "paper" Cartesian doubt. Inquiry always hits the ground running, so to speak, because existing beliefs cannot be removed and replaced by a blank slate just by saying such should be the case.[3] There is a preexisting social element to both scientific and theological inquiry, existing habits that work for our dealings with the world. In this regard, Cobb and Neville have different models of God that come partly from the very different starting points of their theological work. Viewed as Peircean habits, this is simply a fact and not to be questioned. However, when faced with positive reasons to doubt, it becomes evident that beliefs are not infallible and new explanations must be searched for until doubt again ceases. There is much that still works in the different Peircean habits of Neville and Cobb, but there are also problems with each position according to the argument for PCR that will be developed. Those problems provide the opportunity to reach a mediating position through pragmatism that debates centered on Whitehead never achieved.

A Sketch of the Argument

Realism is a common sense position. Skeptics usually violate their skepticism in daily life. One of the greatest among their number in David Hume admitted he had to set aside his doubts about causation when going about his daily business.[4] But naïve realism is easily and decisively refuted by even a cursory glance at the history of ideas. Even giants of the philosophical and scientific canon have been incorrect about what they took to be true features of reality. René Descartes wanted solid foundations on which to carefully build a tower of secured knowledge.[5] Four hundred years later we are still waiting for the indisputable foundations. As a result, the fallibility of any knowledge claim is an uncontroversial position to hold, and epistemology shifted from external realism to constructivism. But what is truth if nothing stable can be referenced? Any claim is approximately true, limited, and open to correction because truth claims are determined in relation to changing historical circumstances. Absolute foundations for theology seem as unlikely as for philosophy, but understanding theology as nothing but the investigation of language seems equally troublesome. Many people who devote themselves to God do so because they understand God to be a reality to which one can be devoted, not a pleasing psychological construct. However, if theologians are to be realists they must also adapt to changing knowledge of the world and admit the indisputable role humans play in that changing knowledge. Peirce understands knowledge as commitment to interpretations of an environment in specific and limited contexts. His pragmatism allows for religious beliefs to similarly be understood as speculative hypotheses rather than assured truths. Creative religious ideas, like novel interpretations of reality in science, can discover religious *realities* in a growing and changing universe. PCR maintains that we are propelled by existing commitments and yet constructive in creatively making sense of new data through novel interpretations of reality.

The chief tools to be employed by PCR in the following argument come from Peirce. Some terminology that will be explained in chapters 2 and 3 will be mentioned up front. His categories of Firstness (qualitative possibility), Secondness (brute fact), and Thirdness (law and generality) mark the real features of the world and their evolution.[6] Abduction (imaginative hypotheses), deduction (logical conclusions), and induction (testing hypotheses through time) are the actions we perform in trying to interpret the world and explain surprising phenomena.[7] Icons, indices, and symbols are the specific features of those interpretations.[8] Thirdness and symbolic reference indicate *synechism*, or the reality of continuity.[9] The transition from Firstness to Secondness, the presentation of shocking new facts requiring interpretation, points to the reality of *tychism*, or chance.[10] Bold theological hypotheses are allowed as abductions, but are also subject to criticism from the rest of PCR's toolbox to ensure they are hypotheses of *this reality* and not some imaginary landscape.

Viewed through the lens of PCR, the debate between Cobb and Neville seems to have three possible resolutions: Cobb may be right that God alongside the world, both mutually transforming the other in the throes of creativity, is the best ultimate explanation; Neville may correctly note a transition from nonbeing to being; or there could be a position affirming that the ground of the determinate world both transcends and yet nonetheless grows in generality with that world. Cobb argues that God is a being with intentions for the world, a point especially important in explaining the features of subjective experience and defending mentality against scientific reductionism. Neville rejects the concept of a divine *being* and instead argues that God is indeterminate, a result from focusing on a transition from nonbeing to being in the divine creative act. Despite the fact that they have restated these differences over and over again in terms of Whitehead's process philosophy, they share many of Peirce's methodological commitments. There is a mediating position capable of being revealed by a deeper investigation of Peircean themes in their work.

Some groundwork will need to be prepared before jumping directly into a creative reinterpretation of two giants of modern theology. Topics like scientific realism and the fallibility of truth claims are well-worn territory. However, covering such terrain, even if just briefly, reveals why current debates such as the one between constructivism and realism keep occurring. Both positions are unsatisfying on their own, and philosophers who have devoted their careers to improving one position or the other have been unable to resolve the tension. The debates are still ongoing. The starting point of this excursus is the debate between realism and constructivism in philosophy, and it is taken in order to problematize both positions and indicate the need to move beyond them. The aim is not to advance analytic debates about realism or constructivism or dig into a deep explanation of either position. The goal is to explain each position well enough to show why neither suffices. This result is less a detailed refutation than a heuristic argument about their usefulness, or lack thereof. Neither is the transition from their problematic nature to PCR presented as a proof. It is an argument that a compelling defensible philosophy that overcomes the problems of realism and constructivism will have features similar to those of PCR. Those features will be more adequate to reality than the binary oppositions it transcends, and those features can be used to criticize and then improve theological work.

Chapter 1 starts with common sense. It is uncontroversial that knowledge is limited to contexts that create inherently partial views open to growth. Even if one argues that genuine truth is correlation between a claim and its referent, knowledge at any moment will be limited by a given context in an evolving world. Dogmatic defenses of absolutely certain claims quickly crumble when novel facts emerge. The limits of context and time make broad consensus difficult to achieve. The possibility of learning the truth about broad pervasive features of reality can quickly be lost to skeptical caution. Thomas Kuhn responded to problems with correspondence theories of truth in philosophy of science through an analysis of scientific revolutions.

The creative role of human agents is laid bare when scientific theories no longer make sense and new explanations must be *created*.[11] Subsequent to this awareness, it could easily seem as if all understandings of reality are constructions, a consequence systematically spelled out by Paul Feyerabend, who moved from realism to constructivism, and then slid down the constructivist slope into an anarchy where anything goes.[12] If that is the only philosophical paradigm, there are implications for theology. Religious ideas are mere projections. Interpretations are fictitious constructions, albeit useful ones, resulting from needs, desires, and fears. Such a view can be found in Ludwig Feuerbach and all hermeneutics of suspicion. However, while created theories do not perfectly mirror reality, the mismatch is only realized when investigators are faced with novel manifestations *of reality* that need explanation. New theories *of reality* must be *constructed*. The necessity of uniting constructivism with realism becomes the inevitable conclusion, even though the two ideas are often depicted as incompatible.

Chapter 2 argues that Charles S. Peirce's philosophy is capable of achieving such a mediating position. Realism can be naïve or based on progressive inquiry. For example, cell biology has *revealed* deeper *previously hidden* structures. Regarding such progression, Peirce argues that signs are the basic units of meaning and interpretation is the basic causal activity of the world. Interpretation is a sign transformation with *causal* connections to the objects interpreted. Signs bring us closer to the objects interpreted. There is a sense in which signs can be constructions and still real. Achieving success in a changing universe requires the right method, otherwise novel interpretations will not be attuned to novel developments in that world and will lack any ability to predict and control. We start inquiry as creatures of habit and only later realize what inferences are truly valid.[13] We learn self-control over previous habits. Signs are also not just a matter of conscious interpretation. From intelligent animals, all the way down to single cell organisms, semiotic relations are found, a point that will be elaborated upon with examples in chapter 8.[14] Even in humans, signs have a basic physicality in which chemical reactions respond to stimuli in an environment. Sign systems also have complicated interrelations. Those chemical connections became necessary for the evolution of more complicated nervous systems. Symbolic codes constructed and learned socially led to evolution in the biological realm. For example, chemical reactions in the auditory system can be signs of a distant, more significant thing such as a crying baby or threatening person. Stimuli lead to interpretations, which lead to intelligence, environmental discrimination, and imagination capable of integrating the initial stimuli into more complex harmonies. It is beneficial that symbols can be projections. Becoming self-conscious of the constructed aspect of symbols allows for the use of creativity and the discovery of previously unnoticed *aspects of reality*.

The appreciation of Peirce in chapter 2 turns to necessary criticism in chapter 3. Peirce was so concerned about establishing the reasonableness and lawlike behavior of nature that he affirmed panpsychism. This is his position that "matter is effete mind, inveterate habits becoming physical laws."[15] An associated questionable anthropocentric doctrine he embraced was agapism, evolutionary love.[16] Matter was destined, since it is also mind, to develop in reasonable, predictable ways in the universe. These associated claims not only explain why our minds are attuned to be able to know the natural world, but our ability to predict and control that world. The natural world is for us, because something like our mind has always been in it. However, to avoid the questionable conclusions that rocks have conscious experiences or the evolution of the world is due to the inevitable development of that mental aspect of reality, it will be necessary to push Peirce deeper into his own philosophical system. His categories of Firstness, Secondness, and Thirdness account for the emergence of novel orders in the world. They can account for the emergence of human experience from inert matter, without reading mind into that matter. Similarly, the development of the universe is a contingent matter open to empirical inquiry. Thirdness is an achievement, not preordained. Only intelligent use of method and collaborative inquiry will further its growth.

Chapter 4 represents a transition in the argument from philosophy to theology. With the method and key features of PCR established, the stage will be set to use PCR to analyze the theological positions of Cobb and Neville. This transition relies upon the work of Sandra Rosenthal, who construes the debate between process and pragmatic thinkers as centering on continuity and time.[17] For Whitehead, each emerging occasion comes into being and in so doing defines its present spatial and temporal scope. Once definite, it stops becoming and is past. The continuity between present emerging and past definite occasions is that the past is prehended in the present. Continuity in this view is the coming together of distinct elements from the past in a decision that then increases the next diversity to be brought together by one by becoming one of the many elements to be prehended in that moment. When it is satisfied and in the past, it has specific spatial and temporal locations. There is therefore disconnect between past (fully definite) and emerging (not yet definite) entities. Pragmatic thinkers like Peirce have an opposite intuition: emerging out of instead of coming together. Peirce expresses this theme in the movement from Firstness to Thirdness. There is growth and extension of what was emerging and will continue to emerge. Emergence is without breaks; it is small accretion in a continuous stream. Causality in this case is from the past to what emerges from it, as opposed to process thought in which the causal power of the present integrates potentials. For pragmatists, the past is relatively definite because it can change as what emerges from it gives it new character. There is a specious present "blooming, buzzing, confusion," as William James would say.[18] Process thought presents separate discontinuous acts of creativity while Peirce presents emergence as continuous creativity. Despite being known as a pragmatic theologian, Neville explicitly sides with Whitehead on this issue. This thematic debate is relevant for moving beyond Cobb and Neville, for understanding a God who creates a world that emerges out of rather than one that comes together.

Later in his life Peirce came to believe that once growth, thought, and reasonableness have become pervasive features of the universe, they become inseparable from the idea of a personal creator. His affirmation of genuine chance mitigates against rigid causation and makes space for mind, even a divine mind, to be inferred from the lawlike regularity of the world. He had already embraced panpsychism, the view that mind is more basic than matter. It is a small step from that to understanding mind as the source of all existence as well. Such recognition of chance and mind, along with his argument that all inquiry begins with existing habits, is amenable to process theologians. That is the point with which chapter 5 starts.

The existing habit, so to speak, for Cobb is Christian theism. When that position ran aground on the shore of experience, work was done to fix problems but save what remains of the ship.[19] Whitehead's philosophy was the life raft, enabling Cobb to understand God as alongside the world, transcending it in the lure of ideas that actual occasions of experience can realize or neglect. The realization of divine ideas depends on the world. This places limitations on dualistic substance theism, limiting God's power and knowledge before actual occasions are completed. Still, God remains a being with intentions for God's creatures. In Cobb's theology, there is hope for theological progress as well as connection to older, possibly cherished, beliefs. Correction, though, seems unsystematic. The ability to adapt comes from the protective belt of the very systematic process metaphysics developed by Whitehead, but appears in theology piece by piece as challenges come where they may. Nonetheless, process thought does allow Cobb to establish new habitual responses to the world by which people are capable of living ethically, pluralistically, and with strong religious beliefs while also being aware of the best science of the day.

Neville is also unsatisfied with substance theism but makes a move opposite that of Cobb in response. Rather than modifying theism to fit the data, he makes a new creative hypothesis for the sort of God responsible for the world, the subject matter of chapter 6. Only after this God hypothesis is in place does Neville consider the formation of religious beliefs. As a result, his theology provides a strong break with some previous ways of considering God's being but is intended to provide a more systematic and thorough connection with the world he considered in developing his God hypothesis. Cobb takes challenges to existing beliefs serially, as they arise, adjusting a piece of a theology here and another there, with a hope for systematic integrity through the skillful use of Whitehead's philosophy. Neville looks at the whole world now and seeks a unifying explanation. His answer is that God is the indeterminate source of the determinate world, and apart from the act of creating that world, God is indistinguishable from nothing.[20] However, God cannot be sheer indeterminacy, nothingness, since there is creation. In the creative act, God is established as the indeterminate source of the determinate world.

Neville's argument for God's indeterminacy is satisfying. Where Neville falls short is in thinking he does justice to the transcendence *and* presence of God. His argument for God the creator provides what may be one of the most transcendent models of God available, and because of that fact Neville has difficulty affirming God's immanent determinate character. In fact, he does not. Any determinate claim about God is a broken symbol that cannot univocally apply to God.[21] God's immanence breaks on God's transcendence. While Cobb's process theology does not struggle with this issue, it does face a problem when it comes to God's transcendence, God's primordial nature. Cobb's God, like Whitehead's, contains the possibilities for the world. Cobb believes they cannot be contained in the past, which is settled. To avoid constructing a philosophy that describes us as being in a box universe, he argues that the possibilities for the world, its Platonic forms, are eternal objects in God. Furthermore, this God must be an actual entity alongside the world, not a being transcending it, to be able to provide these possibilities to actual occasions in the form of initial aims. Explaining then criticizing both these positions happens in chapter 7. My pragmatic alternative then follows in chapter 8.

God can be understood as real, near, and participating in all three of Peirce's categories by binding them together, a theme expressed well in the developmental teleology of Cobb's process theology. God can also be understood as the creative source of the three categories, a theme captured by Neville. If the theme these debating theological positions ignore is given more attention, the emerging out of rather than the coming together of reality, both God and Firstness, Secondness, and Thirdness can be understood as growing *together* in concrete reasonableness. God would emerge from an indeterminate Firstness to a determinate Thirdness with the character given by the act of creating those features. God's character as indeterminate creator remains so in Firstness until specific instances of coming together propel Secondness and Thirdness into existence and give undifferentiated possibility determinate character. An indeterminate God without a fixed finite identity can be determinately extended by the world. Creative interpretations maintain the meaning and reality of God in the world by giving symbolic expression to what cannot be known in any other fashion. Furthermore, far from being flights of the imagination, interpretations are continuous with symbolizations found in the natural world at simple levels devoid of conscious experience. This means that religious individuals work together with God in a crucial way to constantly redeem the reference of that term in unique ways for a world constantly growing in novelty. Symbols of God are not broken as much as they are growing, shifting, and adapting.

The concluding chapter makes a form of pluralism implicit in the entire argument explicit. We do not have uncomplicated direct access to reality given the role of interpretation, nor should we expect consensus as if culture had no role in interpretation. Interests partly determine how and what we engage in an environment. Anyone who understands their religious identity pragmatically immediately understands the nature and necessity of there being very different religious neighbors. That is, they understand that no one can understand or prejudge another religion because members of that tradition are likely making interpretations and engaging values that arise within the codependence of contexts and interpretations. This inherent pluralism of PCR is on display in the way Cobb and Neville are treated as equals to be pushed and challenged on a quest, not opponents to be vanquished. If fallibility is taken seriously, religious traditions will naturally be modified when individuals and communities need to create novel religious interpretations of religious realities when existing interpretations no longer engage. Knowing one's own pragmatic commitments means knowing why others in different contexts with different presuppositions will differ. This pluralism is not due to indifference as can be the case in relativism. Rather, distinct differences and contexts are what shock people, grab them, and demand, or fail to demand, adherence. Doubt and belief are mental states of affairs forced upon us by *external* experiences. Different people in different cultures interpret reality differently. This is a good thing. The only bad conclusion is exclusive dogmatic positions that admit no position other than their own. They self-exclude from pragmatic inquiry by freely choosing positions incapable of being included in and learning from open dialogue. For good pragmatic philosophical theologians such as Cobb, Neville, and myself, we move onward together because of, not despite, our differences.

1 | Realism, Constructivism, and Their Discontents

AT STAKE IN THE DEBATE between realism and constructivism is reality, its nature, and how it is or is not accessible through human language. Philosophical realism is closely aligned with scientific realism and the correspondence theory of truth.[1] True beliefs and statements provide a complete and accurate picture of the world investigated by the various scientific disciplines. Constructivism is more closely associated with idealism and the coherence theory of truth. It is a position that does not necessarily reject the reality of the world, though in such a case it certainly does not make that world easily accessible. Rather than pictures mirroring reality, the truth of statements about reality is a matter of their being logically consistent with one another.[2] Beliefs are reasonable if they cohere with other beliefs, whether or not any of them accurately reflect the nature of reality. In weighing the pros and cons of each side, the implied question is whether inquiry should stop when a coherent set of beliefs are reached in any given cultural-linguistic situation or whether progress toward understanding the "thing-in-itself" is possible.

The present task is not to definitively refute realism and constructivism in philosophy and science. Their advocates will surely continue to debate as if this chapter never existed. Rather, the aim of this chapter is to problematize these two philosophies by poking enough holes in coherence and simple correspondence theories of truth so that anyone currently on board with those positions will abandon ship. Similarly, PCR will not be proven, but presented as a better alternative to the sinking philosophical ships. It is a promising philosophical position that seeks to transcend realist and constructivist extremes by mediating between them, addressing issues important to both. Other plausible philosophical alternatives will share its basic details, even if differing in some specifics. A reinterpretation of classical American pragmatism is certainly not the only viable option, and shares much in common with process philosophy. However, as will be shown in chapters 4 and 8, the core insights of PCR differ from those of Whitehead, especially regarding the role of possibilities in the universe. Once presented as a plausible philosophy, PCR can then be used as a lens for viewing the merits and demerits of theological arguments that seek to be consistent with knowledge of the world. But first we turn to the competing philosophies of realism and constructivism.

Realism versus Constructivism in Philosophy and Science

A basic construal of realism is that objects and their properties exist (e.g., that house is yellow), and they exist independently of what anyone thinks about them. Stars, moons, and planets existed long before anyone perceived or held beliefs about them. True theories accurately describe such phenomena, packaging reality in their concepts. Constructivism, by contrast, typically denies one of two aspects of realism, existence or mind-independence. Forms of instrumentalism deny the existence of objects and their properties, asserting instead that those are convenient fictions necessarily used to get by daily and solve problems in specific fields. Theories are just useful tools on this view, but remain silent as to what we really know about that with which we work.[3] Idealists are constructivists who think theories impose necessary order on chaotic experience. This makes them capable of being realists in the provisional sense that stable structures of experience exist, even though they are unable to define reality beyond the knowing mind.[4] There may be a real world for such philosophers, but there is no way to understand it apart from our concepts. Since we cannot know whether we have ever broken through our conceptual barrier to know reality in itself, the best we can do is make our concepts coherent with one another and fruitful for solving the problems of life.

Realists will bristle at the idealist rejection of mind-independence. Instead of that position, they will hold some form of the correspondence theory of truth, which maintains that true claims correspond with facts of the real world. It is a position affirming the metaphysical reality of the world that is, appropriately, at least as old as Aristotle's formulation in *Metaphysics*: "To say that what is is not, or that what is not is, is false; but to say that what is is, and what is not is not, is true; and therefore also he who says that a thing is or is not will say either what is true or what is false."[5] It is also found in Aquinas's assertion that true judgments of the intellect conform with things in the world.[6] It is by no means only ancient, however. William James defended it. "Truth, as any dictionary will tell you, is a property of certain of our ideas. It means their 'agreement,' as falsity means their disagreement, with 'reality.'"[7] Of any belief, thought, or judgment, it can be asked whether they truly represent the actual state of affairs, with that state of affairs, not the relationship between thoughts, determining truth and falsity.

On the other side of the aisle, George Berkeley has provided one of the classic expressions of idealism, the position that all supposed external objects and their properties are actually mental, ideas in a mind. "All the choir of heaven and furniture of the earth, in a word all those bodies which compose the mighty frame of the world, have not any subsistence without a mind."[8] Realists should at least admit his expression of idealism is poetic, perhaps due in part to religious influences. In order to mitigate against the nonexistence of anything prior to the development of living beings capable of mental activity, Berkeley makes reality an idea in the mind of God. But idealism need not end in theism. Michael Dummett argues for semantic realism, with *semantic* doing the heavy lifting in his argument. For him, a semantic realist acknowledges the truth of a proposition may be independent of anyone recognizing it. Initially, this position seems like good news for realists. However, while a proposition may be true or false, there is no way to determine which. According to Dummett's "constitution thesis," the content of realism is therefore nothing but semantic realism.[9] The only literal content of realistic claims about the external world is the understanding that some claims about it have conditions that would make them true or false, even if we can never determine whether they are true or false.

Michael Devitt has also realized that "semantic" is doing more work than "realism" in Dummett's argument and makes the additional claim that semantic realism may be more compatible with an idealistic metaphysics. He contrasts realism with realist truth, Dummett's semantic realism, as follows. "Realism (as I have defined it), requires the objective independent existence of commonsense physical entities. Realist Truth concerns physical *statements* and has no such requirement: *it says nothing about the nature of the reality that makes those statements true or false*, except that it is objective. An idealist who believed in the objective existence of a purely mental realm of sense data could subscribe to Realist Truth."[10] The basic idea behind Devitt's argument is that as soon as subjective factors enter it is hard to prevent them from dominating, inextricably difficult to determine which judgments are disclosing reality and which are nothing but human judgments, resulting in realism's departure. This is a problem for realists because, as John McDowell notes, once any appeal to the given is abandoned, there is a lurking danger that coherentism loses *any* contact with the world.[11] The one piece of constructivism acceptable to realists is lost. Regarding this loss of contact with the world, realists might rightly wonder how human thoughts come to have any bearing on reality whatsoever if thinking has no empirical constraints. If our representations of any subject matter are determined by factors other than the objective content of that subject matter, faith that we are ever accurately describing anything may waver.

Ludwig Wittgenstein is a go-to example of how human factors can come to dominate philosophy, and for good reason. He technically affirms the correspondence of basic propositions with basic facts, in which nonbasic propositions are explained in terms of the relation they have with the basic facts. As he put it formally, complex statements including positive affirmations of 'p' and 'q' need to be evaluated in terms of the status of the basic components 'p' and 'q.' If both are not true, the complex statements do not correspond with reality, or vice versa.[12] The problem for realists is when rules for a communal way of thinking are taken to be those basic facts. When 'p' and 'q' are determined by language games, correspondence to facts becomes correspondence to a community's rules. True propositions do not conform to facts of the world, according to this view. Instead, certain propositions are facts to which other propositions must conform. What appeared like a correspondence theory of truth has succumbed to coherence with a given set of rules. Rather than reality, privileged propositions about reality are the conditions of truth for other propositions. This allows Wittgenstein to claim "every view is significant for the one who sees it as significant ... in this sense, every view is equally significant."[13] Such privileged propositions are believed, but cannot be shown, to be true. When meaning depends on practice, and no standards outside of communal practice are available, correspondence with reality is not a possible check one can make for any statement. Philosophers are left to describe communal rules, not interrogate them and provide alternative explanations. Similar problems with realism and the slippery slope of constructivism toward relativism can be seen by investigating scientific realism and its critics.

Scientific realism, a subset within philosophical realism, gives epistemic endorsement to the content of the best scientific theories, affirming the reality of both observable and unobservable entities they describe. It is a positive stance toward epistemology that leads to a metaphysical picture of reality made up of those observable and unobservable entities. The models with which scientists work are not only useful for making measurements and predictions, but are objective depictions of reality. An obvious reply from a skeptic would highlight the many drastic changes regarding the dominant theory regarded as "true" in any scientific field through the years. The fact that many scientific theories and models have been improved (e.g., we no longer think of elementary particles as billiard balls) or shown to be outright false (e.g. the eighteenth-century phlogiston theory of a fire-like substance in combustible bodies has been falsified by chemists) does put pressure on simple identifications of theoretical models with objective reality. However, a scientific realist need not be blind to progress in science and think current models perfectly mirror reality. The question for such self-aware realists is then how to determine which theories are to be identified with the truth of the world and which are not. A typical appeal is referencing mature theories that have endured testing and produced fruitful results over time.[14] However, once talk of theoretical development is admitted, that theories gain the status of being true of reality over time, a gap between theory and reality is introduced. Once that gap is present, one can only claim to be a realist of a qualified sort.

Structural realism, in light of the gap between theory and reality, is the position that successful mature scientific theories do not describe the actual features of objects in the world, but their general structure. As a result, structural realists often express skepticism regarding possible knowledge of unobservable entities described by physicists.[15] Supposed unobservable entities are descriptions of otherwise unknown forces or objects interacting. Once the epistemic route to knowing and accurately describing such entities is made suspect, ontologically questioning the very reality of the world depicted in scientific models is not far behind.[16] As Bas van Fraassen has forcefully argued, without access to the real world, the grounds for affirming such a world are also lost. Scientific theories work, are empirically adequate, solve problems, and need not imply anything metaphysically about reality.[17] The underdetermination of theory by data only makes the situation more problematic for realists.

To be empirically adequate, scientific hypotheses must result in testable predictions. Yet testing requires adequate instruments and measurements. It also requires adequate methods and models for investigation, which are informed by background theories, the advancement of technology, and countless other historical and social conditions. As a result, when experiments produce results other than what was expected, it can be hard to determine where the error lies. Alternatively, when conflicting theories arise to explain a set of data and are each consistent with that set of data, as is currently the case with rival interpretations of quantum mechanics, the evidence alone does not force belief in one theory over another. Choosing which theory is true is underdetermined by the data.[18] Willard Quine goes even further and argues that this point applies to the attempt to confirm all knowledge claims, not just those in science.[19] Underdetermination also highlights the socially and historically conditioned aspects of scientific theories, aspects most famously explored by Thomas Kuhn.

Kuhn explains the process by which scientific disciplines adapt to changes in data by contrasting "normal" science with "revolutionary" science. Normal science is characterized by the acceptance of a paradigm that determines the standards, questions, and acceptable explanations used when attempting to understand data. Revolutions occur when an existing paradigm is challenged by data it cannot explain and authority is passed on to a new guiding scientific paradigm with new theories and concepts capable of accounting for the data that the now old paradigm could not. Normal science is interrupted by revolutions that replace an old "normal" paradigm with a new one. An interesting wrinkle in this theory is that sometimes the two normal periods may be so different so as to be incommensurable, making the understanding of reality radically different before and after, all because of theory change.[20] Quantum mechanics is currently overturning fundamental particle physics and reopening the issue of laws and determinism with evidence that observers impact what is observed in a nontrivial fashion. Before the publication of Charles Darwin's *On the Origin of Species,* the immutability of species was largely accepted. However, Darwin's hypothesis more adequately dealt with new data. His new hypothesis was a revolution in that it offered a new understanding of biological life that entailed new deductive possibilities of understanding how species are related and change through time. After the neo-Darwinian synthesis with gene theory, relations could be tracked genetically, providing further confirmation of the new evolutionary paradigm. Still, it is important to note that in Kuhn's framework the social construction of reality cannot be separated from the objective understanding of reality.[21] The scientific story has reached a place similar to the philosophical one. Even if realism is one's goal, once subjective human factors are acknowledged, they are almost impossible to expunge.

Volumes have been, and many more will be, written about the back and forth between realists and constructivists through the years and the ways each finds the other's position lacking. The point of the present argument is that there are legitimate reasons for being dissatisfied with both realism and constructivism. That the debate has been unending should be enough impetus for looking elsewhere for a solution. Responses and rebuttals keep being given because the shortcomings keep making themselves evident. Seeking positions that seek to mediate rather than choose sides is not the dominant philosophical story, unfortunately. Rather than mediation, some philosophers have moved from realism to constructivism, due to problems with realism. From there, due to real problems with constructivism, instead of finding a better third way, some slip into relativism and embrace the lack of any standards. When truth is coherence with a set of propositions, and there is no external reality to help in determining which propositions should be given that special status, all coherent propositions are allowed and anything goes. Paul Feyerabend's career perfectly exemplifies the problems with accepting a dichotomy between realism and constructivism by following that path to a relativistic oblivion. First, though, an introduction to his slippery slope by means of Karl Popper.

Popper argues that scientific knowledge proceeds by way of "conjectures" and "refutations." Simply stated, all knowledge of the world takes the form of tentative conjectures, uncertain propositions that may or may not be true. Those conjectures are tested through refutations, critical attempts to display the falsity of conjectures. Popper understands this to be the point of scientific experiments. Within the interplay of these two processes there is no certain knowledge, only statements that have survived all refutations thus far but should still be tested. Popper claims the purpose of science is to erase mistakes and "understand the difficulties of the problem which we are trying to solve."[22] Within this falsificationist view of scientific inquiry, when theories resist attempts at refutation, they gain further support. Science proceeds by producing and testing deductive inferences of theories.

Feyerabend began arguing in the late 1950s for a realist view of science based on Popper's account of conjectures, refutations, and falsification. Feyerabend contrasts his position with the view that major changes in scientific theories, an undisputed fact that has happened over and over again, will not impact the empirical meaning of terms in scientific theories. He argues that this view, which he attributes to the logical positivists, stands in complete opposition to science and any half-decent philosophy informed by science.

His counterpoint, "Thesis I," is that "the interpretation of an observation language is determined by the theories which we use to explain what we observe, and it changes as soon as those theories change."[23] According to Feyerabend's positivist opponents, all meaning is determined by sense experience and the language of observation, but he reverses the order. When theories change, what we observe and the way we experience things changes as well. Thesis I reverses the dependence of theories upon reality that is typical of realist positions. Though his stated intent was to provide a realistic understanding of science, his position altered the meaning of realism. For him, theories are independently real, not the world and experiences of it. He transitioned from realism to a contextual theory of meaning.

Rather than passively accepting phenomena around us as we experience them, Feyerabend argues that we interrogate and alter phenomena we experience. Contra Kuhn and Popper, he does not believe the interrogation happens with only one dominant theory or grand scientific framework. In his words, "We use a plurality of theories (systems of thought, institutional frameworks) from the very beginning. The theories (systems of thought, forms of life, frameworks) are used in their strongest form, not as schemes for the processing of events whose nature is determined by other considerations, but as accounts or determinants of this very nature."[24] Feyerabend only moves to affirming realism after the critical investigation of phenomena with a proliferation of theories. Theory, not reality, is primarily determinative in any scientific discipline.

According to his account, scientific realism is a general theory of knowledge, just as much about the reality of an independent world as the reality of daily scientific activity. Science is in part about the nature of reality, a partial concession to realists, but it is also about living scientists making predictions. "It is metaphysics and engineering theory in one."[25] Scientists and the theories they develop actively shape what results will be found through experimentation by creating the standards for research. If theories are merely summaries of experience, and therefore not believed to influence observation, he claims there should only be one account of reality. While realists could view this as a good thing, since having the true description of reality is their goal, Feyerabend draws disastrous consequences for realists. Without alternative theories, there is no critical testing in science, and without experimental support in favor of one theory rather than another there is no strong argument that any given scientific theory truly depicts the world. The result is that the realist story about science becomes nothing but a dogmatic myth.

A shift happened in Feyerabend's thinking in the 1960s when he realized the consequences of Kuhn's point about incommensurability in combination with his own focus on theory proliferation. Feyerabend realized the underlying principles resulting in the construction of one theory can go against those of another. Thus, the content of scientific theories cannot always be compared. The result was a great shift in the trajectory of his thought. His focus on the primacy of theory led him from talk of realism to the possibility that there may be no nonarbitrary means of choosing between theories. He basically drove himself from realism to relativism. First, his realism. His understanding of realism is that its value is in spurring the creation of as many theories as possible.[26] This construal of realism makes sense given his approval of Popper's refutation thesis. To be testable, theories need falsifiers, so the more theories the better. If all those theories are all incompatible, even better. Therefore, he affirms a theoretical pluralism in which as many incompatible theories as possible compete, enhancing the testability and empirical worth of all competitors in the process.[27] Feyerabend was fixated on a sort of liminal space, Kuhn's "pre-paradigm" phase after a revolution and before theories have been adjudicated so as to lead to a new normal phase of science.[28] This shift in focus to theory construction would be met with approval by Van Fraassen's constructivist approach to science.[29] Focusing on the relation of theories to one another, rather than their relation to empirical observations and comparison of how theories deal with those observations, would also complete Feyerabend's conversion from realism, through constructivism, to relativism.

In *Against Method* Feyerabend came out as an epistemological anarchist. In it he rejects all scientific methods for being a mix of good rational decisions and political propaganda. Given incommensurability between theories, other factors than observation and rational decision-making become decisive. The battle between Galileo and the Catholic Church is his chief example. It was a full-blown propaganda war, with Galileo relying as much, if not more, on rhetoric than on empirical adequacy to garner support for his heliocentric position. The lesson is supposed to be that, at best, theory choice can be made on aesthetic grounds, and, at worst, it is done for social reasons and compelled by ulterior motives. Feyerabend ended his career so sure bias will always be present in the method for choosing one theory over another that he argued science should be separated from the state, just like religion. He expressed his completed conversation to relativism as follows: "To those who look at the rich material provided by history, and who are not intent on impoverishing it in order to please their lower instincts, their craving for intellectual security in the form of clarity, precision, 'objectivity', 'truth', it will become clear that there is only one principle that can be defended under all circumstances and in all stages of human development. It is the principle: anything goes."[30] Reality is forever obscured, human judgments have no standards, and unmitigated relativism wins the day.

Philosophical Implications for Religion

This same split between realism and constructivism is present within philosophy of religion and theology. Are theological claims true of God and historical events in the world, even if they happened long ago, or is theology only the activity of deducing the consequences of existing Christian beliefs and making adjustments when tensions are found so that all beliefs cohere with one another again? William Alston has offered one of the strongest examples of realism in religion with his direct realism, a position he has also defended extensively on purely philosophical grounds by arguing that perceptions of God are not unlike perceptions of a red building.[31] On the constructivist side stand those within the "Yale School" of Hans Frei and George Lindbeck.[32] For them, religion is first and foremost a communal phenomenon, one guided by the beliefs that form a community's self-understanding. Theology is then just a matter of understanding the grammar of the community, refining its accepted narrative. This makes the task of the theologian little more than that of gatekeeper to determine whether practices or beliefs are in line with that grammar. But God, Brahman, Emptiness, and so forth should not be understood as referring to anything outside that community, as those terms are just refined means of defining meaning within it. With this very basic sketch of how the philosophical debate between realists and constructivists is also occurring among religious thinkers in place, it is worth investigating arguably one of the strongest defenses of realism in religion currently available in more detail.

Alston defends a strong notion of realism concerning data presented in perceptual experience. He argues that perception has a sort of prima facie justification through its intrinsic character of felt objective relationality. How could we question the reality of what we perceive and interact with when they are so obviously *there*? This realism of perceived objects forms the basis for his justification of religious belief in God as perceived object. His strategy is to defend a realist stance toward objects presented in perceptual experience and then defend religious realism on the basis that God appears to subjects in a similar manner in religious experience. As a *direct* realist, these justified beliefs do not depend on arguments based on separate premises.[33] In other words, a direct realist, in both everyday sensory and religious cases, believes that perceptual experience carries with it the justification of belief about how objects are presented in such experience.

Alston defines perceptual experience as the presentation of objects that appear in such experience. Perception is simply the appearance of something to the perceiving subject. Furthermore, the one having the perceptual experience is *directly* aware of the presentation of some object. The object is what is presented, not a mediating sign of something else. Elsewhere Alston marks his approach off from externalist theories of perception that hold that perception cannot be veridical unless causal conditions are met.[34] Such conditions do not concern his argument that perception has prima facie justificatory force, even if the object perceived cannot be proven to exist. The reason perception can play this role is that the phenomena of presentation automatically carry a sense of objective relation from the point of view of the subject, according to Alston. With this switch to the internal nature of perception, perceptual experience can be given the simple formulation "for S to perceive X is simply for X to appear to S as so-and-so."[35] Thus, being a realist about perception means distinguishing between phenomena perceived and things as they are in themselves. The former can be defended even if the latter cannot be proven.

Alston created what he calls the "theory of appearing" for justifying beliefs in light of the presentational character of experience. The theory has a commonsense tone because it upholds the commonsense feeling that perception justifies belief. Regardless of whether the objects of sense experience can be proven to exist, perceptual experience has such a force on the perceiver that it can never really be doubted. The lesson is to trust your eyes, so to speak. Beliefs can be justified because it is at least possible that objects of perceptual experience would present themselves as so-and-so if those objects existed. That is, sense experience has an "act-object" relation in which something appears to a subject as bearing certain phenomenal qualities.[36] Nothing needs to be added to sense experience for the argument that S sees X to be true. The experience of X's presentation to S is sufficient. Alston's frequent example is that seeing a house is different than a memory of that same house. He would experience different phenomena if he closed his eyes and thought of a house and then opened his eyes and saw that house presented in experience. Thus,

Alston distinguishes the presentation of phenomena perceived from any interpretation of what is given. To perceive a house as "directly presented to one's experience" is not the same as interpreting experience as manifesting a house.[37] With his argument for the justification of beliefs about objects presented in perceptual experience in place, Alston proceeds to make the case that the same theory can be used to justify religious beliefs.

Alston must argue for a strong similarity between the way God is perceived and the way everyday objects like tables, chairs, and houses are perceived if perceptions of God are to be perceptions as he has defined the term. But making such a connection is not a straightforward process because any argument for similarities between sensory and nonsensory perceptions of God will be controversial, save the possibility of God appearing as an ordinary object of perception like a burning bush. Nonetheless, given the theory of appearing, Alston locates a similarity at the heart of both kinds of perception: in both cases perceived objects are presented to subjects. As far as presentation is concerned, God can appear just like a chair in the sense that subjects become aware and convinced about the reality of an object being presented.[38] Crucial for his argument is the claim that the possibility of God's presentation does not depend on anyone knowing the mechanisms that could be involved in that presentation.

Not every cause is perceived in the experience produced. For example, planes often cause vapor trails in the sky that can be seen in the absence of the physical presence of the planes. Thus, it would seem a direct realist such as Alston who wants to argue that *God* is perceived, rather than God's effects, needs to account for the right kind of causal connection. However, Alston understands this line of questioning as problematic. No one type of causal connection is adequate for all experiences. Basic sense perceptions like seeing and feeling involve such different causal contributions that firsthand experience of seeing and feeling something is needed before it can be determined what object was causally connected to the perception. "We have no resources for doing it the other way around, first determining the specific causal requirement and then picking out objects seen on the basis of what satisfies that requirement."[39] Therefore, the possibility that God is not the cause of a perception of God cannot be the grounds for ruling out that God really is perceived. Valid perception of an object appearing as so-and-so comes before determining causal relations for that object appearing. So, with an argument for the possibility that perceptual experiences of God can occur, Alston goes on to argue that such experiences can justifiably lead to beliefs about God.

Supposed perceptions of God naturally give rise to beliefs about God. Beliefs about the nature and activity of God can be generated just like beliefs concerning the nature and activity of birds presented in experience. Justified beliefs about God being or doing something arise in virtue of subjects perceiving God being or doing something within a perceptual experience. Alston defines such beliefs as manifestation beliefs, or "M-beliefs."[40] These are beliefs that God is doing something or perceived as having a property in relation to the subject to which God is manifest. However, in terms of justifying beliefs about God, critics could rightly note that many people who perceive God already believed in God's reality beforehand. Alston has a response to this concern, a concern that people do not typically raise about daily sense perceptions: "To be sure, those who perceive God as loving, powerful, and so on, typically believed that God is so characterized long before they had that experience. But the same is true of sense perception, where my 50,000th look at my house doesn't generate any new beliefs."[41] Therefore, beliefs about God being or doing something can be generated or reinforced by perceptual religious experiences in which divine objects appear to subjects. The cognitive significance of these religious experiences is that their phenomenal character, regardless of whether God exists or not, is simply a matter of whether it seems to be the case to a subject that God appears as being or doing something. For such realism to hold in cases of religious experience, there must be a strong analogy between these two kinds of experience. The crucial test for Alston's proposal is whether sense perception involves interpretation. If it does, then his hope of justifying religious beliefs based on direct perception is stopped before it can get started because it relies on similarity between perception in religious experience and *direct* sense perception.

Nathaniel Barrett and Wesley Wildman have critiqued Alston's theory of appearing in favor of a theory they term "dynamic engagement." They argue Alston's one-to-one correspondence between felt qualities and objective quantities ignores the genuine role of the subject in perception. Against Alston, Barrett and Wildman argue that subjects actively explore environments through a process including substantial contributions from the subjects.[42] Interpretations connected to a larger context of other interpreted perceptions play a dominant role in structuring subject-object relations. Perception, rather than the passive presentation of objects to subjects, is formed by a subject's dynamic engagement with an environment. That is, experience is devoid of content, including the presentation of something as being or doing so-and-so, unless there is interaction between a perceiver and the world. Perception in this framework is an active process involving the subject, not merely the passive reception of presented objects.

Barrett and Wildman contrast their dynamic account with what they call Alston's "instantaneous snapshot" approach. The instant presentation of a phenomenon to someone amounts to a snapshot presented as a complete picture to a passive subject. They are correct that Alston emphasizes reception while downplaying intention, which is understandable given his focus on phenomenal concepts. Alston states as much himself: "A *phenomenal concept* is a concept of the intrinsic qualitative distinctness of a way of appearing. When I use 'red' in a phenomenal sense in saying that something looks red, I am simply recording the qualitative distinctness of the way it visually appears to me, and that's all. I am saying nothing about its continuing powers and proclivities, its entanglements with other things, its intrinsic nature, or anything else that goes beyond the visually sensible character of its look."[43] In other words, Alston rejects the argument that there can be no such thing as unmediated or uninterpreted experience. Advances in cognitive science have shown Alston's passive understanding of perception cannot stand.

Living organisms interacted with environments before complex perception mechanisms evolved. Interaction with an environment actually drives the evolutionary development of more complex perceptual systems in organisms.[44] Conscious sense perception is something that arose from and depends on the proper functioning of unconscious instinctual behavior and basic motor patterns.[45] When perception does occur, contrasts created by an individual's focus become part of the perceptual experience so that verification of initial perceptions depends on continued engagement with the environment. Regarding perceptions of color, experiments with projections of black, white, and gray checkerboard patterns have produced multicolored images according to individuals' reports of their perceptions.[46] In such experiments, subjects were clearly not passively letting the phenomena fall on them without dynamic engagement impacting perception. Barrett and Wildman take this line of thinking and use it to directly counter Alston's frequent use of the color red in support of his argument.

If red appears distinctly, as in a specific shade of red, it needs to be marked off from borderline cases of other shades and other colors. The perceiving subject would need to actively engage an environment and compare shades of color for any one color to be presented clearly. However, Alston believes qualitative distinctness arrives automatically with the sense of relating to an object presented in experience. The details of perception arrive all at once according to his argument. As soon as something is presented in experience, every detail of its nature perceived in the presentation is present as well. No interpretation extended through time is necessary because all the details are present immediately. Barrett and Wildman point out that reducing presentation to the distinctiveness of appearances unravels the presentational character of experience. "Presentational character requires more than the positive feeling of distinctiveness and the absence of conscious effort; it requires a positive feeling of the dynamic character of what appears, *and this cannot be given by any content that arrives all at once, no matter how distinctive its qualitative character may be.*"[47] Presentation, despite what Alston claims, includes involvement with what is presented. Seeing something in certain respects, interpreting it somehow, is necessary for seeing it at all.

Perception implies judgment. To see a house as red is already to see it as something rather than something else. René van Woudenberg argues that Alston cannot get away with denying this something as something structure plays no role in his account of perception as appearing. To perceive something as something is not an explanation added to perceptual experience. To perceive some red thing as an apple is to interpret some appearance of a red object as an apple. In religious experience, to perceive God as being or doing something is to interpret the object being or doing something as God. "For the minimal conceptualist will at least hold that in mystical perception, God is being perceived *as* God…. And, surely, in Alston's paradigm cases God is being *identified* as God."[48] Van Woudenberg's rhetorical strategy reveals what Alston really means by conceptualization or interpretation; he thinks they are elements above and beyond perception. However, in so construing interpretation Alston has misconstrued the very nature of perception. Interpretation is not an endeavor apart from perception by which individuals try to prove the existence of something already presented in experience. Rather, it is immersed in perception because it presupposes an appearance for there to be any identification. Barrett and Wildman rely on the work of Alva Noë to show why this is the case and correct Alston's mistake.

Instead of perceiving the details of any perceptual landscape at once, the details focused on are perceived while the rest of the scene remains vague. This is a well-documented scientifically established fact.[49] The way rods and cones work in conjunction with saccades of the eyes results in clear perceptions of the objects focused on as well as vague content perceived at the fringes of perception but not clearly understood as anything specific. Noë calls this vague content "virtual" as opposed to completely illusionary. Naming the content virtual means vague details are experienced and, being vague, are available for exploration and determination. However, that determination only happens through a temporally extended process.[50] Colors like red are never experienced in abstracted isolation on their own. The contrast with other colors noticed by a subject actively engaging an environment constitutes objects as they are perceived. Alston's passive understanding of perception is correct in one respect, however. Subjects are presented with objects and are thus not creating reality out of their imaginations. Everyone engaged in this debate is a realist. However, perception never occurs all at once, but instead occurs through a continuous exploration of vague content. This exploration need not be intentional. Saccades of the eyes are not necessarily consciously controlled, but interpretive exploration of an environment must involve a dynamic interplay between subject and environment. Such necessity is a direct refutation of Alston's direct passive realism. This negative conclusion regarding Alston's theory of appearing is even more problematic for perceptions of God.

If interpretation is not allowed a role in identifying objects perceived as God, then religious experiences would actually fail to produce any perceptions. Since Alston's justification of M-beliefs depends on the viability of extending a theory of appearing regarding sense perception into nonsensory religious experience, a justification of religious beliefs based on perceptions of God is brought to a halt before it can get going since the theory of appearing is false. Alston's argument for phenomenal concepts results in perceptual experiences so isolated that they undermine the very objects he means to defend. Just like in purely philosophical arguments, once the subjective human element is admitted as necessary in explanations, direct realism, in this case the direct realism of God, quickly fades away. As in philosophy, some theologians decided to take constructivism and run with it based on such failures.

Realism versus Constructivism in Theology

Unlike theologians who look for meaning in universal features of experience to which theology can then relate, or conservative approaches seeking literal factual references in the Bible, Hans Frei and George Lindbeck embrace the role of constructivism. Their work led in no small part to the postliberal neo-orthodox approach to theology. Rather than seeking to explain objective divine perceptions, they promote the primacy of the biblical narrative. Narrative is more important than experience of a reality in such an approach. Lindbeck's *The Nature of Doctrine* presents religion as a cultural linguistic enterprise against those who argue it is about understanding experiences or making propositional claims about reality.[51] He understands the narrative of a religion as shaping the cultural and linguistic world in which believers find meaning. Theology should concern itself with using those internal rules to find the meaning present in them—no outside sources needed. "The reasonableness of a religion is largely a function of its assimilative powers, of its ability to provide an intelligible interpretation *in its own terms* of the varied situations and realities adherents encounter."[52] A massive problem with this approach is that it provides no means for insiders to meet any modern challenges to their beliefs. Either you "get" the rules of the Christian narrative or you do not. As the world rapidly moves past the worldview of that narrative, to be content with such a theological enterprise seems naïve at best and, at worst, doomed. Any attempt to give an account of one's faith in this linguistic approach will be presented in terms practically nobody not already on the inside will be able to accept. Besides these walled off cities on a hill not being how actual communities, religious or otherwise, behave in the world, the nonreferential depiction of belief should be insulting to the majority of those it supposedly describes.

The same debate between realism and constructivism in philosophy of religion and theology could be construed in terms of the prior generation, as Karl Barth and Paul Tillich disagreed as to whether seeking extranarrative reference for Christianity is its saving grace or among the worst sins possible. Robert Neville argues that they conceive very different starting points and goals for Christian theology, privileging either religious identity or truth.[53] Barth does theology in a narrative form that privileges the Christian identity. The history of the Christian narrative enacted by God is its singular subject.[54] That story is to be accepted and clarified, not criticized and modified. Such theology will serve the identities of people who already accept the Christian story very well. Christianity need not justify its truth. Theology for Barth is therefore autonomous. It needs no reason beyond revelation and no common ground with other ways of life.[55] The "given truth" of Christianity in revelation is all that concerns him.

Tillich, conversely, focuses on truth in religion over identity. Truth is not obtained if theologians only refer to aspects of a narrative without knowing whether they are true. Tillich's position is that you have to make a case for religious claims. To do this, you also need to know knowledge outside the narrow realm of theology. One's religious identity is not settled by a narrative, but contingent upon what is found after investigating knowledge in other disciplines.[56] The arbitrariness Barth embraces is a problem for Tillich. Putting forth a narrative and only accepting someone as Christian if they fall within the parameters of that narrative can appear parochial and uninteresting to anyone not already invested in the story. Furthermore, it does not consider possibly valid alternatives. Besides not seriously considering other religions, Barth neglects the fact that money, politics, and other forms of social capital are the ultimate concern of many people.[57] In refusing to engage with those concerns and the world in which they exist, Barth paradoxically makes Christianity, which he deems true for everyone, among the most parochial and potentially irrelevant institutions.

Granted, to insiders, revelation will be anything but arbitrary. However, Barth's way of doing theology still reflects arbitrary choices he does not acknowledge. He does not think theology has anything to do with other disciplines, but ignores assumptions of Greek philosophy built into the Gospel accounts of Jesus that he accepts as revelation. Barth admits no such external entanglement.[58] He also pretends nobody else shares similar understandings of revelation, God, or religion. These assumptions might have been revealed as such if he had engaged in comparative theology with other religions. For Barth, theology is to correspond with the story of the birth, death, and resurrection of Jesus Christ. Theologians should clarify the meaning of that story, and then their work will be done.[59] For Tillich, conversely, a desire for truth puts pressure on any narrative. He argues that anyone with a relevant perspective on theological topics is welcome to weigh in on their veracity.[60] Furthermore, he understands that a key feature of the claims of the Christian message is their purported ability to speak to the current historical situation. Jesus came to us in this world. If theologians are to continue speaking his message to the world they need to know what is going on in that world. They must speak *to* the world rather than *at* it. To achieve this goal, Tillich developed his method of correlation, a method that could not be more opposed to that of Barth.

Tillich's method of correlation asserts that for Christians to genuinely engage others with their message that message must be true *for them*. This method implies two dimensions. Imaginatively, the message must engage non-Christians. But those same people must also be capable of interpreting that engaging message as true, or they will reject the message. This second dimension is not found in Barth's work, a key weakness present in his theology that is not found in Tillich's. If the message is not interpreted as true, religious symbols can be reinterpreted so as to be engaging again, according to Tillich.[61] He focused on making classical symbols sing for a new generation. If a symbol is not true in a situation, his system contains the resources for allowing the imaginative reinterpretation or creation of new symbols. For

Tillich there are no clear and easy boundaries for Christian identity in the way that there are for Barth. The message of the Bible should be expressed through acquaintance with psychology, science, and the arts. If this is not done, whoever does not buy into the Christian narrative and Barth's assurance that it can stand on its own will be left in the cold without a God.

Barth could reply that Tillich's approach lacks the coherence and vivacity needed for Christian identity. Barth spells out the requirements for such a unified identity with clarity and force. But once theology is out in the wilderness of the world, as Tillich advocates, who has the authority to decide whether what is found will serve the needs of the church? For Barth revelation comes from God to us, and we have nothing to contribute. We simply accept what God gives. The elements to be accepted are not merely the events of the birth, death, and resurrection of Jesus as recorded in the Gospels, but propositional claims that become doctrine.[62] God is revealed as triune as the Father sent the Son to establish a community of faith through the Holy Spirit. Jesus is a hypostatic union of God and human. As human, he died in our place. As God, he took humanity up to God in his resurrection. Awareness of God and all theological doctrines come from God in revelation. God set the parameters of what in the world can be used to relate to God when the human being Jesus, who was also fully God, was judged and killed to save the rest of humanity from God's judgment. That is the only knowledge Barth needs for Christian theology, and it is only relevant for theology because God made it so. With what authority could Tillich investigate the world then decide some findings are relevant for theology? Tillich would simply accept this criticism and say one's Christian identity is built piecemeal depending on the outcome on critical inquiry into other disciplines. If accepting calcified narrative works for Barth, great. The rest of us can journey onward and do our best.

Beyond the Impasse?

What is the point to take away from this chapter? Both realism and constructivism fly in the face of common sense. To slightly exaggerate the matter to make this point, realists claim that everything depends on the world. There is no role for perceiving subjects other than to get out of the way and let the world impress itself upon perceiving subjects. Anything else we do will distort the world's reality. Constructivists say everything is us, everything has a touch of humanity. There is no direct encounter with the world, or maybe we even make up the world. Apart from our construction of reality, there is nothing. Realism violates commonsense experiences of incorrect interpretations. What is clear and "obvious" is often revealed, upon further investigation, to be entirely different than it was thought to be. Error, and progress in light of errors, has revealed the role of human subjects in learning what is true of reality. Our thoughts inevitably play a role in understanding reality because we simply cannot get out of our own heads and compare thought to reality from some neutral perspective.[63] Immanuel Kant was correct that thoughts have an inevitable role in constituting experience. Even if we desire to know the world as it really is, we cannot leave our thoughts behind. But constructivism equally violates common sense. Phenomena that reveal the errors of our thoughts are often unwanted, coming unexpectedly from the world. They force themselves upon us and we have the choice to either adjust our thoughts to account for such stubborn facts or irresponsibly ignore them. Reality pushes back upon wild interpretations and makes them all but impossible to continue holding.

Paul Thagard has recently tried to refocus this debate in a way that points toward the right direction, moving beyond an either/or binary to seeing the points in *both* realism and constructivism, amid their many flaws. He argues that "if there is a world independent of representations of it, as historical evidence suggests, then the aim of representation should be to describe the world, not just relate to other representations. My argument does not refute the coherence theory, but shows that it implausibly gives minds too large a place in constituting truth."[64] He is correct. He does not deny that the human mind has a role in understanding reality and determining what is true. He just denies it has a fully determinative role. Neither does he deny the role of constructed representations. He just denies that they are of something other than the world. Realists could respond that no constructions are involved in knowing the world, and constructivists could argue coherence is with other propositions, not with the world. Such responses would be recasting the debate this chapter has been summarizing rather than learning from it. Learning from that endless debate and moving on is the goal of the next chapter. Taking a cue from Thagard, it is possible to find a third philosophical way that has learned from the promises and perils that have been described. That third way in this argument is represented by Charles S. Peirce and the American pragmatists.

Pragmatists admit conventional constructed interpretations of reality, but embrace them as means of engaging real objects, objects that would be less well known, or unknown, without those constructions. Human contributions are not a barrier to reality, but a window to it. If they get us nowhere, provide no traction for progress or feedback for improvement, then they are revealed as false constructions. There is no similar progress when internal language games determine what is real. The pragmatic perspective is also more honest about the attitudes of both scientists and religious believers—their beliefs refer in some sense to that which they seem to refer and do so in a way that is true and meaningful, unveiling actual information about reality. Against the use of epistemology to deny that reference is possible, in religion or elsewhere, or to deny any positive role for construction in knowledge, pragmatists affirm that real reference is possible without assuming that human subjects play nothing but a passive role.

2 | Beyond the Impasse

CHARLES S. PEIRCE AND
AMERICAN PRAGMATISM

PURSUING THE RIGHT METHOD OF THINKING means everything for Peirce. Using excellent tools inappropriately will not get anyone very far in any field. He begins from an empirical standpoint, but unlike the British empiricists, he affirms fallibilism over and against skepticism. Beliefs can be mistaken but realizing that fact is an invitation to correct mistaken judgments rather than be pessimistic about our ability to know anything beyond phenomenal appearances. Furthermore, unlike logical positivists who also affirm empiricism and the ability to know the real world, he does not reduce all meaning to sense data. Rather than basing philosophy on science as a means of eliminating most philosophical questions, Peirce accepts this basis as a means of reaching better answers to those questions. To mitigate against individual idiosyncrasies and errors, he also argues for the necessity of a community of inquiry. Within community, rather than in isolation, is where inquiry takes place. By being fallible and responsive to corrective pressures from the world, a community with shared interests will be able to arrive at truth in the long run. The progressively improving interpretations of a community and the real world they are interpreting are intricately woven together. As the interpretations improve, they will gain general applicability. The community will gain better predictive power and self-control when investigating any phenomenon.

"Paper" Doubt and Groundless Grounds

Peirce was extremely critical of artificially manufactured "paper" Cartesian doubt. Even Descartes knew his quest of radically bringing all knowledge into question was something impractical and unnecessary for daily life.[1] From Peirce's perspective, it is absurd to question someone's beliefs or the right to hold those beliefs, much less your own, until they become problematic. His understanding of habits and fallibilism allows him to bypass philosophical skepticism. Fallibilists expect cognitive errors that worry the skeptic and lead some to think realism is mistaken. Fallibilists even arguably welcome errors as opportunities for progress. Conversely, Descartes believed the possibility of one belief being incorrect was reason enough to be skeptical regarding all beliefs. Fallibilism, however, is an attitude that recognizes all beliefs are formed on the basis of a limited degree of evidence and could be shown to be mistaken through the uncovering of further evidence. Peirce is an extreme embodiment of this attitude, going so far as stating "I will not, therefore, admit that we know anything whatever with *absolute certainty.*"[2] No judgments belong to an epistemic class that can rule out the possibility of error.

Because there is no blank slate from which inquiry begins, everyone is always already working with ways of thinking and beliefs about the world that have more or less worked, their existing habits. Because they have worked, there is nothing to doubt. There is no choice but to start philosophy with all the opinions and prejudices brought to any question, not with universal doubt, according to Peirce. Preferences and already formed ideas cannot be questioned then removed just by saying such should be the case. His response to such skeptical suggestions always remained the same: "There must be real and living doubt, and without this all discussion is idle."[3] His argument takes the following form:[4]

1 The starting point in philosophy involves beliefs already held in daily inquiries,

and

2 the belief that we are not in the skeptical situation is one of those beliefs,

therefore

3 the challenge of the skeptic is outside the realm of the accepted beliefs that cannot easily be abandoned and is not challenging for that reason.

The reasoning behind the last point is as follows:

1. We cannot force doubt on beliefs already held by an act of will.
2. Thus doubt has an external origin, which is surprise.
3. That knowledge is denied by a skeptical argument is not surprising.

Doubt cannot be introduced artificially, though it does arise. It comes from the irritation of what Peirce calls Secondness, the brute shock of unknown facts in the world. Once that irritation of doubt occurs, the existing habit can no longer survive and the task is now to move from doubt to belief once again. Habits can be out of tune with an environment. New beliefs that bring new habits can solve the irritation. Closing the gap between doubt and new working beliefs is the start of inquiry for Peirce. "The irritation of doubt causes a struggle to attain a state of belief. I shall term this struggle *inquiry*."[5] We always carry working theories with us, expectations against which surprise is measured, and when surprise is registered, true inquiry begins.

For something to appear as new and unknown, it must be contrasted with a background of settled knowledge. The scientific impulse is to reconcile these two, as the search for knowledge begins by realizing an incorrect expectation as such. Contrast with that existing expectation is crucial. Irregularity itself does not call out for an explanation. Neither does it necessarily have an obvious explanation or need one. To illustrate what he means, Peirce notes that we do not normally ask for a special explanation for the configuration of random trees in a forest because we are not shocked to find them.[6] Since we are not surprised to find them, we do not go on to craft a hypothesis explaining their configuration. There is no clash with expectations, so we move on with life.

In his argument, Peirce is relying on a difference between positive reasons to doubt and positive reasons in favor of beliefs. Positive reasons to doubt beliefs would lead to "living" doubt. However, the same is not true for a situation in which positive reasons to believe are missing. Given that Peirce thinks infallible beliefs do not exist, and philosophy always begins in the context of many accepted prejudices, the certainty with which any belief is reached is overriding except in cases where there is positive reason to doubt.[7] "The only effect which real things have is to cause belief, for all the sensations which they excite emerge into consciousness in the form of beliefs."[8] This claim does not license dogmatically adhering to a given set of beliefs forever, since his fallibilism means better alternatives should always be entertained and accepted when necessary. But when entertaining such alternatives, using the right method for once again establishing belief is of utmost importance.

Peirce understands our lives as governed by existing patterns and habits, and only through their irritation do we gradually discover valid rules of inference. We transition from habit to self-control. Comparing methods is therefore important in determining the best means of fixing our beliefs and gaining that control. Peirce considers the methods of tenacity, authority, a priori, and of science.[9] Tenacity is an individual method that does not involve a community. It focuses on clinging to one's opinions and refusing to admit any counterevidence that would challenge those opinions. It provides a strong sense of security, but is highly vulnerable to social manipulation (e.g., fundamentalism in religion) and becoming so out of touch with reality that it is unsustainable. Authority concerns determining the methods and goals of inquiry by imposing control, often through religious and political institutions. Peirce is especially harsh on those who would settle theological questions by authority, viewing that as perhaps the largest roadblock to inquiry. In either case, politics or religion, the greater the imposing power, the more lasting the forms of control, but the more arbitrary the results. The a priori method is opposite the authoritative one, settling opinion through reason instead of social control. But Peirce argues that supposedly universal truths reached through mere use of reason are always impacted by personal taste. Peirce also rejects immediate intuitions, arguing instead that all reasoning starts with empirical traction with reality.

All three methods Peirce rejects share a common feature: they fail to point to something external to the self or community. They reveal nothing about the nature of reality. Tenacity holds on to a beloved narrative rather than facing a reality that may overturn that story. Authority tries to enforce a narrative through power, but nature can resist control. The a priori method is not even interested in checking its claims with reality. All three methods stand opposed to truth-seeking as Peirce understands it. For Peirce, someone concerned with truth would "not in the least be wedded to his conclusions; he stands ready to abandon one or all as soon as experience opposes them."[10] Thus, Peirce turns to science, a method "by which our beliefs may be caused by nothing human, but by some external permanency—by something upon which our thinking has no effect."[11] Science helps move beyond mere opinion. It admits right and wrong usage of terms. In tenacity, personal preference defines what is true. In authority, the powerful define rightness. But science admits independent constraints on opinions. Reality has features we did not create.

One reason the right method is so important to Peirce is that he affirms *tychism,* or the reality of chance in the universe. Peirce affirms genuine novelty in reality, not just due to human ignorance at any moment but because reality contains chance elements.[12] "The premises of Nature's own processes are all the independent uncaused elements of fact that go to make up the variety of nature, which the necessitarian supposes to have been all in existence from the foundation of the world, but which the Tychist supposes are continually receiving new accretions."[13] Reality is not settled and waiting to be found, but is continually growing. Without the right method and the ability to consciously control hypotheses about novel developments, reality will leave a community of inquiry behind. This right method is also not given, but obtained through intelligent effort. What is given are unconscious habits that we only later learn to control. It is no coincidence that Peirce was developing his philosophy as Darwin was initiating a revolution in biology. The development of evolutionary theory is a wonderful example of the transition from a habitual understanding to a new theory provoked by problems with that previously accepted set of beliefs. A way of summarizing this point is that reasonableness is obtained and grows.

Ideas that work to settle a doubtful situation and reestablish habitual and working understandings do so because they exist in a world that tests them through causal connections. Peirce disagrees with the British empiricists. Ideas are not copies of sensations. Rather, they are interpretations that have already transformed sensations into instruments for the one doing the interpreting. It may then seem odd that Peirce defines reality as that which is unimpacted by us. However, while beliefs are interpretations, not mere copies, of what we experience, those interpretations are constrained by independent objects. Combining these two claims means there is ideal correspondence between human methods, when pursued in a community, and reality. Final beliefs will be independent of any individual. A correspondence theory of truth is attached to a theory of consensus reached over time. The community is the "place" of knowledge, so to speak. But for this knowledge to work, for it to count as knowledge, it must have traction with the world being investigated.

This form of inquiry is about determining what conceived effects are relevant to the objects being investigated. Our understanding of them then moves toward completion in the future as we develop concepts, predict effects, and test them in a community over time. Peirce's well-known pragmatic maxim presents the truth of any subject matter as follows: "Consider what effects, which might conceivably have practical bearings, we conceive the object of our conception to have. Then, our conception of these effects is the whole of our conception of the object."[14] This sounds like the constructivism examined in the previous chapter. But unlike constructivists, the possible effects Peirce has in mind are not just human creations. The maxim immediately drives one to investigate reality as a test of all concepts.

One example Peirce gives of the pragmatic maxim at work is the hardness of diamonds. What "hardness" means is that when you go into the world and find a diamond, you will not be able to scratch it with many other objects. Hardness is not defined antecedently. Rather, we try to scratch something. Then we know if a diamond is hard in addition to all other members of its class, by way of induction.[15] This could lead to nominalism, a diamond never scratched could not be known to be hard, but that is not Peirce's position. He includes the important modifier "might conceivably" in his maxim. Things that would-be can be spoken of as real for Peirce. It is a fact that an unscratched diamond would still resist being scratched by many objects.[16] He also does not want to reduce his maxim to psychology. We all have our preferences, but if we hold on to them instead of developing our beliefs through controlled inquiry, reality will push back on our preferences and force a change. Psychology is not the end and reading the maxim as nothing but psychological is a common popular misuse of "pragmatism."

Realism for Peirce is therefore more like a whirlwind, a nexus of concepts readjusting themselves in order to be true, than it is like a solid rock, the view that "real" claims about the world will be forever settled. He compares realism to walking on a bog, or what could be called having groundless grounds. "It is walking upon a bog, and can only say, this ground seems to hold for the present. Here I will stay till it begins to give way."[17] The important thing to note in defense of realism is that theories are upset *by experience*. Unlike constructivists who take the imperfection of theories to be a lesson about the social construction of reality, holding up our thoughts as barriers to any independently real world, knowledge for Peirce is *constructed* and *reconstructed* when experience *of the real world forces the revision*. Neither is Peirce's realism a Cartesian castle steadily and permanently built piece by piece. Anything could potentially be disrupted in the future.

Triads in Human Inquiry and the Natural World

Peirce's epistemology is grounded in representing external facts in a way that navigates past endless debates between realism and constructivism. In his Cognition Series of articles intended for the *Journal of Speculative Philosophy* he gives an account of mind and reality based on his metaphysical categories, developing a basis for an objective empirical philosophy. His basic point is that everything is an interpretation of an interpretation of an interpretation; nature is perfused with signs. We know reality by interpreting it, and interpretations involve signs, the object to which the signs refer, and the respects with which the object is engaged through the sign by an interpreter. His metaphysical categories of Firstness, Secondness, and Thirdness mark the *real* features of everything found in the world. The three categories are the general features of reality. His method of attacking skepticism reveals how triadic interpretive communication is basic to human inquiry and the reality found in that inquiry. All thinking takes place with iconic, indexical, and symbolic signs, a triadic structure also found in the structure of the categories, and thus the world.

Truth is intimately related to inquiry for Peirce, who spent his life developing a semiotic theory of meaning-making. We arrive at truth through inquiry when using the right method of interpretation, and interpretation involves the aforementioned symbolic, indexical, and iconic reference. For each sign there is an object, that to which the sign refers, and the effect the sign has on an interpreter as a sign, the interpretant. Interpretants are always another sign or set of signs, the respects in which the meaning of an object is conveyed in the act of interpretation. This means the immediate object of a sign is another sign, while the dynamic object is the real thing in the world being signified.[18] In other words, for Peirce the object of a sign "presupposes an acquaintance in order to convey further information concerning it."[19] Objects have to be capable of being interpreted in certain determinate respects by interpreters, which is the role of interpretants, if any information about them is to be conveyed. This is the critique that Barrett and Wildman leveled against Alston. Only by interpreting something in certain respects are interpretants able to carry across any features of reality to interpreters.

Icons relate to objects in terms of likeness, sharing common material qualities. Indices relate to their objects directly, indicating what caused them, like a weather vane indicating the direction of wind or the mercury in a thermometer rising. Symbols have their relation to objects determined by specific characters they are given for general use. They bring to mind their general objects to interpreters.[20] Icons, indices, and symbols also frequently overlap. A stop sign can refer indexically to a specific sign in a specific location, but it can also refer symbolically to a driving law to be followed wherever they are found. While symbolic meaning depends on cultural conventions, signs with iconic reference are taken to be exactly like the object they represent in some respect. As a result, it is possible to conflate icons with that to which they are meant to refer.

A street map represents a certain area of land, but the representation becomes false if its practical purpose is forgotten and the map is taken to literally exhaust the representation of that land. A street map intended to inform drivers may not indicate vegetation or certain topographical features deemed irrelevant to the main purpose of indicating the layout of city streets. However, plants and changes in elevation are certainly part of the real location represented on the map. Icons can gloss over features not important for their intended purpose. Indices can lead to valuable conclusions about the referent to which the signs point in a way that moves beyond simply cohering in a one-to-one fashion. Tree leaves moving along the ground indicate causal relations between those leaves and wind. A wedding ceremony is also an index. It is not a literal union of two people's bodies, though decorations on top of wedding cakes are often iconic representations of the couple. Rather, like a finger pointing toward an object, a wedding indexically indicates real changes occurring in the lives of the partners. A wedding is also a symbol, involving many socially constructed features that vary from culture to culture. Symbols include icons (there are two people being married) and indices (marriage is causally changing the lives of those two people), but the full meaning of symbols is lost if the triadic nature of how they communicate meaning is forgotten and reduced to the level of icons or indices (two people having their lives changed by being literally united).

All such signification of experience is possible due to interpretants, signs of any sort taken by an interpreter to characterize a referent somehow. If objects of inquiry cannot be experienced in some respects, for example, silver, sharp, hard, then they cannot be experienced at all. Furthermore, signs are not like settled monads just waiting to be discovered and forever known. An interpretant is itself a sign that relates to other signs that through their relations carry across meaning to the interpreter in the complex interrelated web they create. The relation of interpretants means no sign can have its meaning set forever. It may need modification when signs to which it relates change. A change in time, place, or understanding can change one interpretant with ramifications for other signs understood in relation to it. Again, a Cartesian building-block picture of the universe is rejected. Truth and meaning are found through interpretation at specific times and places. Different understandings *of reality* will emerge as time and place change.

The epistemological process through which we arrive at beliefs reveals something about the truth we seek in that process. Peirce rejects simple correspondence theories of truth, insofar as they seek to relate truth to a thing-in-itself that supposedly lies *outside* our experience of it. Truth and falsity are matters of corresponding with a real world for him, but can only be defined in terms of doubt and belief, the uncomfortable and unexpected disruption of habits and their consequent resolution in true beliefs. Knowing a proposition is true means knowing its consequences for doubt and belief, knowing what perceptual occasions would satisfy or disappoint. He calls the simplistic version of correspondence that he rejects the "transcendence" theory of truth because in it truth transcends experience, making the true understanding of anything so irrelevant to human inquiries that nobody will be able to determine the truth or falsity of anything.[21] In this regard, he agrees with constructivist critiques of realism. Since we know not what to expect in the "transcendence" theory, we have no way to experience doubt or belief. Truth as correspondence, positively understood, becomes the aim of inquiry for Peirce, but as something that a community will arrive at in the long run.[22] It is that which would never lead to disappointment, to further doubts prompting further inquiry.

Peirce's semiotics are embedded within his method of inquiry, which involves three stages of abductive, deductive, and inductive reasoning. The abductive phase generates explanatory hypotheses for unexpected experiences one has of the world, with the deductive phase building logical elaborations based on those hypotheses. Induction is a corrective means for the first two steps, as future experience will confirm or falsify the initial explanatory hypotheses or the deductive elaborations of them, or both. There is nothing new in explicative knowledge. Deduction spells out the consequences already contained in a theory and implies a probabilistic induction by which examples of those consequences are sought. Abduction is the only form of reasoning that goes beyond the given, as the imagination is involved in explaining unexpected yet inexpungable experiences. It involves a jump from a novel experience in the world to its explanation.

Abductive inferences provide hypotheses for testing. As Peirce describes their working, "We find some very curious circumstance, which would be explained by the supposition that it was a case of a certain general rule, and thereupon adopt that supposition."[23] We observe surprising fact X. We note that if A were true, X would be an expected regular fact. Therefore, there is reason to believe A.[24] Peirce sometimes uses abduction and retroduction interchangeably as the only forms of reasoning that introduce new knowledge. Whereas induction is the act of concluding from some observed cases that cases not yet examined will be similar, abduction concludes that there is something different and real from which something observed would result. Induction moves from particular to general law. Abduction moves from effect to cause. Their difference is one of classifying like things versus explaining unlike things. Abduction moves from puzzling observations to a theory that would explain them.[25] It is as bold and perilous as it is exciting.

While Peirce often writes about abduction and retroduction as if they were identical, there are good reasons to distinguish them. If an abductive hypothesis is so bold that it is disproven by a further look at the facts, it can be salvaged by means of retroduction. A novel hypothesis that is found to be problematic in light of new information can become fruitful again when appropriately modified through retroduction. Abduction allows making a wildly imaginative guess, and if components of such a guess are refuted then retroduction allows the game to continue, so to speak. If necessary, an entire idea can be abandoned for another abductive hypothesis, but as long as a new hypothesis with testable deductive consequences can be formed in its place, inquirers have the right to play the game. The defeat of a hypothesis is not the end. It is an indication that other routes should be considered when further developing that hypothesis.

The natural world, like progressive communities of inquiry, is also an evolving system of signs growing in generality and self-control. The growth of concrete reasonableness is Peirce's way of referencing the real world, of taking on the general character of signification as the laws of nature are established and we learn about them. The field of biosemiotics, dealt with in more detail in chapter 8, lends some scientific backing to this assertion by Peirce.[26] Both the natural world and our interpretations of it develop self-control, become reasonable. This concept of real generals is important for understanding Peirce on these points, and needs some unpacking.

Generals are entities indeterminate with respect to some property. A triangle could be obtuse, acute, or isosceles. The interpreter finishes the determination. Generality is also not vagueness, something having a determinate character of which we are just ignorant. Edward Moore presents generality as an empirical hypothesis in the following way: "There are real objects which have properties which extend over a range of interpretations any one of which may be selected by an observer. Such objects are real general objects."[27] He appeals to the Lorentz equation, the length of light varying by the velocity of the observer, for support. On the microscopic level, he appeals to the Copenhagen interpretation of quantum mechanics. Another example could be taken from biology. The Baldwin effect shows how gene determination has a range of possibilities that can be affected by environmental factors like temperature and chemicals present. In some species of lizards and turtles, the sex of individuals born depends on ambient temperature in their environment.[28] While it is still debated, the claim that natural kinds are real, not just human constructs, is at least a live option in the philosophy of science.[29] That is precisely one of the ways Peirce raised the issue of generals, by asking whether horse and other natural classes correspond independent of our thought. He answers in the affirmative.[30] Ideas can give existence to individual members of a class, not by conferring material existence upon them, but through the power of bringing about results in the world.

Generals are real through a sort of final causation, as ideas find vehicles for transforming reality. In short, while there are examples of chaotic disruption on this planet and throughout the cosmos, not everything has been the result of blind habit or chance. The order, relations, and laws of the universe indicate that nature is also reasonable, just like our ever-improving significations of it. Unlike constructed subjective generalizations, a real law of nature is an objective generalization from observation supporting verifiable predictions. There is objective reasonableness shaping phenomena, and it has also shaped our own reasoning.[31] The correct method of knowing reality is also embedded in the subject matter of that reality, which exhibits a growing, reasonable, triadic interpretive character.

Just as Peirce affirms the truth of general interpretations of reality, his philosophy moves to describe the general features of that reality. The world of chance and continuity known by communities of inquiry is marked by three general features mentioned previously: Firstness, Secondness, and Thirdness. His paper "On a New List of Categories" lays the groundwork for the relation between his categories and sign usage. The universe evolves toward forms of connection, exhibits self-control as general laws take hold. The categories cannot be reduced to one another, and sign activity cannot take place without reference to the categories. Those three categories relate to possibilities, actualities, and intelligible representation in experience. They also describe the continuous evolution of the universe from Firstness to Thirdness, a process marked by varying degrees of chance, necessity, and mediation. Mere possibility is Firstness without Secondness. Secondness is existence, causation, compulsion. Necessity is Thirdness, rational general necessity.[32] Forms, facts, and relations are the universal categories of reality for Peirce.

His early description of Firstness, Secondness, and Thirdness is expressed in terms of pure feeling or quality, action-reaction, and thinking. Feeling is when something is present to the mind without compulsion or reasoning, which he describes as considering a red color without asking questions about in what determinate thing it is instantiated or even considering its possible pleasantness as a color. However, feelings can be broken by other feelings, like when a sudden noise breaks someone out of a daydream. Such experiences are of Secondness and are proofs of realism. It is brute facticity, cause and reaction, a teacher showing us when our concepts are false, and a teacher Peirce describes as often harsh and indifferent: "Open your mouth and shut your eyes / And I'll give you something to make you wise."[33] While Peirce uses the analogy of a harsh teacher, causal relations in nature are neither good nor bad. They are brute facts. They are forced upon people and resistance is felt. Their unexpected givenness is the proof of a reality not caused by our ideas of it. "Her favorite way of teaching is by means of practical jokes,—the more cruel the better. To describe it more exactly, Experience invariably teaches by means of surprises."[34] Secondness is not yet thinking, however, in which the phenomenon impacting us due to the brute facticity of Secondness are found to be governed by certain rules and behaving in ways that can be anticipated. In Thirdness actions become known as means for bringing about certain results. Understanding entails prediction and control with some degree of regularity.

Peirce is a realist, meaning objects of knowledge are really existing things external to knowers. We are involved in uncovering knowledge about them in a crucial way, but the objects do not depend on us for their existence. Firstness is the quality of being in itself, everything just enjoying the quality of being what it is. Secondness reveals the existence of such objects, while Thirdness relates to knowing those objects. Affirming Thirdness amounts to agreement with Georg W. F. Hegel that thought is part of reality, while Secondness makes it clear that reality is also made of that which thought cannot produce.[35] Secondness is like a common-sense defense of reality, while knowing Secondness through the rational process of forming and testing hypotheses is how we come to fix beliefs about that external reality.

Peirce attempted to clarify the categories by expressing them in terms of each other. All the categories can be described in terms of their Thirdness. This provides feeling, signs of Firstness, action and reaction, signs of Secondness, and learning or mediation, signs of Thirdness. In the form of Secondness we have qualia, or the sheer fact of Firstness as it is alone, relations, or facts of Secondness with others, and signs, or facts of Thirdness indicating others. The categories in terms of Firstness provide Peirce's ontological structure for reality. Firstness is qualitative possibility, Secondness is the reality of independent facts, and Thirdness is relations governing facts.[36] Of the three, Thirdness always seemed to be Peirce's overriding concern.

Thirdness is triadic, meaning connections encountered in experiences are always a matter of Thirdness. Peirce's obsession with Thirdness is indicated by his rejection of the view that reality is just matter bumping into itself without purpose. Prediction, control, and understanding (Thirdness) are more important than individual reaction (Secondness). Perceptions correlate to Firstness and Secondness as both are givens imposed from without. They do not represent. Rather, they are about themselves, and therefore cannot be false. Falsity requires representing something being otherwise in certain respects. Perceptual judgments correlate to Thirdness. They are representations of something and can be false, even if seemingly performed automatically or unconsciously. The sense of color of an object can be separated from the judgment "that is a red car" even if the sense perception and judgment all arrive at once. Comparison of judgments highlights the role of interpretants, requiring "a mediating representation which represents the relate to be a representation of the same correlate which this mediating representation itself represents."[37] It is the role of interpreter to translate foreign interpretations and verify they are the same as her own, to verify two currencies add up to the same amount or that two models of God are really about the same subject matter. Interpretants make signs publicly accessible.

Thirdness unites Firstness and Secondness, but there is an inverse hierarchy of dependence. Firstness depends on nothing else to be what it is. Secondness could not be if not for Firstness from which it emerges. Thirdness needs both Firstness and Secondness to communicate meaning. Peirce's epistemology is antifoundational but his ontology has asymmetrical priority:

> Out of the womb of indeterminacy we must say that there would have come something, by the principle of Firstness, which we may call a flash. Then by the principle of habit there would have been a second flash. Though time would not yet have been, this second flash was in some sense after the first, because resulting from it. Then there would have come other successions ever more and more closely connected, the habits and the tendency to take them ever strengthening themselves, until the events would have been bound together in something like a continuous flow. We have no reason to think that even now time is quite perfectly continuous and uniform in its flow.[38]

Thirdness is essential, but only governs by action, which arises in feeling things in their interaction. Thirdness depends on action (Secondness) and feeling (Firstness). As will be shown, this development from Firstness to

Thirdness led Peirce to identify a cosmic plan in the world, possibly a divine one, even if it can only be vaguely felt.

Possibilities are also real for Peirce. He explicitly connects Firstness to questions of origins and argues that Firstness makes itself manifest in unlimited variety. "Before any comparison or discrimination can be made between what is present, what is present must have been recognized as such, as *it*, and subsequently the metaphysical parts which are recognized by abstraction are attributed to this *it*, but the *it* cannot itself be made a predicate. This *it* is thus neither predicated of a subject, nor in a subject, and accordingly is identical with the conception of a substance."[39] But his "substance" of Firstness will demarcate Peirce from Neoplatonism and its insistence on a primal One beyond the multiplicity of the world. Rather, the qualities of Firstness are free-floating possibilities with no internal structure of purpose or intelligibility. It is in Thirdness that they become conscious to interpreters, purposive in the world, and intelligible to interpreters as such.[40] The relation of Firstness to Thirdness is therefore related to the reality of chance.

All is not determined. Possibilities are not just mental fictions that vanish as causes behind them are discovered. Scholastic realists like Peirce argue they exist objectively. Those who think they are mental constructs only speak of them in the absence of adequate data. But for Peirce there is real novelty. The future is open and tied to our conduct. That future is also available now insofar as we struggle over what will be in that future. We find ourselves before an open future and a partially determined past. Both interpreters and the world they interpret have the status of being "not yet" with traces left in the past and present. Mere description, two-term representational thinking, cannot distinguish a real world and fictional world. Indices are needed to do that. This makes Peirce what Max Fisch calls a "three-category realist."[41] Peirce's theory of signs (icon, index, symbol) and theory of categories (Firstness, Secondness, and Thirdness) are associated with three kinds of facts (an object by itself, two objects in causal relation, and several objects in synthetic relation). The reality of all three categories also comes in three grades: possibility, actuality, and generality. What actually is and has been does not exhaust reality.[42] They are only covering actuality. Whatever would be and can be is also real. The interplay between our partially determined past and open future is also reflected in the relationship between what Pierce called "dynamic" and "immediate" objects.

A sign can be looked at as an object but an object can also be looked at as a sign. Context matters. Robert Corrington points out that if the issue at hand is structures of intelligibility and communication, it is appropriate to use "sign." If there are hidden and dynamic aspects in the situation, use "object." "Objects are 'behind' signs, yet they also live 'in front' of them, goading them toward an increase in scope and meaning."[43] Peirce calls the depth dimension of objects the "dynamic object" and the present aspect the "immediate object."[44] The two grow toward convergence in the infinite long run. Unlike Kant's thing-in-itself, Peirce insists inquiry can get us closer to the true dynamic object. Corrington perfectly captures the interplay between the two aspects. "The dynamic object does not simply 'hang out' awaiting its eschatological appearance, but actually lives as a goad to sign activity, compelling it to honor the antecedent *and* emergent aspects of the object."[45] The sign serves the object by unveiling the actual traits of the object. Signs clear the way for objects to appear. Remaining always and only with the immediate object and focusing on signs only as linguistic constructions prevents reaching into objective structures of reality, without which there is no immediate object. Perhaps surprisingly, given that explaining how it is possible to get closer to the truth about dynamic objects and the real world is the topic at hand, Peirce places anthropocentrism at the heart of his metaphysics.

Not brute force, but reasonableness, love, is at the heart of growth in Peirce's universe. Reasonableness subdues chance and efficient causality with "its sceptre, knowledge, and its globe, love."[46] Out of love comes continuity, growth, and the evolution of Thirdness in the universe. In scientific explanations, the fact that our human minds appear tuned to know nature's mysteries, Peirce locates a testament to the fact that something analogous to human thought is present everywhere in the universe. "The one intelligible theory of the universe is that of objective idealism, that matter is effete mind, inveterate habits becoming physical laws."[47] Objective idealism is the position that the world is real, and to be real is to be part of some experience.[48] As a consequence, Peirce adopts panpsychism to explain the reality of Thirdness. This conclusion that mind was always real and always developing entails a teleological view of the world and led Peirce to affirm a rather traditional form of theism, depending on who you ask.[49]

Peirce's Musings on God

Interpretive inquiry and Peirce's categories are pushed to their limits in his understanding of musement. This is a sort of license to let the mind play, let it wander until it arrives at a satisfying explanation. In the case of God, musement involves pondering the origin of the world of the three categories. This gives the mind the following things to contemplate: mere ideas, brute facts and reactions, and active connections. He speaks of "pure play" as a license to let the mind come up with any and every connection, no matter how implausible, between the three categories. The connections involved in Thirdness are crucial for Peirce, binding otherwise isolated facts together and accounting for the developmental teleology he locates everywhere.[50] He concludes God is a power explaining the categories, especially Thirdness, and their relation. Whatever else God may be, God is real, near, and in communion with the three categories by binding them together.

A sketch of how the universe could be understood as moving toward Thirdness in such a way as to lead Peirce to God is as follows. The situation begins with pure possibility, Firstness, that is active rather than passive. From active potentiality comes existence, Secondness, out of which habits develop. Habits develop into laws of nature, and the entire movement from possibility to controlled behavior shows that chance *and* purpose are needed to explain the universe. A divine mind is an abductive hypothesis, which would explain this purpose, and the affirmation of chance gives Peirce an opening to affirm such a God. Without complete causal determination, with real chance, Peirce can insert his panpsychism and argue that mind is more basic than matter. Final causes related to this mind play a role, along with efficient causes, in bringing the universe together. As a result, the universe exhibits developmental teleology, the growth of reasonableness in the universe. So rather than a God needed to explain the raw existence of the categories, Peirce needs a God to explain their togetherness, the inevitable drive toward Thirdness. Evolutionary divine love leaves its mark on all the categories.

As Corrington summarizes Peirce's somewhat fractured views on God, they are a mix of rather orthodox Trinitarian thinking and panentheism. God is meant to account for the world's possibilities without overruling them. Possibilities that become fact participate in God's dynamic spirit. This way of thinking raises a question. If God does not override possibilities by divine plan, is God free to change and grow with those possibilities? Corrington argues Peirce is divided on this issue, but almost moves toward process theology despite himself. Peirce's God is wedded to the world and lives in all three categories. God participates in Firstness in terms of cosmogenesis, manifests Secondness in terms of eschatology, and empowers Thirdness with the emergence of the good at the end of history.[51] But the teleology leading Peirce to this view is in tension with the very parts of his philosophy that led him to such a conclusion, synechism and Thirdness.

That natural world could have developed according to Peirce's understanding without recourse to divine teleology. His synechism can account for Thirdness and reasonableness in the world. Continuity and Thirdness guarantee a reasonable nature more than Peirce himself realized. By simply affirming Thirdness, that relations perform real work, Peirce gets the development he wants.[52] Nature is already teleological for Peirce, even before he was led to thoughts of a divine source for such directionality. This potential problem in Peirce's thought opens him up for reinterpretation, which will be performed in the next chapter. However, at this point it is worth discussing the two major interpretations of Peirce's philosophy of religion that brought clarity to his fractured thoughts on God, aligning him roughly with either process theology or ground-of-being theology.

Donna Orange has provided *the* interpretation of Peirce that aligns him roughly with process theology. She identifies Peirce's God with concrete reasonableness, the ideal perfection of knowledge. God is not an independent absolute ruler of the universe, but the supreme ideal of the universe.[53] This is a somewhat Whiteheadian, and very Hegelian, God—the truth at which science is trending and the final goal of the universe. Evolutionary love leads to God at the end of the evolutionary rainbow, so to speak. Expressed in terms of truth as the final opinion that a community of inquiry would agree upon in the infinite long run, Orange argues that God appears as a "highly confirmed hypothesis" for Peirce.[54] That confirmed hypothesis is an endpoint the world is approaching. Viewed in light of this interpretation, Peirce's lifelong sense of conflict between science and religion, and quarrels with religious people, could stem from the fact that so many people took God as an obvious, already established, and forever settled fact.

God as an ideal end is tied up with the growth of concrete reasonableness, Thirdness, and generals more than antecedent facts. This interpretation tends toward anthropomorphism and allows God to be called a person, persons being a general type of intelligible symbol of which God can be one. Orange appears to be correct that Peirce's understanding of God rests on his categories, and that his emphasis on Thirdness led to a teleology that he identified as stemming from a somewhat personal theistic God. However, that Peirce may have held this view does not mean it is the only one necessitated by his philosophy. Michael Raposa has emphasized the other theological pole in Peirce's thought. While there may be a God epitomizing the reasonableness of Thirdness, there could also be a God deeper and more indeterminate than the cosmic nothingness of Firstness.

Michael Raposa has provided *the* interpretation of Peirce that aligns him roughly with panentheism. His interpretation of Peirce's panentheism also brings Peirce closer to Tillich's ground-of-being theology than some forms of panentheism that shade into process theology. Rather than understanding God as the ideal of the world, Raposa argues that Peirce understood the world as the manifestation of God. An intuitive grasp of the cause of the categories leads one to God as their source, like Tillich's unconditioned God is the natural resting place for contemplation of conditioned existence.[55] God is not a stranger to be met in the future, but more intimate to us than we are to ourselves. As Raposa puts it, we are, for Peirce, intimately connected to God "as Mind to mind."[56] While Orange emphasizes Thirdness in her interpretation, Raposa's emphasizes synechism, or continuity.

Raposa does not deny that Thirdness matters in understanding Peirce's thoughts on God, but emphasizes the question of where it comes from rather than where it is going. It is true that Peirce saw evolutionary love, his teleological view of evolution, as the only view of evolution compatible with Christianity.[57] Raposa simply emphasizes where that teleological movement comes from. Evolution, like God, moves from the vague to the ideal and complete. "Out of that vast nothingness, an infinite world of definite possibilities emerges, and this world also evolves; this Mind grows."[58] Peirce would claim that biological diversity and growth in the natural world is never sheer chaos, but marked by law and reasonableness, or love. The world therefore shows signs of coming from an ultimate mind, that of God.

This divine mind is not first and foremost related to specific laws of nature but with general feeling, with Firstness. As this feeling grows or evolves, connections are made. "The Absolute Mind would represent a kind of all-embracing 'supersystem,' with its habits of thought and feeling constituting the natural laws that regulate all of its coordinated subsystems."[59] Peirce's belief that God was creator of the universe means he was not a pantheist, as Raposa notes. The divine "supersystem" is not the total collection of all the world's parts, in their completion, but that from which they emerge. "If the Absolute Mind is an all-embracing continuum, its reality, its enormous potential, must be greater than the combined reality of any number of its actualized parts. It is the whole that 'calls out its parts,' without ever being reducible to them."[60] Peirce's model of God is therefore roughly panentheistic, with the world being in God without God being reducible to that world. God's mind infinitely transcends and infinitely informs all things.

God is panentheistic on this account by being both the source of semiotic activity and that reality bringing interpretive activity in line with divine purposes. God is the ontological source of the three categories and cosmological guide of semiotic activity within them, urging the world toward the realization of concrete reasonableness. Divine purposes are worked out through signs, which, in the same manner as all signs represent something else, represent God in the world. In this sense, abstract musement is concretely connected with common acts of interpreting signs. For Peirce, the success of science is proof that our minds are attuned to reality, at least when following the correct method. Thus, the way we interpret God in musement should also be trusted.

While panentheism can be amenable to process theology, and Orange admits Peirce can interpreted both as a process theist and traditional theist,[61] Raposa casts the process elements in Peirce aside.[62] Peirce explicitly rejected pantheism and a finite God. He also rejected any model of God that is not omnipotent or which makes God subject to time, ruling out the process model of God.[63] Raposa gives Peirce an interpretation along the lines of Tillich and Neville. He argues that "it would be a mistake on Peirce's account to apply his categorial scheme to an analysis of the idea of God (Hartshorne's prescription), since God transcends those very categories. God is the primordial, pre-categorial 'No-thing.' I suggest that Peirce developed at least the blueprint for his own version of a negative theology."[64] Peirce lends support to this claim, noting God "eludes every attempt to grasp it."[65] Thought of God is through signs, not a direct grasping of God.

While there are unresolved problems with Peirce's understanding of God, he has shown in musement that abduction is not only allowed but necessary for finding explanations on such a general level. Induction cannot perform this function because it does not advance knowledge. Neither can deduction, which would amount to the ontological argument for God. In musement Peirce argues that it is possible to focus on the creator being manifest in the created, the origin and synechistic connection of the three universes. Perhaps most importantly, he has shown highly imaginative abductive activity that seems detached from empirical inquiry is still at the heart of his method that was, after all, developed in light of science. In terms of how Orange and Raposa have assessed this theological scheme, Orange makes a compelling case that Peirce held some rather traditional beliefs.[66] However, Peirce was clearly wrestling with those beliefs and struggling to fully embrace the religious implications of his thought. As Peirce noted, God is "prior to every first."[67] God is deeper than Firstness, that from which the world arises. The question is whether his strong affirmation of panpsychism means God is also some sort of Absolute Mind evolving out of that deep reality, or just a symbolic human construction. The notion of God being completely other than the world, yet being the germ of the world and therefore growing with it, will be crucial when returning to PCR and theology in mediating between Cobb and Neville in chapter 8. God may be accessible only through signs and interpretations, but signification is how Peirce defended access to reality as it *really is*.

3 | Pragmatic Constructive Realism

WHILE THERE IS MUCH TO COMMEND IN PEIRCE, his philosophy is not perfect and requires updating. Thankfully, he was a fallibilist, so this judgment is neither surprising nor damning. Panpsychism is a conclusion that is troubling to many people who affirm scientific realism. The associated doctrine of evolutionary love, which Peirce admits is anthropocentric, is also not the clear and obvious interpretation of evolution Peirce thought it was. The work of John Dewey and Robert Corrington will be used to reject these ideas and affirm the instrumentality of reality. There is more dynamism in the world than Peirce thought, without having to read mind into everything. How the world develops is just an empirical matter, what happens to occur within the dynamism of things, and not through the inevitable march of evolutionary love. This resistance to panpsychism and anthropomorphic teleology is still rooted in Peirce's realism, though. It is based in the realism of his categories, which can perform those functions on their own. This argument also resists the slide into constructivism that modern neopragmatists have made on the basis of constructivist elements in the work of the classical pragmatists. However, the neopragmatist revival of pragmatism, at least in name, has been an important alternative voice to analytic philosophy. It is with them and their differences with classical pragmatists, especially Peirce, that this chapter begins before moving on to modifying Peirce's philosophy.

Peirce and Neopragmatists

Robert Brandom calls himself an analytic philosopher who makes clear distinctions about the phenomena of experience and a pragmatist in that he nonetheless thinks systematically.[1] He accepts the "myth of the given" articulated by Wilfrid Sellars.[2] Categories are always already implicated in our experiences and inferences. Of course, Peirce already made this point in the nineteenth century in his rejection of intuition, even intuition of the self, and acceptance of habit over absolute doubt.[3] At any rate, for Brandom, developing these existing cognitive habits leads to patterns of inference presupposed in communication. Thus, he tries to navigate between externalist epistemologies that only judge thought by its results and internalist ones that aim to illuminate the inner life of consciousness. But he is still primarily working on an analysis of thoughts, prescinding discursive thought from the objects with which it is engaged.

Classical pragmatists identify more transaction between intellectual order and the environment. Brandom can name a great amount of order and clear analytic distinctions because he has so abstracted thought from its objects, whereas an alternative view would only see as much order as is found in the world. It is often not found, as things are messy out there. His ideal of clear justified arguments in clear justified language always presupposes a context justifying and contextualizing that language. With reference to Wittgenstein and hermeneutic contexts, he calls this a sort of pragmatism. Brandom shifts focus from relations among meanings to relations between meanings and use.[4] However, insofar as these idealized contexts of meaning and use still separate us from reality, his work has little connection with classical pragmatism. The shift from meanings to meanings and use still does not make the turn of classical pragmatists to meanings, use, and a real world that both hinders and furthers such use. Language and conceptual norms are still determinative in Brandom's philosophy, not an independent reality. As Richard Bernstein notes, current neopragmatists have basically abandoned Peirce's category of Secondness, rejecting experience as a category and admitting no unexpected feedback from reality.[5] Peirce's pragmatism is about engagement, not just inference. It involves a robust cosmology rather than just clarifying hermeneutic contexts. This contrasts sharply with Brandom who, instead of nature, speaks of "vocabularies" and the medium of thought rather than knowing real things by improving use of that media.

Analytic pragmatism is classical pragmatism cut short. While beliefs matter, they are also understood to be beliefs about something. They result from engaging the real world. If the context or environment of beliefs is merely hermeneutic, about the meaning of given meanings, then the classical pragmatic pushback on beliefs is lost. As with constructivism, relativism will eventually follow, and the only thing pragmatic remaining will be that beliefs have consequences for conduct. However, since there are not external standards for those beliefs, anything goes. Richard Rorty's work is a perfect example of this slippery slope away from realism in modern pragmatism.

One of Rorty's initial assessments of Peirce and pragmatism shows how unhinged Rorty's understanding of pragmatism is from reality, from any feedback from Secondness. He admits Peirce was the best representative of pragmatism in its burgeoning phase, but praises his achievements in rather non-Peircean ways. Essentially, Rorty reads the later Wittgenstein into Peirce, praising only those features that mesh with Wittgenstein and misconstruing those that do not. First, Rorty praises Peirce for rejecting nominalism just as people resist reductionism today. Second, he praises that rejection for correctly identifying the error in nominalism, attempting to transcend language into metaphysics. Third, he supports this claim by noting that Peirce defends universals as real existent things. There is no need to transcend experience to find them. Finally, he claims both Peirce and Wittgenstein are concerned with use rather than inherent meaning. The only relevant meaning is possible effect on conduct.[6] However, other than his first point about Peirce rejecting nominalism, Rorty's interpretation goes far off course.

Peirce did not reject nominalism in an effort to avoid metaphysics, but actually expanded metaphysics as a result. Rather than restricting meaning to sense data, Peirce's universe is teeming with more reality than Rorty is willing to admit. This is clear from looking at the reasons behind Rorty's third point. The reality of possibilities and universals comes from Peirce's categories, his grand metaphysical scheme. Paul Weiss, one of the original editors of Peirce's collected papers along with Charles Hartshorne, was among the first to correctly note that the theory of categories is at the heart of Peirce's philosophy. Peirce was always a metaphysician, even if part of his modern resurgence has to do with his rediscovery within mathematics and logic.[7] Firstness, Secondness, and Thirdness are rooted in his overall understanding of reality, not simply affirmed because they are relevant to the language that communities use to interpret phenomena. The "outward clash" of Secondness that constrains thinking is more basic than the authority of lawlike claims that are the markers of Thirdness. Mastering a language game is not the same as having to give an account of something forced upon us. Secondness is not the same as knowledge; it is brute facticity that is not self-interpreting.

However, Secondness is a metaphysical fact that we have no choice but to deal with. Rorty left all these realist elements behind. He makes this clear, claiming pragmatism "is the doctrine that there are no constraints on inquiry save conversational ones—no wholesale constraints derived from the nature of the objects, or of the mind, or of language, but only those retail constraints provided by the remarks of our fellow inquirers."[8] His neopragmatism is constructivism that never transcended its binary opposition with realism to affirm pragmatic constructive realism.

For another example of how neopragmatists can be constructivists in such a way that leads to relativism, consider Hilary Putnam. While not known as a pragmatist, he was attracted to pragmatism throughout his career, praising it for eschewing skepticism, affirming fallibilism, uniting facts and values, and making practice primary in philosophy.[9] However, he follows Rorty in rejecting metaphysical realism. Putnam takes his cue from Dewey, rejecting one real view of the world in favor of interrogating views to discover how they are better or worse at solving specific problems. Rather than practice being related to truth, Putnam basically makes them one and the same. He argues truth is not "simply a mystery mental act by which we relate ourselves to a relation called 'correspondence' that is totally independent of the practices by which we decide what is and what is not true."[10] Rather than follow a minimalist pragmatic realism in which truth corresponds with reality in the long run, even if fully denying we will ever get there, he denies truth can be defined as having anything to do with verification. Stated negatively, he has moved from coherence and internal realism to conflating truth and practice.[11] In his own words, he "rejects James', Dewey's, and Peirce's theories of truth on the ground that all three thinkers believe that a proposition cannot be true unless it is 'fated' to be verified in the long run."[12] He tries to avoid the complete relativism implied in this view by accepting an essentially Kantian model of human inquiry.

Putnam claims he maintains normativity in his scheme, but evidence to support that claim is lacking. In his defense, he states "we are *thinkers,* and that as thinkers we are committed to there being *some* kind of truth, some kind of correctness which is substantial and not merely 'disquotational.' That means that there is no eliminating the normative."[13] Still, it seems the norm for Putnam is simply whatever humans happen to do. "My own view is that truth is to be identified with idealized justification, rather than with justification-on-present evidence. 'Truth' in this sense is as context sensitive as we are."[14] Relativism is still present, as there is no clear definition of "we" in his position. Is it "obviously" good informed academic liberals like himself, or right-wing extremists who would dismantle the former's world? On his account, both seem equally justified in applying their norms. He provides no reason to protest the resurgence of KKK and neo-Nazi rallies in the United States since 2016. Worse, his philosophy might justify them just as much as the protesters. Truth is context sensitive, after all.

To give Putnam some benefit of the doubt, there are liberal, conservative, racist, sexist, and so forth pockets of countries. There are many different contexts in which people are born, educated, and in which their thinking emerges. Peirce's criticism of Cartesian doubt would find a home in Putnam's appeal to Dewey against foundationalism, his assertion that "we can only start from where we are."[15] Of course, Peirce agrees, without adding the troublesome qualifier that where we are has no pushback from independent sources. Putnam could retort as follows:

> From a metaphysical realist point of view, one can never begin with an epistemological premise that *people are able to tell whether A or B*; one must first show that, in "the absolute conception of the world," there are such possible facts as A and B. A metaphysical-reductive account of what good is must precede any discussion of what is better than what. In my view, the great contribution of Dewey was to insist that we neither have nor require a "theory of everything," and to stress that what we need instead is insight into how human beings resolve problematical situations.[16]

If we cannot tell whether A or B, whether racist nationalism is bad and protests against it are good, it is at least just as open a question whether the philosophy supporting such agnosticism is worthwhile. Any sense of shared common reality is lost in Putnam's philosophy, but David Hildebrand notes he cannot have it so easy, at least based on Dewey. "If Putnam is going to succeed in undermining the realist/antirealist controversy by using the pragmatist insight that practice is primary, he must not reiterate the old intellectualist fallacy by characterizing experience as somehow derivative of language. Language, on Dewey's view, arises in the course of experience and contributes to experience."[17] Not being separable, language cannot predetermine the range of possible experiences. For the classical pragmatists, the need to respond to unexpected developments in reality is more basic than the need to respond to rules of language use.

Peirce and Classical Pragmatists

Among the classical pragmatists, Peirce, James, and Dewey are engaged in a very similar project in that they begin with empirical inquiry. Peirce argues there is no cognition not determined by previous cognitions.[18] After forming concepts from experience, one should deductively spell out the consequences of the concepts then test them through induction and see if they are verified in experience. If they are not verified, by retroduction one should modify concepts and clarify inferences and then return to experience. The whole process is one of making our understanding of reality through experience more and more clear. James's radical empiricism makes philosophical baggage of the past, like the split between mind and matter, about felt relations in pure experience. There is a stream of pure experience from which all concepts are derived in the form of different perspectives on the same stream.[19] Dewey's immediate empiricism is closely related.[20] He claims all things are simply what they are experienced as being. A scientist searching for fundamental particles might find a quark where a nonscientist experiences a table. This is fine, since neither has a privileged stance according to Dewey. Both are true, based on different aspects of experience.

Dewey understands realism in terms of common sense. Individuals encounter things in the world, some already known and some unexpected, as objects of knowledge. He contrasts this commonsense notion with idealism. Yet against the realists of his day, Dewey sought to show that truth is a process rather than something to which one simply has immediate access. Perception is an active process by which one gains insights into the world. Dewey contrasts the terms "had" and "have" to disclose this shift by which an understanding of reality gained in experience comes to be known differently. He argues there is a difference between primary experiences and later experiences that require reflection, considering the new experience of reality in connection with the relevant signs employed to understand reality.[21] Reality is found through encounters with the world, but only in an active process of interpreting those encounters that accounts for the idealist insight that reality changes as new interpreted experiences change.

Concrete differences in subsequent experiences can reveal how earlier experiences were false, although no less real. For Dewey, inquiry starts in an indeterminate situation and ends when it has made matters clear again. As for Peirce, there is no point in discussing which relevant means should be used to reach a certain end when everyone is satisfied and nothing needs to be changed. In a psychological bent, James also argues beliefs only need to be changed when they run aground on opposing beliefs and are thus seen as problematic for the first time. Any debate in absence of this situation would be merely verbal and pointless, irrelevant for the conduct of life, exactly the sort of things his pragmatism was meant to eliminate.[22] Rather than focus on how individuals resolve doubts, Peirce emphasizes the role of a community when beliefs become problematic. He does this because he wants to settle upon beliefs independent of the desires of any single individual. He accepts the role of human knowledge in the world, but hopes the idiosyncrasies of any individual will be eliminated as a community converges on reality.

Change is an obvious component of altering existing beliefs and finding solutions in problematic situations. Peirce was very clear that someone following the scientific method will not be wedded to their conclusions and will not be surprised when they need to modify those conclusions. Dewey's concept of the reflexive arc captures the fact that means employed to bring about a certain change may be improperly understood or incorrectly applied.[23] Concepts will need to be clarified and methods refined before trying again. The classical pragmatists are all engaged in a common project together. They start inquiry in the empirical world with existing beliefs that are only changed upon their frustration. When frustrated and in need of modification, unless you adopt the more individualist view of James, the fix is performed in community over time. When change is needed again, the process reboots until goals are reached, facts known, and ideals satisfied. From this empirical realist starting point, all three philosophers make a place for realizing the human element in the world. Thirdness is the embodiment of purposes in the world for Peirce. By knowing and being able to predict regularities, we can better bring about our purposes in the world. James's refusal to consider pointless debates can lead to personal satisfaction where there could be useless arguing about beliefs. Dewey's instrumentalism is about working to change the world to one better suited to our purposes. But despite both following the scientific method to reach their goals, Peirce and Dewey have very different goals.

Dewey, like Peirce, takes philosophical lessons directly from Darwin. For a long time in philosophy, as well as natural science, final form is all that mattered. Changes were regarded as unreal. Knowledge of final ends is what counted. After Darwin, form and adaptation were understood as that which is worked out in concrete struggles. There are no longer predetermined beginnings or ends. There are specific problems and specific solutions. Any sense of finality beyond that context is superfluous and unverifiable. In this sense, Dewey is certainly influenced by science, but views it as more of a heuristic tool than does Peirce. Theory and practice go together. Knowledge is action in the world. Dewey is future oriented. Whatever problems arise determine the context for what counts as a solution. Whether our concepts or beliefs are true or false will not be raised in contexts where they work, because working is enough. Dewey is a commonsense realist, but was neither a metaphysical realist nor antirealist when it came to science.[24] In short, we engage problems with existing habits. When the situation moves from settled to indeterminate, we make inferences and adopt means to resolve the problem. If they fail, we reflect on what went wrong and make a better attempt at a solution.

Dewey's experimentalism, which puts concepts to work in the world, does not entail realism or antirealism. Rather, concepts are verified when they work, and no further questions need be asked of them. For him, experimental inquiry starts in a problematic situation. It is concept-led and not concept-driven. As such, inquiry aims to correct inferences regarding the correct means to an end and stabilize the situation by reaching a determinate conclusion. It is also future oriented. What counts as a solution will be determined by the problem. True and false are not issues that will be raised when a concept works in bringing about a solution to that problem. Furthermore, concepts foreign to the situation cannot be imposed on it simply because they are deemed to be true. The fact that true or false are not relevant when there is verification in experience is an expression of Dewey's immediate empiricism. If someone walks along a trail and finds an object they identify as a stone with an interesting shape, but someone else walks along that same trail, finds that same object, and identifies it as an arrowhead, both individuals are correct. Each inquiry into that object was satisfied. It is the same for mind and matter, or concepts and reality. They are different ways of looking at the same experience.

As a consequence of his experimentalism, Dewey could be called a naïve commonsense realist. He seeks verification in experience. Whether concepts have greater ontological status does not interest him.[25] One person, due to the aim of their inquiry, can experience a buzzing swarm of particles practically devoid of the sense of solid matter, while at the same time another could experience a solid object. Neither is truer or more privileged than the other. One was looking for a table and found it. The other was trying to find out if something was composed of more fundamental particles and confirmed this fact. Peirce, on the other hand, is greatly concerned about reality. He classifies metaphysics as depending on normative sciences.[26] He spells out the three general categories of the world and how true meaning can be found in them. The affirmation of Secondness and pushback from an independent reality on interpretations makes Peirce a realist rather than a constructivist. But his argument that all reality is semiotic, that there is no access to reality independent of interpretations, admits elements of construction that direct or naïve realists will deny.

To arrive at genuine understanding in a world marked by Peirce's categories, it is important to know the intended interpretation of a sign. An interpretant is the respects in which an object is represented in a sign to an interpreter. The fact that interpretations of an independent reality are fallible means, as Peirce noted, that "reality consists in the future," at least to some extent.[27] Reality is what communities of inquiry would conclude in the long run of their investigations, after eliminating personal eccentricities or biases and fixing errors. To say that inquiry must happen in community and what that community agrees about an independent reality is to "assert emphatically the reality of the public world of the indefinite future as against our past opinions of what it was to be."[28] Reality therefore entails community without limits. Even Dewey, in an aspect of his philosophy often overlooked in favor of his instrumentalism, argued that community is where experimental inquiry occurs. Individuals adjusting means to certain ends will not have much success. Rather, a stable and cooperative society is needed for attention to be devoted to such problem solving. This is a wider sphere than even a community of scientists or ethicists. The nation is involved. But for Dewey it is not an independent reality that the community strives to know and control, but the strictures of any given problem. For Peirce, on the other hand, the real and unreal consist of those which will eventually always be affirmed and always be denied. What is real and unreal is independent of individual opinion yet only reached through individual opinion collectively worked out according to the right method, constructivism and realism united in the pragmatic method. These are all logical elements that can be applied in any situation to arrive at meaning, the exact opposite of Dewey's contextual approach.

Peirce's pragmatism is not a consensus theory of truth asserting the truth of any matter is merely what a certain community agrees upon. While the concept of a community of inquiry is crucial to his realism, that community is not detached from and independent of reality as in completely relativistic postmodern philosophies. Peircean communities are embedded in and use the method of pragmatism to discover reality. Community *and* the world are found by participating in communal inquiry. Peirce was clear that it is reality, not merely the solution to a problem, that is reached in successful scientific inquiry. "There are real things, whose characters are entirely independent of our opinions about them; those realities affect our senses according to regular laws, and, though our sensations are as different as our relations to the objects, yet, by taking advantage of the laws of perception, we can ascertain by reasoning how things really are, and any man, if he have sufficient experience and reason enough about it, will be led to the one true conclusion."[29] Peirce therefore has a correspondence theory of truth, though that claim needs qualification. Peirce affirms correspondence not just of our words about reality and that reality, but the correlation of words, reality, and our interpretive processes. This happens dialectically as each informs the other. His formulation is "each increase of a man's information involves and is involved by, a corresponding increase of a word's information."[30] Interpretations grow when more complex interpretants are included within their scope. We grow as interpreters when we let new signs shape us in our inquiries. This does not, as some neopragmatists like Rorty claim, mean interpreters are just texts. As Corrington points out, there is a vector dimension to Peirce's pragmatism, constantly driving all postmodern aspects of his thought into reality as their final test. He notes that for Peirce "the self must select those interpretants that reinforce its survival value and power in a naturalistic context."[31] Inquiry is like evolution. Self-control means all interpretations must pass a test.

What makes Peirce so unique compared to the other classical pragmatists can also be highlighted by comparing him with William James. James is clear that he wants to avoid outdated philosophical dualisms, but still affirms a dyadic understanding of experience. Conscious experience consists of flights and perches within a more primary stream of sciousness, undifferentiated continuous experience.[32] Conscious experience arises and gets entangled with binaries abstracted from more basic feelings of unity. Peirce affirms triadic, rather than dyadic, experience. The sign/object/interpretant triad is basic for all experiences. James also has a pluralistic philosophy in which things are what they are experienced as, with no hierarchical unity imposed from outside such experiences. However, compared with Peirce such pluralism almost looks like a monism in which it almost does not matter whether anything is experienced as this or that. James also lacks the concept of an interpretant, the understanding that flights and perches from the stream of sciousness are necessary if anything in the stream is to be experienced as anything at all.

James and Peirce differ on the meaning of pragmatism at their cores. While sharing many features, their different renderings of the pragmatic maxim reveal different goals for their work. Peirce wants to understand reality and conform human reason to reality. His categories are general features *of the world*. He developed a logical method informed by science to control thought in order to understand that world, and hated nominalism and a focus on the particular without any connection to generals and laws. The maxim at the heart of his philosophy is embedded in nature and scientific in method. In James's terms, James is a tenderhearted pragmatist while Peirce always insists on the hard-hearted test of an independent reality.[33] For Peirce, the more method strays from science, the more any given inquiry will flounder. James was not interested in logical rules like Peirce. James applies pragmatism to important human questions more than an understanding of the universe. The pragmatic maxim, for him, becomes the means for leaving behind the failures of scientific materialism for more adequate explorations of human interests.

Peirce's pragmatic maxim is concerned with what conceivable practical effects a concept *might* have, whereas James merely wants to uncover the practical consequences in conduct to learn the meaning of a concept. The difference between the two is subtle, but important. The core difference can be presented as follows. If C is true, what will I experience? If C is true, what will I do? These two questions capture the pragmatism of James.[34] He is concerned about conduct. Peirce is different, and would ask the question in the following way. If C were to be true, what would I experience if I were to do A? Peirce's focus is on controlling thought, discovering general patterns, and developing the ability to predict. James is a pragmatist in the vernacular sense of the term. He is concerned about what people do in their day-to-day lives, regardless of whether their choices are ultimately true or not. Peirce is a logician and a metaphysician trying to understand reality. Compared to James, Peirce is looking to the future. The final interpretant is one about which every mind would agree. James is always thinking of the way people happen to act now.

James's tenderheartedness also opens the door to neopragmatism. Pragmatism, in many ways, looks like a total break with many traditional philosophical problems. James frequently presented pragmatism as a way of moving past idle philosophical debates about the principles and categories of thought. Peirce takes pragmatism as a tool for refining those philosophical debates in ways that everyone in the trajectory from Descartes to Kant could not. Principles and categories are at the heart of his work. Thus, Rorty can identify James, and pragmatism in his sense, with the shift from modern to postmodern concerns, while viewing Peirce as too traditional and therefore unpragmatic.[35] But Peirce moves past debates about realism and antirealist constructivism since it is experience of the world that unveils reality in semiotic activity.[36] It is possible to experience reality without making the naïve assertion that the "thing-in-itself" as it will forever be known is what was experienced. The fact that reality is experienced as changing highlights the role of the interpreter in experiencing reality. However, *reality* is still experienced and not a mere fantasy of a subjective mind. As they have been presented, Peirce is the strongest realist among himself, James, and Dewey. It may seem ironic, then, that to a fuller realism that does justice to all three of his categories is where Peirce needs to be pushed.

Peirce without Panpsychism

Despite affirming the reality of three categories, Peirce's concern with Thirdness led him to read it into the others. Rather than equally affirming possibilities that are never realized and random occurrences that never become lawlike, Firstness and Secondness, Peirce claims everything is effete mind. Rather than admit there are more possibilities than generals and more facts than laws, Peirce read Thirdness into Secondness and Firstness. In an unexpected twist for someone who wants truth to be independent of any mind, he makes mind the defining feature of all reality. Peirce must be taken back to his own pragmatic intentions, to let reality be what it is and use the best method to know it as such. As Sandra Rosenthal notes, pragmatists have, or at least should have, a "radically nonspectator" theory of knowledge.[37] Experience is always a product of what is really independently there in the world, even if we always experience it with concepts that will more or less match or clash with that reality. Reality is still what is engaged in our interpretations, the purposes with which we interact with that world. These two factors, our purposes and that which we engage based on those purposes, also undercut the dichotomy of realism and constructivism that has been presented. There is no pragmatic aim to seek absolute foundations or give up that search for an equally absolute nonfoundational skepticism about talk of reality.

Peirce's philosophy has the resources to understand the emergence of laws, mind, and intelligent controlling levels of reality, but he insufficiently applied those resources. Abduction is where all progress in knowledge is made. Deduction is conservative and makes no progress, but spells out the consequences of abductive theories. Induction is where the deductive consequences are placed in the world to test the hypothesis. The process works like this. Suppose there is a surprising phenomenon C. It is surprising because no current theory predicted its occurrence. However, C was not an isolated occurrence and continues to appear over and over again. Peirce would solve this problem as follows. There is a surprising fact C. If theory A were the case, C would be an expected matter of course. Therefore, there is reason to think that A is true. This is how abduction is prompted. Novel phenomena require novel explanations that make them expected phenomena. This way of thinking is readily applicable to current scientific controversies. Neuroscientists and philosophers of mind are debating the relation of mind to matter. With stronger concepts of mind and emergence, mind's emergence from matter would no longer be such a shocking phenomenon.[38] Such a theory is a novel abduction, not reading Thirdness into everything in the form of panpsychism. There is a middle ground between assuming everything has something like a human experience and that such experiences are merely by-products, epiphenomena. This could have been noticed by Peirce if he followed the emergent method contained in the evolution of Firstness to Thirdness instead of unduly focusing on the achievement of Thirdness.

In a sense, Peirce anticipated critiques of reductionism in science from process philosophers and theologians. As will be noted in chapter 5, Cobb has been critical of biologists for studying the emergence of life without changing their corresponding philosophy of nature. Their actual scientific work does not require an associated materialistic philosophy.[39] However, both he and Peirce go too far in reading the features of intelligent life into all of nature. If materialists make the error of assuming the physical matter they study defines all of reality, panpsychists or panexperientialists make the opposite mistake by assuming that the human experiences they focus on are present in everything. Against both views, levels of emergence should be allowed to be just what they are, without making any one them a defining feature of *all* levels.

On the issue of emergence and reductionism, Philip Clayton has distinguished three general levels of emergence in the world. The physical level has very low levels of indeterminacy, perhaps only at the quantum level, and is otherwise lawful. At this level, physical laws dominate. Next is the biological level in which information and the function of physical forms is crucial. Purposefulness is present, but only at this level, not at the physical level. Against the insistence of process philosophers that purposive action is found in all things, Clayton notes that "process thinkers do not respond adequately to what we have learned about the emergent structure of the natural world."[40] The same is true of Peirce. Conscious experience can be real without holding a frankly embarrassing doctrine that entails that rocks have experiences.[41] Finally, on the level of humans, and likely in varying degrees in other animals, Clayton locates mental activities that are distinct from other behaviors and exert different causality.[42] Clayton argues that his three distinctions actually allow for more novelty in the world than process thought since what emerges at each level is truly different, whereas process thinkers and Peirce read subjectivity into everything. If the same ontology applies everywhere, references to novelty are little more than lip service. Rather than downplaying a potentially embarrassing aspect of Whitehead's thought by claiming that subjectivity is negligible at the physical level and merely repeats what is given, it is important to agree with Clayton that science is incompatible with such a claim.

What remains unclear is whether all three levels of emergence that Clayton describes are necessary. It is an open question how neuroscience will progress in reducing conscious experience to physical events in the brain. That is, weak emergence, the view that properties at higher levels are still the result of bottom-up causation and do not affect what happens at lower levels, may still make great progress. Clayton is not against scientific progress on the subject. He has just made his bet on how far it will go. His bet is on strong emergence, the view that emergent properties do exert top-down causation and will never be fully explained away. Perhaps, it just seems plausible that neuroscience will continue to encroach on that territory. No matter, the most important point presently is that if you want to affirm purpose and the reality of human experience, as Peirce does, accepting panpsychism is not necessary. His acceptance of panpsychism is also unfortunate because he has a theory of emergence in his philosophy. He affirms continuity as well as discontinuity when something novel emerges. There is Thirdness *and* Secondness, without needing to read the former into the latter. There are some genuine leaps that create breaks with what they emerged from, even while obviously connected to what they emerged from. Where panpsychists and panexperientialists like Peirce, Whitehead, and Cobb locate emergence in every interaction, complex subjectivity emerging from simple/negligible subjectivity, a position like Clayton's in which subjectivity emerged from a world in which it did not exist carries less metaphysical baggage. However far emergence goes, its achievements are genuinely novel and need not be fully present in the conditions from which they arose.

Emergence theories grant downward dependence but reject that there can be complete downward explanatory reduction. This also works the other way. Downward reduction fails because there are features at lower levels that are not present in higher levels. Panpsychism is a flat ontology in which the same explanation can be given of everything, just with differences of degree. From an emergent point of view, new features do not emerge without causes on which they depend, but once they have emerged they have their own reality that can be quite unlike that from which they emerged.

Not unlike Clayton, Terrence Deacon also identifies three orders of emergence, three distinct layers to reality. First-order emergence involves new properties in the aggregate that are not present in the individuals. It is akin to Peirce's triadic structure of interpretation in which information flow between sign, interpreter, and interpretant would be missing without any of the pieces. In second-order emergence, new causal effects not seen in first order are found. Structural features—forms and not merely causally interacting particles—can affect the further growth of individual pieces. Third-order emergence shares the features of second-order, but now information and not just form is passed on.[43] For example, self-replicating cells display features not present before their existence—information for building cells like themselves. Third-order emergence is like Peirce's notion of creeping Thirdness and concrete reasonableness. Cells interpret the world as information is shared, embedding systems within one another.[44] Or, as Peirce would say, self-control grows.

With Peirce, PCR can affirm that reasonableness is capable of controlling brute physical forces and influencing the direction in which the universe evolves, but without reading that into every aspect of reality. Reasonableness is an achievement, not a given fact since time immemorial. Firstness, Secondness, and Thirdness can occur together, but not necessarily. In such cases, like the laws of nature, they occur all at once, though they can be prescinded from one another in analysis. But there is also loss in the world; supernovas explode and the majority of the cosmos is full of random happenings that never create connections and become general features of the world. Despite affirming the reality of chance and the mere facticity of Secondness, Peirce flew away from them to Thirdness before adequately considering the implications. This move by Peirce was a mistake. Thirdness emerges increasingly over time. The early moments after the Big Bang were a cosmic soup more like pure chaos in which Secondness and Thirdness were entirely absent. Random genetic mutations can be understood, but are not themselves an example of reasonable self-controlled behavior.

Peirce without Evolutionary Love

Closely related to Peirce's panpsychism is his notion of evolutionary love. His concern with the reality of Thirdness led him not only to read mind into matter, but to affirm a strong teleology in that mind-matter, which inevitably leads to Thirdness. Peirce believed in synechism, or continuity, in the world, but balanced it out with his notion of tychism, of absolute chance. Because there is absolute chance but the world displays reasonableness, there is evolutionary love, what Peirce calls agapism.[45] There is real providential force that brings about Thirdness and makes our reason capable of communing with it. This is not far off from being a naturalistic sort of intelligent design argument in which chance is not accepted as sufficient for explaining the world we have. It certainly runs counter to science as it stands today, and can be deemed unnecessary with panpsychism already rejected.

Human thought and behavior can develop randomly, necessarily, or by agape. We can be flooded by random thoughts, follow deduction and induction, or be attracted to ideals and purposes. Corrington argues it is not as clear as Peirce thinks that this analysis of methods of thinking can be read into the structures of evolution. Peirce's only support is panpsychism and a neo-Lamarckian view of evolution, viewing nature as a mental process. Corrington argues, and the present argument follows him on this point, that anthropomorphic and anthropocentric bias led Peirce to focus on mentality and understanding to the extent that he needed to assure himself of intelligible signification prior to human life. This strategy actually drove his pragmatism away from nature, not into it.[46] Purposes can be fragmented, belonging to specific contexts and achieving just what they happen to achieve, or even failing to bring about anything at all. They need not have a preexisting reality marching inevitably toward realization.

Murray Murphey also noted that Peirce, despite his fractured musings on God, does not *need* recourse to divine purpose to explain possibilities, their development, and their continuity, which leads to Thirdness. Tychism allows Peirce to say the universe evolves out of chance rather than necessity. Spontaneity and connection between the categories can explain the movement of the universe toward Thirdness. Therefore, Murphey argues, a divine will is not necessary to explain such progress or the existence of novelty that led to such growth. "The original continuum of possibility is differentiated by acts, which, as acts, are free and arbitrary."[47] That is how the universe evolves, with real growth through chance and some chance connections without that growth necessarily going in any one direction. Repeated acts are generalized into habits as some of the original possibilities within the continuum are excluded. Pockets of the universe gradually become reasonable rather than chaotic. But they do so out of chance, something primordial prior to the existence of general laws and their determinations. Peirce's affirmation of generality is important for understanding the development of possibilities.

Recall that generals are indeterminate in some respects. An interpreter completes the determination. An interesting conclusion that flows from this is that potentiality exists as part of reality. Edward Moore makes the point by giving the example of sugar and its ability to dissolve: "What is there in sugar right now that I am trying to characterize when I say sugar has solubility? I do not believe that you can define a present potentiality in terms of future actualities. A present potentiality exists right now. It may or may not become actualized in the future. But if it never becomes actualized it still exists now as a potentiality."[48] The importance of generals is not about acting, actualizing a potential by putting the sugar in a liquid. Sugar has the potential to dissolve right now, even if it is never placed in a liquid. As Peirce says, "every general idea has more or less power of working itself out into fact; some more so, some less so."[49] Among such processes he included even those purely physical processes that are irreversible and "tend asymptotically toward bringing about an ultimate state of things. If ideological is too strong a word to apply to them, we might invent the word finious, to express their tendency toward a final state."[50] Physical force and efficient causation are not enough to explain the irreversible character that Peirce is trying to explain. However, T. L. Short has convincingly argued that Peirce does not need such a strong teleology as to invoke theology. Peirce is basically just trying to explain the development of natural laws. "All that is required is a knowledge of some theorems in the mathematical theory of probability. Therefore, it is such laws, and not the particular forces involved, that explain the diffusion of gases. Such a law, being a law, and purely mathematical at that, is not a force. It is, as Peirce says later in the same passage, 'an intellectual character.'"[51] Since for Peirce the final cause is a general type, it can be actualized in many ways, making the invocation of final cause less threating to evolutionary science. Invocation of final causes need not implicate mind in the matter.

Giving examples of efficient *as well as* final causation is insufficient to conclude everything has mind, according to Short. "To say that an organ or artifact exists because of what it does or can be used to do is to say that it has been selected because the usual results of its operation are of a type that satisfies some general principle. Thus, all teleological explanation refers, at bottom, to finious processes defined by variation and selection."[52] Cases of final causation are found when the principle of selection is grounded in an individual entity, but this can simply be a matter of chance and the workings of internal physical organization. The self-promulgation of amoeba and bacteria is an obvious example.[53] As for Whitehead, Peirce understands direction guided by purposes of a conscious agent only as the most common example of causation by general principles. However, even if one affirms continuity between consciousness and other seemingly purposeful teleological processes, it is not necessary to assert that there is mind everywhere. It is possible to simply emphasize the similarity in the process and assert, with Short, "human mentality is constituted by processes which may be found in lower grades elsewhere in nature."[54] Peirce's panpsychism and strong teleology also led him to consider the question of God's reality, considerations that must also be modified in light of PCR's rejection of panpsychism and evolutionary love.

In his musings on God, Peirce distinguishes God's existence from God's reality. He discusses the latter, not the former. Existence is only for what reacts in the world, Secondness, while reality applies to generals that are manifestations of reason. Far from being brute facts of existence, sometimes they are constructions of the human mind, though nonetheless real on Peirce's account. We make reliable scientific predictions. We have some sense of the reasonableness of the universe. For Peirce, this implies we have insight into the mind of God. For him, God is real and partakes in generality as the reality holding together the world's evolution from a less to more determinate state. God is creating the universe now, not a deist clockmaker who set up the world and then left it alone. The development of the world due to God's influence means any valid prediction of the future is a fragment of God's mind. Not unlike Plato, forms of the world are in the mind of God and creation manifests them as they gradually emerge. Or, as Corrington describes the way development occurs in both God and the world, there is movement from greater nothingness (potencies) to lesser nothingness (possibilities) to generals (forms).[55] Peirce never definitively stated whether he thought God was an agent behind all natural processes or a product of those same processes, but he had certain leanings toward God being somewhat fragmented and evolving in quality. After all, he wrote that God fully appears to us *and Godself* only at the end of history.[56]

The reality Peirce describes is one in which once growth has been accepted as part of the universe, it becomes inseparable from the idea of a personal creator. Peirce thinks viewing everything as a result of mechanical, impersonal relations gives no clue as to how growth and Thirdness came about. But as Corrington notes, this personal creator will only prevail in a universe in which Peirce's strong developmental teleology of evolutionary love is real.

God's personality and an open future must obtain together. This fact raises questions Peirce never fully answered. How does God relate to developmental teleological structures and an open future? If God's future is as underdetermined as ours, it is open to something greater than God, new potentials for God or potentials that even transform or transcend God?[57] Otherwise stated, Peirce's personal God is not as necessary as he thinks, but is open to alternative models of God such as prepersonal grounds of reality or growth and change in the personal God, changes Peirce never considered. Furthermore, Peirce does not *need* a personal God to explain teleology. There can be development without reading a preordained teleology from God into the universe. God will be affirmed as source of the universe as well as that which grows along with it in chapter 8, though that argument will place severe limitations on Peirce's anthropocentric view, which confuses structures of evolution with processes of human thought. Again, this is consistent with the resources of Peirce's philosophy, even if it is not what he affirmed.

From Constructivism or Realism to Pragmatic Constructive Realism

Neopragmatists accept Peirce's criterion for truth, that "the rational purport of a word or other expression, lies exclusively in its conceivable bearing upon the conduct of life."[58] However, they have unhinged truth from its metaphysical and mind-independent moorings. Peirce accepted the Scholastic realism of Duns Scotus.[59] Things are what they are regardless of what anyone thinks, and general terms have a reality independent of language. Peirce is a realist through and through. Chance, necessity, and everything else he affirms have their basis in reality. But what makes PCR pragmatic constructive realism rather than simply realism or constructivism is that human strivings, our constructions with language, are a necessary part of reality. They are not to be rejected as impediments to reality or understood as free-floating islands that keep us away from reality.

For Peirce, what is most important about the universe is not actions within it, the reduction of reality to the actions and reactions of physics, but where those actions are leading, the evolution of the universe. At higher levels this happens through self-control, not just a mixture of chance occurrences and continuity. Therefore, humans enter the continuity of the world, learning from and further developing natural processes, and in turn furthering the development of the universe. Constructivism is not only a means of accessing reality, rather than a barrier, but further develops what is real.

Signs are incomplete and always capable of further interpretation by other signs. They leave interpreters to supply part of the meaning. The universe is perfused with signs. Interpreters enter the world of signs that surrounds them. They intersect, and people get by with vague habits that may work and may need improvement. The development of habits makes them reasonable as they participate in the growth of self-control. Corrington summarizes this pragmatic union of constructivism and realism that is being argued for in the form of PCR in his introduction to Peirce. "Under the aegis of self-control, the habits of the universe become our habits."[60] This has important consequences for thinking about our habits in relation to God.

In a series of articles intended for publication in *The Monist,* Peirce makes several key points that have potentially startling consequences when thinking about PCR and theology. Nothing arrives at the intellect that is not first in the senses. Here he agrees with British empiricism, though he supplements their thought with the undergirding of his Scholastic realism. He also goes beyond nominalism in asserting that our perceptual judgments contain generals, which leads to the affirmation of universal propositions. An interesting, and potentially challenging, point for theology is that he also claims abduction shades into perception with no absolutely sharp distinction between the two.[61] Some of the obvious theological consequences that flow from these claims are as follows. Theology cannot start with the assumption of God and read that assumption into the world. It cannot privilege Barthian narratives over empirical facts. In fact, it must begin with empirical facts. But rather than quickly fleeing to God and the transcendent realm, the move to God must be earned. God can enter in from an empirical starting point, but not just because a theologian wants to bring in that hypothesis. An abductive move to God must offer an explanation.

Abduction and retroduction mean theologians get to keep playing the game, so to speak. Atheist scientists, especially those who write best-selling books, like to claim they have refuted theism, but theologians can offer different concepts of God and continue to play the game. Process theologians have abandoned the God of substance theism, and their God is not designing or controlling the world directly. Such a God will not be refuted by the same scientific arguments against substance theism. Neville affirms a strong concept of God's transcendence and otherness, but his argument does not fall prey to criticisms of the idea of a transcendent eternal *being*. As long as theologians can specify new ideas offered as clear hypotheses with consequences, their work continues. By reason (P) we interpret (C) reality (R). The world is real and presses itself upon us (Secondness). It is self-interpreting in the sense of being full of signs and triadic systems that so force themselves upon us, but not exhaustively so. We also interpret reality. But Secondness is not yet understanding (Thirdness), and feeling/intuition (Firstness) is not exhaustive of reality. Reason (P) is supplemented by experience (R). Reason and experience can be understood as somewhat opposed, as neopragmatists will readily point out, but a more accurate picture is one in which lines extend from each pole toward the other, reaching their fullest union in our constructive interpretations. Without our interpretations (C) holding the balance, we end up with either idealism or deterministic materialism in both philosophy and theology. To avoid this conclusion, a position with the basic features of pragmatic constructive realism is necessary.

4 | Emerging Philosophically and Theologically

GIVEN HOW THE BACK-AND-FORTH debate between realists and constructivists has been described, someone familiar with the work of both Neville and Cobb might place the former in the realist camp and the latter with the constructivists. Neville provides a grand metaphysical system meant to give an account of all reality. He yearns for the medieval unity of thought that has become unfashionable in postmodern circles. His work, in a sense, is to make it fashionable again, or at least the best, most unfashionable affront to postmodern sensibilities possible. God the creator is his ultimate explanation needed to understand such a grand picture of reality. Cobb, on the other hand, affirms the relativity of truth claims and focuses on the contextuality of worldviews. Claims of reality change as contexts change. Similarly, his model for the relation between God and the world has both in active relation and constantly reconstructing one another in relation to one another. His affirmation of the reality of that God does not focus on certain bedrock features, like indeterminacy for Neville, but more on the constant surpassing of all features, creative transformation. Simply stated, each theologian deals with God's transcendence and immanence, but emphasizes one over the other. This one-sidedness is as unsatisfying as choosing either realism or constructivism in philosophy.

Neville's work focuses on the transcendence of God, while Cobb's focuses on divine immanence. Neville's theory of an indeterminate divine creator is perhaps one of the most novel and strong models of transcendence that has been offered. Cobb, latching onto and developing Whitehead's insight that God is the source of novelty for the world, focuses on creative transformation in the world. While both affirm the other side of the equation, neither does so as strongly as the other. The primordial nature of God cannot compare to the transcendence of Neville's indeterminate creator, but Neville's God, which gives itself the determinate character of creator in creating, is immanently nothing compared to the God incarnate in every instance of creative transformation. While both theologians have dealt supremely well with the aspect of God that is their main focus, both positions are unsatisfying and one-sided if left merely in opposition to one another, just as choosing either constructivism or realism is an unsatisfying binary option. Rather than opposing one another, they can progress with each other by thinking through each other via PCR. Despite the disagreements between the two theologians, this effort to creatively synthesize their insights touches upon the heart of both theological projects.

Two Giants of Modern Theology

For Cobb, worldviews are to be put into dialogue with one another so each can be creatively transformed. Science is a worldview, as is Christianity. Since one of the virtues he identifies in Whitehead's philosophy is its ability to put Christianity in agreement with scientific knowledge of the world, the different worldviews cannot just be allowed to continue existing along separate tracks. However, when they do engage in dialogue, creative exchange should go both ways. Rather than giving up aspects of process thought to accommodate the dominant scientific worldview concerning minds and subjectivity, Cobb urges the scientists to modify their position on such points.[1] The same applies to how Cobb engages in interreligious dialogue. He has spent considerable time in discussion with Buddhists, and, as the title of one of his books on the subject shows, all participants should move *Beyond Dialogue* into actively transforming their own tradition in light of insights gained from interreligious comparison. Failure to transform in that way would mean participants did not really engage in dialogue, but merely talked at one other.

Neville understands the theological situation rather differently, but at his core shares similar concerns as Cobb. Neville does not develop a contextual worldview, but one comprehensive worldview that takes stock of philosophy, the best current science, and numerous religious traditions. It is in relation to that overall picture that he then seeks a unifying explanation, his indeterminate grounding for it all. That subsequent understanding of an indeterminate creator is meant to be in harmony with science and bring world religions together rather than drive them apart. However, it does that in their current form. The world's religions are not creatively transformed in dialogue so much as they are shown to be possible syntheses for a suitably complex and unified life.[2] Cobb's method begins within the highly specific context of Christian theism, basically taking a Peircean notion of common-sense working habits very seriously. Beginning theological work in this Christian context contrasts sharply with Neville's search for a deeper and universal unifying explanation.

In defense of his specific starting point, Cobb contends that much of the liberal Christian theological tradition has appealed to a God that makes sense to the modern mind but does not create devotion or any interest among the general population. The God of that liberal tradition tends to do nothing. Tillich's God beyond the God of the Bible and appeals to divine mystery just make it clear that such a God is or does nothing, making it even easier for modern people to do without such a God.[3] On the other hand, process philosophy enables some features of the God that once died for Cobb in theory and practice to be resurrected.[4] He is a theist, an ontological realist, affirms the unique presence of God in Jesus, performs natural theology of a qualified "Christian" variety, and affirms this all with a philosophy that does not shun real achievements of the modern world. The interests he shares with Neville, such as not shying away from metaphysics, dialogue with science, and interreligious dialogue, are all in favor of a much narrower goal than in Neville's work. Cobb's hope is that rather than viewing God as a powerful ruler, arbiter of eternal moral law, or a philosophical absolute, God can be viewed once again as tender love presented through the lens of Jesus. "I am hoping that the time may finally have come when Jesus can again have priority over the Christ of the creeds."[5] Cobb's focus on the immanent side of theology proclaimed by Jesus is not about an eschatological call to a kingdom at the end of time, or the expectation of another reality once this one ends. Jesus was proclaiming a reality, God's ideal loving community, that is a real immediate possibility right now. Cobb's work is a proclamation about that God immanent in our world. Neville's understanding of the immanent side of religious life is where he creatively extends Peirce's theory of interpretation. Peircean indices, when used to engage an indeterminate reality, must be broken. They point to, but do not literally depict, the God engaged in their usage. Even when turning from metaphysics to the daily lived aspects of religion, Neville's gaze is turned toward the transcendent indeterminate

God. However, neither Cobb nor Neville ever really considered pragmatic philosophy as a genuine alternative framework in which their work could be developed. Neville ignores Peirce's categories of Firstness, Secondness, and Thirdness in favor of his own analysis of essential and conditional features in determinacy. Cobb, following Hartshorne's negative assessment of Peirce, never considers pragmatism as a viable form of process thought, though it is.[6] This is unfortunate, because Peirce's metaphysical scheme has resources capable of rounding out each theological system. Peirce's categories are capable of giving more robust immanence to Neville's indeterminate God, a development that would bring this aspect of Neville's thought closer to Cobb and process theology. It also allows asking big ontological questions rather than settling for cosmological principles, a feature of pragmatism that can bring Cobb and process theology closer to Neville's position on God.

Tillich's Realism and Barth's Constructivism in Theology

Having set up well-known differences between Cobb and Neville once again, it should be noted that both Neville and Cobb stand on the realist side of the dichotomy set up earlier between Barth and Tillich. In being on that realist side, both are also with Peirce, in spirit. The method of science, rather than tenacity, authority, or the a priori is the one that puts us in touch with something external to ourselves and our communities. It seems Cobb makes a move akin to that of Barth in starting theology with the structures of a Christian understanding of existence.[7] Conversely, Neville starts by privileging an ontology meant to be true and relevant for anyone, not just Christians.[8] His position is agnostic regarding which specific religious symbols are used by humans in engaging God. But neither will Cobb restrict theology to self-examination. It must be an adequate expression of Christianity, to be sure, as that is the context in which Cobb begins his work, but it must also illuminate and be consistent with the world in which we live to be deemed credible. For Cobb, this entails an explicit rejection of Barth. "For Barth, Christian theology has as its subject matter, ultimately, only faith as the work of God. Christian faith no longer illuminates anything but itself."[9] Just as the realist and constructivist positions can be reconciled in philosophy, religious belief can have both truth-seeking and identity-forming dimensions, though Tillich's truth-seeking concerns must come first.

Besides the fact that it should be possible to learn truths about the world and find ways to orient one's life in light of what is found, rather than only investigating subject matter that will not likely disrupt beliefs important to one's identity, there are sociological reasons to not prima facie accept privileged narratives. Beliefs that provide narrative meaning and personal identity are not neutral. The theistic narrative of substitutionary atonement in Jesus Christ has been used to support wars, oppress women, and deny gay people their dignity and rights in the name of self-sacrifice.[10] Not only is it philosophically questionable to simply accept a given set of religious beliefs and assume they are immune from correction and coherent with knowledge about the world without even checking, it is morally problematic. However, simply amassing factual knowledge will not do much to fully express the meaning of anyone's being. Truth-seeking is the ontological component in religion, Tillich's primary concern. Narrative is the existential component, Barth's only concern.[11] The two components conform by default in Barth because the narrative of Jesus Christ laid out in God's revelation sets the ontology within that narrative. Meanwhile, Tillich's understanding of the revelation of God to one's inner awareness does not predetermine what in the world will be relevant for expressing being so grasped by God. If both the ontological and existential dimensions are important, it is more responsible to follow Tillich and check the identity being expressed with claims from other disciplines. Being engaged by a narrative is not sufficient. The Nazis were engaging, but demonically so. The same could be said of right-wing nationalist movements rising in popularity across the world. While Tillich's theology is not representative of the position that will be reached by navigating between Cobb and Neville with PCR, it illuminates the need to unite cosmology and ontology, constructivism and realism, transcendence and immanence.

Tillich's discussion of the ontological and cosmological approaches to philosophy of religion in his well-known "The Two Types of Philosophy of Religion" argues that the cosmological approach to God fails unless it is based on the ontological approach. Moreover, his discussion is more than a tool for analyzing how philosophers have talked about God. Tillich prefaced his famous article by mentioning his presidential address at the 1944 meeting of the American Theological Society.[12] The two types of philosophy of religion are ways of *approaching* God.

Tillich equates the ontological method with overcoming estrangement and the cosmological method with meeting a stranger. Regarding the first method, the religious meaning of estrangement is separation from God and thus from one's true nature. More generally, its philosophical expression is a separation of true unity, be it subject from object or the estrangement from one's essential being. The implication of noting that separation stems from an original unity is that speaking in terms of separated parts becomes paradoxical. It is a wonder as to how it ever occurred. Since the true unity always existed and is essential, a feeling of separation is merely accidental and can be overcome. The question is how to escape this puzzling situation and return to original unity. Meeting a stranger, by contrast, is to meet that which is essentially separated from you and whose meeting will be contingent.[13] You may never meet, and, if you do, it could be a mere accident.

The problem Tillich identifies in the methods just sketched is the competition of two absolutes. Mythic stories throughout human history have placed divine powers in the universe, making God one being among others or even just one divine being among a vast array of beings with divine powers. There was then a religious conquering of that multifaceted world through the idea of one true God, as well as a separate philosophical conquering that made all the principles of the world manifestations of one overarching governing principle. Because the existence of two absolutes is a contradiction, there must be a connection or even identification between the two. The relation between God and a philosophical understanding of being is therefore the basic problem Tillich faces. Can God and the ultimate philosophical principle be two sides of the same coin? It is against this backdrop that Tillich speaks of two types of philosophy of religion. He argues that the ontological type will correctly overcome the problem of two absolutes while the cosmological will only heighten the tension. However, overcoming the problem also reveals how cosmology and ontology are necessarily related.

Just because Tillich distinguishes cosmology and ontology does not mean they are separate. Rather, they imply one another even though there are differences between them. Tillich's stranger language helps clarify what he has in mind. He is thinking of objects and where they are found. In the cosmological method, God is the problem and we are not. The issue is how to go about finding the stranger God. The ontological method is exactly the reverse. We are the problem and God is not.[14] Ontologically, God is beyond distinctions between the subject's location and God, the object, being located somewhere else. God is always already the answer, we just need to realize this fact.

The ontological method, rather than searching outside ourselves for something else, is an internal process of realization in which God becomes immediately present to one's awareness. As Tillich expresses such interiority, "the Truth is dwelling."[15] It can become apparent that truth equals the very nature of being itself, which is the same as God. Thus, to return to an issue from the first chapter, awareness as direct realism in perceptual experience, as argued for by William Alston, becomes direct realism through inner awareness without perception for Tillich. Both are immediate, but perception is no longer involved in becoming aware of God, a reality *not found as an object outside oneself*. The way of overcoming estrangement, the correct way in Tillich's view, realizes that God is somehow always already present. "*God is the presupposition of the question of God:* This is the ontological solution of the problem of the philosophy of religion, God can never be reached if he is the *object* of a question, and not its *basis*."[16] God is the ground of being, not a being, even an ultimate one, found in cosmological analysis. Awareness of this point always takes the form of a paradox.

Tillich's philosophy is almost Kantian in that it concerns the condition for the possibility of thinking we relate to objects. Tillich's answer is that subject-object distinctions presuppose an unconditional reality. There cannot be a difference between subject and object that is not already a difference *of* something. This type of thinking is not alien to Neville's assertion that everything determinate is a harmony in need of an indeterminate context explaining the togetherness of that harmony.[17] As a consequence, the essence of being can be understood in two ways. Being can be either an actuality or the very power of being that allows something to exist. That latter power of being is transcendental, going before all that has being, and is affirmed by Tillich to be the true God.[18] Everything that exists, that has being, is created by virtue of this power of being and, as a consequence, it cannot be said that God exists as *a being* among others. God, as that which is unconditional, would then also create God as a being. Therefore, God is not a being. This distinction between being and the condition for the possibility of being also creates a sense of contingency in need of answering.

The possibility of being can be inferred from what has being. "To be" implies that it was possible "to be" and therefore possible "not to be." Since there is something rather than nothing, and in order for God to make all things possible, God's reality must be beyond that distinction. Otherwise, God would not be the condition making the distinction possible. God must be present wherever something with being exists, as that grounding its reality. Given such necessary presence, it must always be possible to be aware of God.

Awareness of God is an existential occurrence in which something at the depth of our own being that was always there is realized as such. This awareness is rarely clear, however. God is usually not at the front of our minds as we go about our daily activities, but it is nonetheless possible to realize the unconditional as our own identity according to Tillich's account.[19] This inner state is not mere emotion, but the consciousness of being related to something that is beyond possible distinctions of the will and intellectual objects that can be created at a whim. It is awareness of something we did not create and yet which conditions us, a realization of our contingency and dependence upon its reality.

This awareness of God is not something to be logically deduced from a set of premises. We depend on God for what we can know of God. We would have no being without the power of being. Here is the point where Tillich's realism breaks with realists like Alston. Awareness of God dawns by realizing the condition of the possibility of all that is experienced, including one's own perceptual experience. Still, Tillich is in Alston's realist camp. This awareness is not merely subjective. It is awareness of something real that makes the possibility of our very actuality possible. Nonetheless, Tillich would reject other aspects of Alston's work for employing the cosmological method without ontological support.

It might seem like a categorical mistake to continue the realism versus constructivism thread of the first chapter by claiming Tillich would reject Alston's approach. After all, Alston argues for the justificatory force of *non-sensory* perceptions of God. It might also be the case that Alston's notion of religious perception is an *inner* experience in the same manner as Tillich's ontological awareness. However, the real problem has to do with the permanent separation of subject and object by Alston. Tillich argues the first theological step should be to become aware of God as that which comes before such a division. Only then can subject-object statements about such awareness be used, though always in a paradoxical fashion.[20] For Alston, awareness of God comes packaged with the perception of God as the object presented in religious experience. In this context, Neville's theory of broken symbols falls in line with Alston, with the crucial difference that the broken perceptual/determinate aspect is praised by Neville. It is actually Cobb, despite working out of Whitehead's *cosmology*, who affirms a deeper unity between God and creature in the form of initial aims and subjective responses. In all four cases, the issue is the relation between awareness of God's reality and the contingent manner in which that reality will be realized in experience. For Tillich, as for Neville and less so for Cobb, awareness of God must involve a paradox.

Ontological awareness of the unconditional is defined by what it is not. It is not experience, intuition, or knowing because all these are tied to space and time. They are all ways of knowing conditional reality. But the unconditional and conditional are different in kind.[21] Consider what this means through a mathematical example. That a series exists is not a fact that is instantiated as a member within that series. That is to say, affirming a series exists is not the same as giving another example of the series or one of its members. Tillich's unconditional God is similar. It is presupposed by conditional reality. Written as a series this point would look something like the following: God {x, y, z ...}. As the condition for there being a series, God is connected to the series. Thus, God is the condition for the existence of being and is therefore necessarily connected to what has being. God is connected to conditional reality. However, God as the presupposition of being can be understood by thinking in the other direction. Without being, the notion of there being a condition for being makes no sense. But there is being, therefore there is God.

For Tillich, nothing exists apart from God since God is the condition for the possibility of existing. God is already present before the issue of questioning or affirming God can even be raised. Thus, a necessary ordering becomes clear. It is possible to identify or perceive the unconditional in the conditional, but only if you are aware of the unconditional first. To reverse this order would result in elevating some conditional reality to the status of the unconditional. However, the problem is that the realized identity between God and existence is always expressed in philosophical terms that violate that identity. Tillich's solution, *Deus est esse,* God is being, uses "to be" twice in its formulation. Saying "God is" only heightens the problem and makes God a being in the world just like anything else. However, "God is being" should indicate that God is the power to be, the power without which nothing exists. *Deus est esse ipsum,* God is being itself.[22] Only after this statement is accepted is it possible to say "God is" or that anything exists. As a consequence, awareness of God does not arise from specific experiences. Nobody becomes aware of God through a special perception in experience, but from the very fact *that* they are. Only for this reason is Tillich able to say that God is the presupposition of the question of God. Given that awareness of God is only possible because there are things with being and all things are constituted by the unconditional, it becomes possible to perceptually identify God in conditional reality as long as awareness of God is first in one's mind.[23] But any statement about one's inner certainty of God's connection to all reality will use language that makes the unconditional God what it is not, an object.

Tillich, in seeking to unite the cosmological and ontological approaches to God, ends up with a position very close to Neville's theory of symbolic truth. "When it is said that the self grasps within itself the Unconditional as the basis of its own self-certainty, the opposition of subject and object is contained in the very form of this statement. But the import of the statement stands in direct contradiction to that, for the Unconditional is neither object or subject, but rather the presupposition for every possible antithesis of subject and object."[24] Nathaniel Barrett argues that this aspect of Tillich's thought, that cosmological inquiry can never reach ontological ultimate depths, separates Tillich and Neville. Neville affirms four cosmological ultimates found everywhere and which connect the determinate world with the indeterminate God, overcoming Tillich's failure.[25] Neville's one ontological and four cosmological ultimates will be explained in chapter 6, but it should be noted now that Barrett's interpretation is not quite right.

Cosmological ultimates are determinate created features of the world and, as Neville is clear about this issue, all determinate symbols of God are broken.[26] In Tillichian terms, once God is expressed in object language, the result is either the separation of that unique object from the rest of the world or complete idealism in which the idea of God can ground one's self-identity though it will never be found as an object in the world. However, if the awareness of God is understood as the transcendental condition for the possibility of distinguishing between subject and object, instead of a duality there is a condition without which dualistic statements could not be made. Symbolic expressions can then be used to express awareness of God in everyday experience. Tillich's test for the vitality of religious symbols could have been written by Neville. "A real symbol points to an object which never can become an object. Religious symbols represent the transcendent but do not make the transcendent immanent. They do not make God a part of the empirical world."[27] Since Tillich's attempted synthesis of immanence and transcendence ends up privileging transcendence, it is worth showing, for the sake of balance, how the case would look different, and more like Cobb, if subsets instead of a series were used as an example of God's relation to the world.

In set theory, B is a subset of A, or A is a superset of B, if all of B is contained in A. This would mean all the elements of B are also elements of A. B can coincide with A in its entirety, while there can be more to A than is found in B. A could be thought of as a large circle with the smaller circle B entirely inside its circumference. If every element of B is also an element of A, B is a subset of A denoted by $B \subseteq A$, or equivalently $B \supseteq A$, A is a superset of B. For example, $B=\{x, y, z\} \subseteq A=\{x, y, z\}$. If B is a subset of A, but they do not share all elements, B is a proper subset of A, written as $B \subsetneq A$. For example, $B\{x, y\} \subsetneq A\{x, y, z\}$. Regular polygons are a proper subset of all polygons, to give an example less abstract than mathematical symbols. There can also be nested inclusive subsets. If $C \subseteq B$ and $B \subseteq A$ that means $C \subseteq A$. This could be pictured as A being the largest circle, B being a smaller circle within A, and C being the smallest circle within B. With mathematical notation out of the way, it can be shown how different the relation between God and the world can look using subsets instead of Tillich's series.

Pantheism is a subset in which every element of the world is also in God. Given World{everything about God} and God{everything about God}, World ⊆ God. There is no difference between the two, complete immanence. I suggest that the position of Tillich and Neville is a very extreme proper subset in which only the barest detail of sharing in the act of creation is shared by the world and God. World{being/created determinacy} and God{power of being/creator of everything determinate, everything else about God} results in World ⊊ God. So far this is not unlike construing Tillich's God using a series, as World ⊊ God is a strong model of transcendence. Consider the statement "God is" and Tillich's remarks on the paradox of that statement. "Religion is aware that no theoretical pointing to the ground of all theory can make the Unconditional alive within consciousness.... If the statement 'God is' is likewise theoretical in its import, then it destroys the divinity of God. Meant as paradox, however, it is the necessary expression for the affirmation of the Unconditional, for it is not possible to direct oneself toward the Unconditional apart from objectification."[28] Affirming that religious symbols must objectify, even though that is always inappropriate, makes the world a rather meager proper subset of God. But nested inclusive subsets open up an option, similar to Cobb's position, that offers more balance between transcendence and immanence. In the case of God{everything else about God, properties of God revealed in creation}, World{God revealed in creation, everything else about the world}, Human Inquiry{God revealed in creation, everything else about the world} actual knowledge of God could be revealed as a creator is displayed in their creation, while the entirety of God would nonetheless transcend the world. Human Inquiry ⊆ World and World ⊊ God so Human Inquiry ⊊ God. The important difference with this inclusive subset framework is that the subset of human inquiry and the world includes actual knowledge of God as revealed in the act of creating, versus the Tillich and Neville proper subset, which only affirms the act of creation but not knowledge of God gleaned from it.

Understood in terms of subsets, Neville's indeterminate God emphasizes a proper subset in which God and world share little in the way of actual knowledge. Cobb's creative transformation emphasizes immanence, a subset in which, in its ideal configuration, God and world more perfectly share knowledge. The point of bringing up subsets is to show that more balance can be achieved. God can transcend the world and remain unknown, while also being immanent in the world, facts about which *can be known in the course of human inquiry,* without eliminating either pole. The task of PCR will be to take Cobb and Neville to such a position.

Transcending Whitehead

From the different starting points of their theological methods, both Cobb and Neville offer novel abductive hypotheses about God. For both, the fact that the model of God contained in their abduction is rather unlike the God of classical substance theism is a sign that their work is moving along the correct path. Both agree such a God has been disproven by science, historical consciousness, and awareness of other religions. Cobb and Neville, despite their strong differences on God, also share core methodological concerns. Neville stands in the lineage of Whitehead as someone who views metaphysics as viable again, as long as it is fallible and sensitive to contextual problems. Neville, despite departing from Whitehead when it comes to God, notes "however one assesses Whitehead's theory of God, he and his followers have shown that the way to solve conceptual problems in theology is by getting better ideas. Precisely because the basic symbols of the religious traditions require interpretation in current terms, metaphysics as a trans-traditional discipline has an ongoing task of conceptual imagination."[29] Despite disagreeing with Whitehead's model of God, it set new standards for clarity in metaphysics.

Neville and Cobb agree nature is prior to history and can handle many different interpretations. The death of God movement was correct that holding up the God of one culture as salvation history for every culture is dead.[30] Both affirm value is bound up with everything we do. Whitehead makes the selection of value fundamental to all processes, the first step in the self-making of every actual occasion. Cobb accepts this view. Peirce argues that interpretation is bound up with value. The respects with which interpretations engage their objects is related to the way those interpretations promote chosen values. Neville accepts this view. In extending beyond their initial contexts, signs grow in richness. Cobb argues that the way to be true to Christianity is to creatively transform it, perhaps beyond all currently recognizable forms. Interpretation does not loosen the grip of reality so we can freely play with it. Rather, it drives us more deeply and widely into reality. In that sense, both theologians are radical empiricists in James's sense. Reality is infinitely richer than our attempts to grasp it with concepts. Despite all these similarities, their respective emphases on the transcendence and presence of God remain drastically different. As will be shown in chapter 7, in which the history of their dialogue is reviewed, a conversation between Cobb and Neville framed in terms of Whitehead's philosophy has run its course. It is time to look at them, and God's transcendence and immanence, though a different, and pragmatic, perspective.

Process philosophy focuses on occasions coming together out of many previous occasions, making a decision, then offering that decision to many other occasions to be unified again. The bringing together of disparate elements is exemplified well in the primordial and consequent natures of God.[31] For Peirce, on the other hand, emergence is first and foremost continuous, even though something quite different can emerge from something else. This makes it possible for pragmatists to affirm even stronger notions of growth and change than process thinkers. For example, when it comes to God, Peirce is open to a deep unknown God that also has a growing determinate character.[32] In an emergent framework, they can be intimately related while different. Process thought starts with the discrete and actual and tries to develop continuity out of individually related things,[33] while pragmatism focuses on continuity and then tries to explain how individual differences emerge.

Sandra Rosenthal lends support to this attempt to form a new kind of mediation between these theological camps through employing pragmatism by noting that Neville is a process philosopher who shares an epochal theory of time with Whitehead, and with Cobb by extension.[34] While Whitehead's philosophy focuses on individual occasions encountering one another, pragmatists, at least the classical ones, focus primarily on continuity. Whitehead provides an excellent account of atomic moments of experience but struggles to provide enough connective tissue between them.[35] Continuity on this account is achieved by the past being experienced in the present, as each occasion harmonizes the many elements of the past and makes its own decision in reaction to them, which is then offered to the next occasions to be experienced. Neville sides with Whitehead on this issue. Pragmatic thinkers like Peirce understand things differently. Rather than discrete entities coming together, entities are understood to emerge from more basic connections and, in that process, there is simultaneous influence between what emerges and what it emerged from. The result is what Peirce called concrete reasonableness, the transition from Firstness to Thirdness, the growth and extension of possibilities. And on Peirce's view there is *continuous* connection, meaning the past is only relatively definite because what emerges from it can give it new character. Despite being known as a pragmatic theologian, Neville explicitly rejects pragmatism on these points.[36] He now goes as far as claiming he must "profoundly reject" Peirce's metaphysics.[37] Charles Hartshorne also seemed to be aware of this dividing line between process and pragmatic philosophy, claiming Peirce's biggest mistake was affirming continuity.[38] His authoritative word on the matter only further indicates Rosenthal has correctly placed her finger on the divide between the two ways of thinking, which is in part why it is interesting to reexamine Neville's engagement with process theology through the lens of pragmatism.

Since PCR sides with pragmatism on this issue and will be used to reinterpret Cobb and Neville, a few key features of pragmatic continuity that Rosenthal highlights should be mentioned. Specifically, the affirmation of continuity means we are always living in a specious present tinged with past, future, and novelty all at once. As Rosenthal summarizes, "The habit-takings of humans and nature are part and parcel of its temporal features.... Thus, habit-taking, interpretation, and temporality are ultimately intertwined in pragmatic philosophy."[39] This is true of even highly habitual responses to our environments like walking. As we walk, our bodies adjust to the contours of the surface upon which we travel, novel responses even if we are not consciously aware of them. "A situation in need of no ongoing adjustment whatsoever could not be truly temporal. Every experience, even the habitual, is tinged with novelty and a sense of accompanying adjustment due to the very nature of time."[40] A brief examination of the way our brains process sense experiences will support Rosenthal's claim.

Our sense experiences are always delayed by around 0.25 seconds due to the time needed for information to spread through the body's nervous system. For example, elite tennis players will report seeing the ball heading toward their racket and deciding to hit it, but the time it takes for a serve over 100 miles per hour to hit the opposing racket and be volleyed back is less time than it takes for the visual signal of the ball hitting the racket to travel from the retina to the cortex.[41] The tennis player is seeing the ball hit after it has been hit. What Whitehead takes to be a series of atomic moments with an irreversible arrow of times are actually past, present, and future intermingling in a continuity out of which the separate components gradually emerge. These present components only emerge, as Rosenthal notes, "because of the way in which continuity allows for traces of the past as possibilities for present creativity, possibilities that are 'there' in the present and stretch into the future."[42] In this sense, Barrett and Wildman's argument against Alston also applies to Whitehead. There is a specious and wider functional present involving interpretation, stretching the present into the wider context of the activity being undertaken at any given moment.

Rather than seek integration of separate units into continuities, pragmatists do not begin by acknowledging ultimate divisible parts. "For pragmatism, the key intuition concerning temporality and the habit-takings that partake of temporal features is that of 'emerging elements within' continuity rather than the 'coming-together-of' discretes."[43] In this continuous situation, it is from ongoing interaction that past, present, and future and discrete individuals emerge. There are breaks within continuity, not of continuity. This focus on continuity also means pragmatists admit play, degrees of freedom, between past and present. "From the pragmatic perspective, there is nothing absolutely finished, fixed, and final except the events of actualization, but the event as a metaphysically discrete determinate individual, as a moment of temporal/ontological atomicity, is an idealized abstraction from a history and process of becoming other."[44] For pragmatists, the concrete is not fully determined. There are always dynamic possibilities that are not settled and that remain open to further actualizations.

In process thought, actual entities are indivisible and become themselves in momentary processes. Once finished, they are fixed and do not change. What changes is subsequent members in the series in response to preceding members. As related to time, this means the distinction between past and present requires that something perish, which in turn requires that the past remain absolutely fixed. Thus, the irreversible arrow of time. But this creates a new problem, according to Rosenthal. With all completed actual entities fixed in the past, something other than the actual world is needed to account for the fact of novelty. Thus, Whitehead must affirm eternal objects, and they must be located somewhere other than the settled past.[45] Whitehead needs recourse to possibilities not in time to account for novelty. The conclusion is that they must be in God.

Ivor Leclerc has also developed an argument against Whitehead that agrees that these differing process and pragmatic intuitions are real, and the specific pressure he places on process philosophy reflects similar pressure that will be placed on the theological projects of Cobb and Neville in the following chapters. He argues that process philosophers have correctly named the death of materialism and its associated sensationalist epistemology but have yet to develop a philosophy entirely adequate to the new organic view of nature. For Whitehead, every actual occasion is self-making, having the power to be within itself, meaning all occasions are self-sufficient and independent from one another.[46] Leclerc contrasts this view with his organic understanding of nature in which the discontinuity of individual things or entire orders of nature, from matter to mind, are understood as entirely related within nature.⁴⁷ For him, we should just let what happens to emerge in reality emerge, without letting extra concepts get in the way. Concrete is not the same as fully determinate, as no ongoing living reality can be fully determinate. In that sense, pragmatists are actually more concerned with the process of growth than those who follow Whitehead. Actual entities are pregnant with possibility. Those possibilities in what is actual, plus chance and continuity, can account for novelty in the world. This opposite intuition also opens the door for a theory of God without eternal objects, since the natural world can fulfill their role, which means God will no longer be necessary, as Whitehead and Cobb think, for explaining novelty.

5 | John Cobb's Creative Transformation

A Theological Peircean Habit

Cobb began his career working out of a rather traditional Christian context. He was born of Methodist missionaries and through the early years of his life held traditional theistic beliefs. God was a supernatural being to which one could pray and on which one could depend. Cobb expected to enter higher education, learn to defeat modern criticisms of that God, and leave ready to defend the faith. However, as Gary Dorrien tells it, things did not work out that way. "His idea was to strengthen his faith by facing the fire of modern criticism. Cobb believed that God created the world, Jesus was God's divine Son and Savior of the world, nothing is more important intellectually than religious truth, and God can be known personally in prayer. Six months later he had no Christian beliefs at all."[1] The theism with which he was working had become problematic, in Peirce's sense. Cobb needed to find resources to salvage it, or give up his Christian identity.

Cobb had no alternative but to try and work his way out of this situation. A sweeping alternative philosophical and theological architectonic like the one Neville creates was not an option for Cobb, as evidenced by his early work. Cobb denies unhistorical reason. He has long since abandoned claims to finality present in his earlier work, that anyone could provide *the* Christian or *the* Buddhist structure of existence, but still maintains that there are truly different structures of existence out of which religious visions of reality develop. It is these structures with which theologians must struggle.[2] All philosophies and theologies develop out of historically conditioned visions of reality. What one affirms still must be defended on its merits as philosophy, but there is something inevitably given about the situation. If traditional views about God become problematic, as they did for Cobb, that vision and structure cannot simply be dropped and new ones created. If they cease to exist, so does God, and, rather than alternatives being open, life just goes on without Christianity. Cobb had to retroductively attempt to salvage his religious identity.

Advances in science and philosophy brought on Cobb's crisis, meaning theological positions like neo-orthodoxy that retreat from modernity were not live options for him. He needed a way to accept the achievements of the modern world while specifically transcending its materialist worldview to one that made Christianity possible again.[3] He was influenced by the "death of God" movement, especially Thomas Altizer, and believed there were reasons God was fading from the consciousness of many people. Structures of existence are doomed without a supporting vision of reality. Consider Altizer's assessment of the task for theology, offered in the context of assessing Cobb's work: "Can God be the compost of our imagination, and compost in the sense that his decaying body is both the source and the consequence of whatever life our words may possess? If we can forget God and leave him to the night, then if one day he happens to return in our language, it should be without our connivance and so disguised that we do not recognize him when we see him again. Is this not a precise formula for our theological task?"[4] Since Cobb construes visions as precognitive ways of ordering experience, a religious vision will not last long without support from other cognitive beliefs about the world. The modern vision from which God was fading took what is real to be what is encountered in sense experience. Its problematic aspects to be overcome are the associated positivist view that this world of sense experience is not meaningful, the phenomenal view that there are only appearances and no reality, and the reductionist view that sense experience is exhaustive of reality. If these are the only options, there is no room for God's action and God really is dead to the modern world. The essay from which the Altizer quote came is titled "Spiritual Existence as God-Transcending Existence." Cobb takes that literally. The modern world that ruled out God moved from the metaphysical dualism of Descartes, to the sensationalism of Hume, and ended in the epistemological dualism of Kant. God and theology get to stick around in Kant's world but have nothing to do with knowledge or reality. To resolve this, Cobb moved from a vision of reality in which isolated subjects and their sense experiences are the locus of reality, with an associated isolated transcendent God, to a vision in which relations are the locus of reality.

In *Christ in a Pluralistic Age* Cobb investigates art historian André Malraux's study of Christ disappearing from modern art in order to find possible seeds of positivity in movements like Altizer's. If he can "wrest from the work of an art historian who sees Christ as having disappeared from Western art the evidence that Christ is the power that is expressed through it," then he will have found a clue to transcending the modern worldview that made his Christianity problematic.[5] He found it. Malraux understood art as getting over one dominant style and moving toward an internal pluralization in the acceptance of all great styles, but thought that same move was impossible for Christianity. For Cobb, that is precisely where Christian theology should go. Christians should proclaim "Christ is no more bound to any particular system of religious belief and practice than is the creative power of art to any particular style," since both embody a power or activity rather than being vehicles for one exclusive form.[6] Cobb saying yes to a world that has gotten over the Christian God is the start to him recovering a better understanding of that God. Malraux's conclusion on modern art is telling for Cobb's vision for Christian theology. Creativity, not form, is the absolute standard by which meaning is found. The resource that enabled Cobb to achieve this goal was Whitehead's process philosophy. Specifically, Cobb was inspired by Whitehead's principle of creative transformation that Cobb would come to identify with Christ.

Challenges from and Challenges to Science

Cobb not only wants theology to be consistent with scientific knowledge, but challenges what he deems problematic aspects of the scientific worldview. He expresses little wonder that Christians are not attracting well-educated people to their churches, but argues things could be different if, conveniently, more educated people adopted a different worldview like Cobb's in which science and theology are not in conflict. "This situation would change if those at the cutting edge of the sciences adopted a worldview that was supportive also of some form of Christian faith. This is a change for which I have been hoping and working throughout my career."[7] That worldview is the nonreductive cosmology of Whitehead, one profuse with subjective experience and with a metaphysics robust enough to affirm God. The title of a volume Cobb edited on the relation of theology to evolution makes his agenda clear: *Back to Darwin: A Richer Account of Evolution.* Science is getting in its own way by reducing everything to physics and genetics but can make real progress in speaking of subjective experiences and relating to religion if outdated metaphysical baggage is dropped in favor of Whitehead's philosophy. "These revisions would account for evidence that the current theory neglects. It would also allow for integration with humanistic and religious concerns, including a role for God. The book suggests how such integration is possible without any distortion of the scientific evidence."[8] Without this challenge, Cobb believes the modern reductive vision of reality will keep pushing God to the margins until forever lost, with ethics and any sense of moral responsibility not far behind. To prevent this, he must show that the reasons for the modern worldview associated with the advances in scientific knowledge are not inevitable. They can be rejected in favor of an alternative worldview without rejecting scientific knowledge and its achievements. He wants to overcome the modern dualism of mind and matter without reducing all matter to sense perception or mind to matter. His suggestion is that all reality "participates in both mentality and materiality without in fact being either."[9] Real things are events, experiences, that in their activity display both mind and matter, as Whitehead argued. "Consciousness presupposes experience, and not experience consciousness."[10] Accepting this panexperientialist position becomes Cobb's key to an alternative understanding of the scientific worldview.

Cobb wishes scientists would give up substantialism as their *assumed* philosophy. He argues there is no evidence for substances. Science deals with events. Events happen and play a role in subsequent events. In living creatures, events involve behavior, purposive behavior. Ignoring these points, a charge he levels against materialist scientists, does not count as a positive argument against Whitehead, value, and religion—it is just willful ignorance. Against reductive materialism, Cobb identifies values in the way every actual entity is self-creative. For example, birds with certain types of beaks are able to reach worms and insects in trees that birds with other beaks cannot. *Purposive* behavior is related to what trait is naturally selected for survival, according to Cobb. "The evidence is that the behavior of living things, omitted from neo-Darwinian theory, plays an important role among simpler organisms as well."[11] He finds support in the symbiotic theory of Lynn Margulis, initially developed in consideration of the formation of the first eukaryotic cells.[12] Natural evolution involves symbiotic relationships, not just random mutations. Cobb states things even more strongly in his rejection of attempts to reduce mind to the firing of neurons in the brain. "But common sense does not agree that because some subjective experiences are caused by neuronal events, this is true of all. This is what the defenders of orthodoxy want neuroscience to prove, and they assume that it is just a matter of further research to complete the task."[13] He argues neuroscientists should explain subjective experiences by what can be observed in the brain, because that is what they do. But there is no need to assume that is the whole story. Experience shows subjective states affect the brain. Subjectivity is a key to Whitehead's philosophy, and without the subjective decisions of occasions, the philosophy falls apart, along with its corresponding model of God. Again, defending experience against materialism is crucial for Cobb.

Process Philosophy and a Loving God

Since Whitehead's process philosophy is the key that allowed Cobb to reconfigure and reclaim his Christian identity, the God of the Bible revealed in Jesus against scientific critics, some of the features of that philosophy relevant to Cobb's theology should be mentioned. Everything in the actual world is in process according to Whitehead. If anything is not understood as a process, that understanding is an abstraction from a process. Religious and philosophical beliefs that the fully real is unchanging, substance philosophy and theism, are examples of such unhelpful abstractions. This means that what we normally call individuals, things that endure, are actually societies of actual occasions.[14] The occasions themselves are always in process, and concrescence is Whitehead's label for their process of becoming concrete.

In a concrescence, each occasion enjoys subjective immediacy. Only when the process is complete does an occasion become objective, a settled piece of external data for other occasions to encounter.[15] Subjective immediacy is not consciousness of pain or pleasure, but individuality. Each occasion, from humans to particles, is a real experiencing subject. The experience they enjoy is being actual entities in and for themselves. They experience the other occasions in the world, feel and respond to them individually, before that response becomes something other occasions can subsequently feel and to which they can respond. To reiterate Whitehead's succinct expression of panexperientialism again, "consciousness presupposes experience, and not experience consciousness."[16] Everything has experience, even if only some experiences rise to consciousness. This is the basic picture, though specific details are a bit more complicated.

It is only necessary that concrete singulars have experiences, according to Whitehead. Concrete particular entities feel and respond to the past, even if primitively, while any given collection of them, what Whitehead called a nexus, might be totally inert and exhibit lifelessness.[17] Thus, a rock is not conscious, but its basic constituents studied by particle physicists do respond to the past in some fashion. Similarly, a process thinker might argue that plants are not sentient beings while affirming that their cells have feelings and respond to the past with some degree of novelty. While this picture is more complicated than simply noting all things have experience according to process thought, insofar as this more nuanced description explains the emergence of these collective stable features from more concrete components exhibiting feeling and responsiveness, experience is still a fundamental feature of all reality.[18]

All actual occasions undergoing this experiential process are related. Gottfried Wilhelm Leibniz had a philosophy of entities in process that are entirely unrelated. The history of substance metaphysics is trying to understand how unchanging substances can have relations. Whitehead's alternative view is that actual occasions, the basic realities taking the place of substance in his philosophy, are events that do not endure—they arise, become, and reach completion. Their experiencing is done, but they can be experienced by others in the next moment. Relations with the past are primary for actual occasions, from which a becoming occasion makes itself. These relations take the form of prehensions or feelings. Occasions prehend/feel previous occasions and become concrete by unifying them in their own decision, their response to the world.[19] Leibniz also understood reality as nothing but experiencing processes, but for him all occasions experienced nothing beyond themselves. They were windowless, and their perceptions were projections that were only accurate because his God created a preestablished harmony. Conversely, Whitehead's occasions begin as open windows to the past, are closed as they form themselves, then open and give what is formed back to the world.

Whitehead's cosmological shift from independent to related events makes all the difference in the world for an understanding of religion. Past and present are interrelated in his philosophy. Past experiences can be incorporated into present experiences through limited selection. Each occasion must receive the past, but how it responds and incorporates a feeling of the past into its own unified experience is not determined by the past. The past is objectively immortal in the sense of continuing on in such reception and incorporation, yet it is also felt in a new way in the present where becoming occasions respond to it with novelty.[20] The past is objective as a real achievement and as an object for an occasion's subjective experience in which the past can be incarnated in the present. But the past does not determine the present. We do not live in a block universe, according to this view. The past starts the process of concrescence, but the free self-determination of the occasion finishes it.

No hard line can be drawn between individual and environment for Whitehead. What is objectively in the environment can enter or be excluded by individual subjective aims by which entities self-create. No environment can be so perfectly configured to guarantee success in any given endeavor, because all occasions are, in the end, self-determining. As Cobb has written with David Griffin, this is also the case for God. "The divine reality so relates itself to us as to heighten the probability that enjoyment will be enhanced. But God does not compel us to enjoy. The individual experience finally determines, within the limits made possible by God and the world, what enjoyment it will realize."[21] Aiming at such enjoyment is how an individual achieves unity, finishing its process of becoming in every moment and offering that final decision to the world. The conclusion at which each occasion aims cannot come entirely from the past, since occasions have their own subjective aims. Not being fully determined by the past world, aims from God can also enter into the experience of concrescence. "The attractive possibility, the lure, in relation to which its act of self-determination is made, is derived from God. This lure is called the 'initial aim.' God is the divine Eros urging the world to new heights of enjoyment."[22] The importance of the past for the becoming present occasion also makes room for Jesus, just as all historical figures of the past are objective elements that must be dealt with in the present. The message Jesus preached is also congenial to Whitehead's philosophy for another reason. Jesus proclaimed a message of love, a lack of force rather than coercion. He preached a God immanent in the world through concrete actions, not abstract thought separated from the world. It was not a message concerned with specific political or philosophical debates of the day as much as it was an attitude for life. Whitehead believed this meant the life and thought of Jesus can still function as a gauge or test for any society. "So long as the Galilean images are but dreams of an unrealized world, so long they must spread the infection of an uneasy spirit."[23] God is revealed in the most immanent intimate calls forward into currently unknown novel spaces, in the self-creative decisions that occasions make that will impact the future.

God's Revealing in God's Concealing

Whitehead credited early Christian communities with latching on to what he called the first major metaphysical insight since Plato,[24] and Cobb's work spells out the implications of that insight. Rather than imitations of reality, early Christians were seeking direct immanence of what is ultimately real. Cobb finds this immanence of God in creative transformation, which he identifies as the defining feature of Jesus's life. Related to his highly contextual starting point for theology, Cobb claims belief in God is not at first abstract belief in a concept, but a concrete experience of someone who was concerned for others. That experience can enter anyone's experience right now and impact the decisions they make for others. That concrete experience of being in relation with Jesus is also the key to a better concept of God. Cobb sees a profound difference between being concerned with the revealed saving presence of God in us and our world and being concerned with a transcendent absolute and its supposed conditioned appearances in the world. One calls attention directly to what is happening in the world, while the other takes us far away from the world. "Our relation to God is not a relationship to a supreme Being, absolute in power and goodness, which is a spurious conception of transcendence, but a new life for others, through participation in the Being of God."[25] The assumption must not be that there is one reality underlying all experience. Such metaphysical grounding already prejudges and predetermines the sort of order and disorder we will allow reality to make manifest to us. The same applies to the history of Christian theology. Even as God is disclosed there is concealing.

One reason Martin Heidegger wanted to strip away philosophical layers and go back to the Greeks was they had an openness to being undistorted by years of recorded history that is hard for us to achieve. Cobb's turn back to the God of the Bible, Abba, echoes this strategy of getting over unhelpful abstractions to get at the truth witnessed in Christ. Therefore, Cobb's recovery of Christ and Christian theology is not so much an answer for the world today as it is a challenge to the world.[26] Jesus proclaimed the God of post-exile Judaism, the God who acted in the past but was felt only remotely in the present. His message was that even though divine action seemed lacking, it was truly immediately present once again.[27] It is present again as a challenge to the world, a call to transform the world.

Cobb's Christology, worked out most fully in *Christ in a Pluralistic Age*, is not *just a* Christology. Cobb arrives at the understanding of both God and God's relation to the world through Jesus. "The thesis is that Christ names the creative transformation of theology by objective study which has broken the correlation of faith and the sacred and made pluralism possible."[28] For Cobb, creative transformation (Christ) reveals a model of God and a model for the proper style of theological work. He refers to "Christ" as an image uniting entity and concept. It is neither a literal reference to a historical person and his work, nor a free-floating symbol that can be modified at will due to lack of a concrete referent. "The unity of entity and concept that 'Christ' names is creative transformation—or Christ."[29] This means "Christ" does not refer to the historical Jesus, but Jesus as the incarnation of God. "'Christ' does not designate Jesus as such but refers to Jesus in a particular way, namely, as the incarnation of the divine. It does not designate deity as such but refers to deity experienced as graciously incarnate in the world."[30] Cobb's point about what is revealed in Jesus can be understood by considering how he contrasts his view with mysticism. Mysticism contains a worthy impulse to seek intimacy with God in the present moment. However, insofar as that impulse leads to earthly renunciation in favor of some supposedly pure awareness of God, that impulse is misguided. "If it is in Jesus that we perceive what God's immanence is and does, then it is from Jesus that we should learn what God is like. We can and must reverse the long history of retaining ideas of God uncongenial to what is apparent in Jesus."[31] God does not relate to the world by forced obedience or transcendent austerity, but by calling everything toward the realization of new possibilities.

Transformation goes further than making God present again. Jesus proclaimed a God that transforms our relationship with the world, calling us to broader possibilities than current standards may admit. Transformation is the insight Cobb took away from Altizer and the death of God movement.[32] Altizer could speak of images of Christ in literature and modern consciousness with beauty and conviction, making his case even more compelling that the God revealed in Jesus was fading. Theologians were too abstract, dull, and irrelevant to the world almost by design. Cobb sought to reconfigure Christian images and recapture a power that abstract metaphysical concepts often lack.

Cobb agrees with Neville, as will be shown in the next chapter, that Christian identity is developed according to the understanding between creator and creation. However, Cobb argues that for it to be a *Christian* identity, the kind of creative action involved must be what is revealed in Jesus. "Love, rather than compulsion, is God's mode of creative action."[33] Cobb admits that Neville's strategy is more typical than his own. By "God" people have often meant a transcendent unitary actuality worthy of worship, that which grounds all the diverse parts of reality. This God on which everything is dependent for its being is also entirely other than what it explains. Cobb's main problem is not that this is bad thinking. It may be excellent philosophy, but it is not Christian in Cobb's sense.

Since Cobb's Christian God is not the God of the philosophers, but the God revealed in Jesus, it is the life of Jesus that pushes Cobb to identify God with novelty, the call forward beyond the given. "We cannot go back to Jesus if that would mean simply repeating his beliefs. We can only go forward in a way that somehow corresponds for our time to the meaning of his life and message for the men of his time. My proposal is that we can do this best by attending to what I am hereafter designating as the *call forward.*"[34] Cobb takes an argument from Henry Nelson Wieman about the independent reality of ideals that is crucial for his theology. For Wieman there is no inference to God that is different than the data from which the inference is made. God is an empirical description of the growth of good in the world, not a good substance outside of the world.[35] The key to understanding God is in entertaining the truly novel, not by abstracting or projecting from what is directly experienced. The core of the meaning of God is therefore not being substantial or beyond experience but being the source of good in this world. God's nature is being creative of all good, and we should devote ourselves to that which is responsible for all good.

Wieman's God is not simply identified with any source of good. Good teachers and parents are not God. His God is identified with human good in general and the processes at work whenever that good appears, the ultimate good and the processes by which it is brought into being. Good has qualitative meaning as the immediacy of the present gives way as an instrument to the future, or enriching the present through remembering the past.[36] Since goods are concrete actualities, that is also where we look for God. It is not a matter of projecting an ideal and seeking means to achieve it, but pinpointing processes that produce the most good and working to bring about conditions necessary for the occurrence of that good. It is in that sense that we should serve God. We abandon false ideals to serve the actual source of good.[37]

Wieman names the process by which this occurs "creative interchange," or the totality of any event in which people encounter other people or other possibilities with sensitivity and openness. Even an encounter with evil can be an occasion for growth. This point is especially important for Cobb, who suggests childhood exemplifies the process of growth well. Adults need to reopen themselves to the process that too often calcifies in adulthood. Jesus exemplified creative interchange, transforming his disciples through meeting others. That event is still alive, or at least should be, in the community of the Christian church. In that community, creative interchange is continued.[38] This does not mean we control God, however, for nobody is wholly responsible for all the growth and good in their lives.

The influx of novelty is a surprising process that we cannot control and predict. "It works in us and among us already in infancy, for it is the process of human growth itself. It works through the creative interchange among persons in which each is transformed in ways which none can foresee or control."[39] Whitehead goes further than Wieman in giving possibilities their own independent reality, a crucial move that Cobb also makes. Pure possibilities in God are encountered in the world; they are the pregiven in each and every experience. God orders the possibilities so as to be relevant to actual occasions, makes them *our* possibilities rather than possibilities in general. However, all occasions are free to do with that ordered set of relevant possibilities what they wish. The philosophy of possibilities shades into theology and need of God in the context of their need to be in some sense concrete if they are to be capable of realization by concrete beings like ourselves.

Wieman's creative interchange becomes Cobb's creative transformation within Whitehead's framework, which Cobb directly contrasts with John Dewey's instrumentalism. "The question arises especially because the power whose objectivity has thus far been affirmed is only that of relevant ideal possibilities. These are abstract and diverse, whereas we can properly speak of God only when we refer to a unitary actuality."[40] Cobb accepts Whitehead's ontological principle of "no actual entity, then no reason."[41] Thus, affirming independently real possibilities is not sufficient. For them to be effective, rather than human projections, they need to be made actual so as to have transformational power. "The difficulty with attributing the requisite agency to possibilities is that in their own being—as merely possible—they are abstract.... Hence, if possibilities unrealized in the past world have effective relevance for new occasions of experience, this is by the agency of something actual."[42] The actual agency by which possibilities gain relevance is God, which, like everything actual, is subject to experience and experienced by others. God orders the possibilities and offers them to becoming subjects for potential realization. "The one who dedicates himself to ideals does so out of the correct judgment that these ideals have objectivity to him, that they lay a claim upon him. Yet he can hardly provide for himself an intelligible explanation of how this is so. If he rejects God as the ground of their claim, then he is driven toward describing them—with Dewey—as projections."[43] The possibilities given by God are not simply a random collection. As the source of order, they are felt as ranked or prioritized. That means that while never forced upon actual entities, they do have the power of a call or lure. They are felt as a real impulse from outside each becoming occasion, urging them toward novelty.

Rather than being determined by antecedent conditions, the present faces disruptions from real possibilities. The future is open rather than fully determined. The present is the place of a decision to let the past be fully determinative, or let in novel possibilities that do not fully conform to the past. The question is whether there is something else calling us into these novel possibilities, or whether they are just projections on human experience. Cobb invokes Dewey's distinction between the ideal and actual, and their active relation. Ideals have an active power.[44] But Cobb thinks Dewey is too limited, as ideals are not independently real for him. "He must interpret them as nothing more than generalizations of features of the actual," as products of human imagination projecting from actual conditions into the future.[45] They can provide a plan of action for achieving a goal, but still come from nothing other than what is already actual.

God the Container of Possibilities

Cobb's God incarnate in Jesus Christ is a God of love, meaning a hope that love will make a difference in the future is the defining feature of creative transformation. For this hope to be real, for the future to be different, there must be possibilities for the present. Possibilities are the means by which entities find purpose in the present and the ability to transcend beyond the given. The future does not have to be fully determined by efficient causality of what came before, though that is a possibility. Past conditions play a large role in shaping present purposes, but not a final role. Present purposes chosen in light of some possibility can also reshape those determining conditions as a response to them, a response to be otherwise. Cobb locates this call in Christ.

> The call of Christ can be understood mythically as the command of God. But it can be demythologized without reducing the actual role of Christ. The call consists in introducing into our existence, moment by moment, possibilities for our self-actualization that lead to good for ourselves and for others. These involve a tension between what simply is and what might be and should be. They involve some urge or impulse to the realization of desirable possibilities. By doing so they introduce a space for human freedom. We are free to create ourselves in relation to both the actual world

from which we come and to these new possibilities for our existence. The effective working of these liberating and challenging possibilities is the presence of the creative and redemptive Christ. Christ is present as the life-giving call to be more than we have been both for our own sake and for the sake of others.[46]

The reality of unrealized possibilities is crucial for Cobb, and for process thought in general. It leads to God as the necessary place, a sort of container, for these possibilities, so they can be of such a status so as to be capable of interacting with concrete events.

What is new, by definition, transcends the given in some sense, but that leads to a problem for Cobb. "How can what is found in the analysis of experience genuinely transcend the experience?"[47] Traditionally the Logos is the transcendent reality incarnate in Christ. Cobb identifies this Logos as the source of order and purpose, the ground of meanings we experience. "Whitehead has called this transcendent source of the aim at the new the principle on concretion, the principle of limitation, the organ of novelty, the lure for feeling, the eternal urge for desire, the divine Eros, and God in his Primordial Nature."[48] It transcends the world and its creatures but is only expressed in them. That is the Logos, a specific force for the creative transformation of specific occasions in specific places at specific times. This is also the reason Whitehead concluded God was needed in his philosophy. God was necessary in order to achieve three tasks in relation to possibilities and the actual world. "These are: first, the envisagement of eternal objects; secondly, the envisagement of possibilities of value in respect to the synthesis of eternal objects; and lastly, the envisagement of the actual matter of fact which must enter into the total situation which is achievable by the addition of the future. But in abstraction from actuality, the eternal activity is divorced from value."[49] That last sentence is crucial. Creativity is not a substance with independent reality. It is the ultimate reality actualized in the activities of actual occasions. However, creativity is neutral regarding forms. Thus, the basic philosophical situation applicable to everything is the relation between actual occasions and eternal objects.

God and occasions in the world are not static objects. They are events constantly undergoing experience. Thus, Cobb argues that the objective achievements of one occasion can enter as subjective possibilities for another, as elements for possible inclusion or rejection. "The unrealized possibilities that present themselves as lures for aims do not exist only in their effective entertainment in the appetitions of a single occasion of experience. They are felt as potentialities that, as potentials, are real in themselves, whether or not they are actualized in the world. They are lures to action, thus exercising their own persuasive agency upon the world."[50] Raw potentiality is just that, "infinite and unordered."[51] To provide actual direction, as opposed to confusion, wonder, or maybe even terror in the face of the infinite chaos, possibilities need to be ordered in relation to one another. Only then can they be relevant for concrete events. This ordered relevance is God incarnate, or the Logos present in Christ. "It is the ordered givenness of relevant potentiality. Ultimately it is the transcendent ordering from which derive the novel order and the ordered novelty in the world."[52] God is necessary for possibilities to be real, and for there to be novelty in the world those possibilities must be made actual in the world. God must be an actual entity whose possibilities can be made incarnate in the world by actual occasions.

If a present occasion is only presented with the objective past, then the present conforms to the past exclusively. Conversely, if something in the present moment is given, but not by the past, then the options for realization in the present are not exhausted by the past. There are possibilities not yet realized yet relevant to the present occasion of experience. For Whitehead, relations to past occasions are "physical feelings/prehensions" while relations to the unrealized possibilities are "conceptual feelings/prehensions."[53] The physical feelings are causal, determined by the past. Conceptual feelings, as they are integrated with the physical, are alternative ways of responding to the past. They are lures of feeling. However, if each occasion merely chooses whatever it wishes among the possibilities given, chance and chaos would likely reign. While there is plenty of evidence for chaos in reality, there are plenty examples of complex order. For Cobb, this "points to the fact that the possibilities are not ordered only in terms of immediate relevance but ordered also so that there are established limits that ensure some correlation among the many decisions that jointly make up the settled world. The principle of novelty is also a principle of order."[54] Thus, Cobb concurs with Whitehead and affirms the primordial nature of God, the primordial envisagement of possibilities apart from their connection with particular occasions.

This God has been referred to as a sort of container, because according to Whitehead and Cobb God is necessary as a sort of warehouse to contain all possibilities. Think of one of the many massive wholesale retail stores if it sold literally everything possible, Amazon turned into an actual physical store. Equally necessary to the warehouse containing all possibilities is the world full of shoppers to come in and choose from among the available goods. In this scenario the layout of the warehouse is tailored for each shopper. The most valuable possibilities are up front near the entrance and highlighted with a nice display, God's initial aim. Regardless of what God has chosen to highlight, each shopper is free to choose anything in the warehouse and make a subjective choice. Upon choosing they leave and take their chosen possibility into the world where they can show it to others. Immediately upon their departure from the warehouse, everything is restocked and reordered for the next shopper to go through the same process, the arrangement of goods now tailored for them.

To be effective in the becoming of any occasion, God and possibilities must be actual. Therefore, God acts upon others in the form of the lure of possibility for a hopeful future and, like all actual entities, God is in turn acted upon, receives the world. In the process of becoming, every actual occasion synthesizes these possibilities with all other objective entities given from the past and offers the result back to the world to be synthesized by others in the future. God cannot be made an exception to this principle.[55] The difference between God and other actual entities is that for God this reception of others is done without limitation or selection. God feels the decisions of all occasions. Even destructive or evil elements of the world are received by God, who then, in light of all the good and bad decisions made by actual occasions, offers the maximum harmony possible in the next moment.

As Whitehead and Cobb paint the picture, without God, creativity and the world would never achieve anything new. As Whitehead says, "this creativity and these forms are together impotent to achieve actuality apart from the completed ideal harmony, which is God."[56] God orders eternal objects according to their relevant value for actual occasions. Without such divine limitation on the possibilities, an ordering where there would otherwise be infinite possibility, there would be no enduring order in the world. Furthermore, because this God is an actual occasion, many traditional attributes can still be ascribed to God. Cobb highlights how this model of God allows affirmation of divine purpose, knowledge, vision, wisdom, consciousness, and love. This God will differ in lacking changelessness, transcendence, and absolute creative power.[57] These features of classic substance theism are affirmed, in a sense, but only when properly qualified and limited in relation with the world.

Cobb explicitly refuses to identify God with being, the depth, source, or the ground of all being. He rejects the move Neville argues that all philosophers and theologians must make. If being is God, Cobb argues that God must at the same time be the being of all beings and the supreme being, fully transcendent and fully immanent. However, the inability of ground-of-being theologians to adequately affirm both transcendence and immanence leads him to accept the distinction between ultimate reality and God. God is a manifestation of the ultimate reality, creativity, and not a name for it. "If God is the one, cosmic, everlasting actualization of ultimate reality on whom all ephemeral actualizations depend, God's non-identity with ultimate reality in no way subordinates God to it, for God is the ultimate *actuality*. God as the ultimate actuality is just as ultimate as is Emptiness as ultimate *reality*."[58] Besides God and the world being co-dependent on one another, Cobb separates God and creativity. Therefore, there are three ultimates in Cobb's theology: creativity, God, and the world.

With Whitehead, Cobb understands being as beyond all forms, but not as their substantial ground. Whitehead breaks with philosophical tradition and identifies being with cosmological creativity. This means being, creativity, is realizable in any form, lacking any character of its own. So as to be relevant for actual entities, creativity is never experienced apart from an ordering of possibilities to be actualized in instances of creativity. This ordered relevance from God is the initial phase of the subjective aim of all things.[59] Of course, process thinkers wish to avoid the conclusion that things like rocks *choose* to continue being rocks. Thus, Cobb affirms with Whitehead that for many entities this impulse toward actualization is just the reenactment of an occasion's immediately given past. This claim is meant to account for the observation of enduring physical patterns, but in living beings we find degrees of novelty rather than simple reenactment. For all these concrete actualities that have experience Christ is not just the name for the possibilities accounting for such novelty, but the Logos incarnate in and through the world. The result is God's universal presence. "The implication of this analysis is that God as Logos is effectively, if unconsciously, present and felt in all events. The Logos is truly incarnate in the world. Christ is a reality in the world."[60] God is present to everything and everyone, even in their rejection of that immanent reality, and the only norm for judging Christian authenticity is relating to the past in the mode of creative transformation. The question is not what we were, what we thought and did in the past, but what we are, how we think, and what we do in relation to that past now. Rejecting it, rethinking it, and behaving differently may be the best way to be true to a tradition.

Creative Transformation

Cobb is aware that in the history of Western theology God is normally identified with whatever is most ultimate. However, he and Whitehead understand the true object of religious concern to be goodness, not ultimacy. If God is the ground-of-being, the foundation of the basic activity that characterizes the world, or identified with that activity, then God must also be identified in every act of evil. Whitehead was very intentional in identifying God with the principle limiting possibilities, rather than creativity, to avoid this association. "If He be conceived as the supreme ground for limitation, it stands in His very nature to divide the Good from the Evil."[61] The process scheme immediately bypasses the traditional problem of evil, which Cobb takes to be a decisive refutation of substance theism. Consider Aquinas on divine impassibility and love. If there are no passions in God, does God love? Human love involves passion, but not so in God according to Aquinas.[62] A God that loves without passion does not respond to us, but indiscriminately enacts the divine will. Similarly, Anselm denies compassion in God. God saves sinners, and is therefore compassionate in a sense, but is not moved by and has no sympathy for sinners.[63] As for Aquinas, God works indiscriminately.

For Cobb, the problem of evil immediately disproves the God of substance metaphysics that is also a cosmic moralist and all controlling power, a God controlling all and willing maximum enjoyment for God's creatures in a world in which evil nonetheless exists. It is an irresolvable problem for substance theism that simply does not arise for Cobb. Not only is his God deeply affected by God's creatures, God cannot force them to do anything. Actual occasions make themselves, and evil is part of our creation. God's lures contain the maximum goodness and beauty possible, but occasions do with those lures what they wish. The real evil, the real theodicy challenge, according to Cobb, is that everything perishes. If death is the final word, nothing we do ultimately matters. If there is not a solution to perishing, then the process God would not be worth worship and devotion. "The ultimate evil in the temporal world is deeper than any specific evil. It lies in the fact that the past fades, that time is a 'perpetual perishing.'"[64] However, everything and everyone matters to God in Cobb's process theology, and they all become eternal objective facts that live on in the life of God. God prehends everything, and in doing so everything lives on as part of God's reaction to the world.

Cobb's process theology negotiates around supernatural theism and naturalistic pantheism. He does this by affirming the standpoint of God. God is not everything, with the things of the world simply divine parts. But neither is the world everything, with God being just another name for describing its entirety. When actual occasions are understood as concrescing subjects, and objects only upon completion, they can enter into one another without violating each other's individuality. God's all-inclusive standpoint, for Cobb, means God and creatures interact as separate individuals, while God nonetheless includes the standpoints of all creatures. All occasions are parts of God, yet possess truly unique identities. "The world does not exist outside God or apart from God, but the world is not God or simply part of God. The character of the world is influenced by God, but it is not determined by him, and the world in its turn contributes novelty and richness to the divine experience."[65] God influences becoming occasions just like any other entity. God envisions purposes not enjoyed by past occasions, offering the potential for novel directions to becoming occasions. "He seeks to lure the new occasion beyond the mere repetition of past purposes and past feelings or new combinations among them. God is thus at once the source of novelty and the lure to finer and richer actualizations embodying that novelty. Thus God is the One Who Calls us beyond all that we have become to what we might be."[66] And in God's own becoming, the world of independent self-determining entities influences God. God influences, and is in turn influenced, taking all experience, the good and the bad, back into the divine life. This is how God redeems the world.

It can be difficult to determine whether Jesus was Cobb's window into a process model of God or if the order was reversed. In good Whiteheadian fashion, it is more likely the two mutually support and presuppose one another. Cobb's Christology proceeds from his understanding of divine and human processes. It proceeds from his arguments in *A Christian Natural Theology*, *The Structure of Christian Existence*, and *God and the World*, not just *Christ in a Pluralistic Age*. Christ is an exemplification of God's reality as well as an exemplar of what is possible within human transformation. His Christology unites realist concerns over accurately depicting the world, in all its beauty and terror, with idealist interests in alternative images and dreams of a better world, what Cobb calls "the union of actuality and possibility."[67] Christ is creative transformation, the movement between and beyond what is and what could be, if we only accept the possibility.

In the life of Jesus, Cobb identifies not so much doctrinal claims as a new way of life. That way is always transformative, calling people forward into a novel future. The process of changing, rather than a settled list of beliefs, is what Jesus was calling his disciples to embrace. "Christ, as the image of creative transformation, can provide a unity within which the many centers of meaning and existence can be appreciated and encouraged and through which openness to the other great Ways of mankind can lead to a deepening of Christian existence."[68] The central problems of life have been different at different times. The meaning of Christ has also varied. Just what needs transformation and what novel solution will be arrived at varies by context and from problem to problem. This means Christ, like God, can also be found everywhere. "Original thinking in science and philosophy, original art in all its forms, original styles of life and social organizations, all witness to the peculiarly effective presence of Christ."[69] Christ, as creative transformation, is not limited exclusively to religious experiences. The presence of creative transformation can be more or less effective in all our actions, affirming or denying Christ through those actions. "Creative transformation is discoverable in nature, in history, and in personal experience. In this sense Christ is fully immanent. But the exclusive alternatives of immanent and transcendent reflect a dualistic mode of thinking that is antithetical to Christian understanding. Christ is not simply identical with each and every instance of creative transformation. Christ is also that in reality by virtue of which each of these instances occurs. As such he transcends all instances."[70] We should follow Jesus in being self-transcending, to become more open to love of God and neighbor.

Jesus is Christ because in him there in no tension between the incarnate Logos and himself. He embodies it in every aspect of his life. He does not choose for or against it, but simply is the Logos incarnate. And since past events can literally play a constitutive role of other events in the future, the church can be the body of Christ. It is a matter of *how* they will be constituted by the creative transformation of Christ. This construal of the relation between Christ and the world is not unlike Tillich's method of correlation, though Cobb thinks the world has moved beyond existentialist concerns. There are more pressing, and potentially more disastrous, economic and ecological perils. Furthermore, Christ relates to hope. Creative transformation is not Christ if it leads to nothing.[71] Christ depends on possibilities contained in God, and those possibilities are nothing if not made actual in the world through Christ, through creative transformation.

6 | Robert Neville's God the Creator

Another Theological Peircean Habit

Neville comes at theology from a very different angle than Cobb. While Cobb begins with a theistic God and repairs that concept as necessary, Neville constructs an entire metaphysical system and only then turns to considerations of the place of God and lived religion within it. Consider his advice in the opening pages of *God the Creator*: "Rather than begin with a proof for the reality of God, the better part of wisdom is to develop the speculative system and at the end point out that God's reality has been demonstrated along the way."[1] Neville has followed his own advice ever since. Aquinas only makes sense within an Aristotelian worldview. Anselm's arguments only come across with force if it is accepted that necessity and dependence are basic characterizations of everything. For Neville, rather than starting theological work with a model of God, it is better to construct an entire worldview adequate to knowledge of the day, then turn to God, not the other way around.

Neville has an overriding interest in the problem of the one and the many that he took from his teacher at Yale, Paul Weiss. While Neville never adopted Weiss's modal distinction between the being of God and that of the world, he adopted the unshakable conviction that *the* test of any philosophical system is how it addresses the problem of the one and the many.[2] A philosophy without an answer to it is incomplete.[3] More precisely, any system without an *ontological* solution to the problem of the one and the many is incomplete. There are many cosmological solutions to that problem, but all lack the explanatory power of an ontological solution.[4] "The problem of the one and the many appears in many guises: as the one for many men in a state, as the unity of man's many needs, and in countless like guises; but these are not instances of the *ontological* problem of the one and the many. What we are after is the ontological one for the many determinations of being."[5] Ontological questions drive deeper than cosmological ones. When Neville frames the cosmological situation in terms of determinacy, the deeper answer to that situation will be indeterminate, an answer that frames his understanding of religion.

Neville's large-scale methodological view is also related to his fallibilism. He wants his position to extend over as many domains as possible to be maximally open to correction by inviting feedback from anyone who could conceivably have a perspective on the topics he treats. "The public for the philosophy as developed here for theological issues includes thinkers who come from any religious or secular tradition with ideas to contribute to the first-order theological issues or to the second and higher order issues of analysis and methodology. The public also includes thinkers from any of the philosophical, literary, scientific, and practical disciplines who might be interested in the arguments necessary to make cases for claims about the first-order issues."[6] This desire to be open to feedback from anyone helps explain his method of comparative abstraction most clearly found in *Behind the Masks of God* and the three-volume *Comparative Religious Ideas Project*. It is also found in *Boston Confucianism* and the fact that he allows for religious syncretism. Just to what extent that mixing and blending can occur depends on one's context and skill at harmonizing diverse symbols and practices. To offer a philosophical system to which anyone can contribute, and an ultimate to which any religious person can relate, requires abstracting enough from their specific contexts and ideas so as to rule out none of them a priori.

The downside to this approach is that concepts so vague as to be capable of receiving feedback from any perspective are potentially too vague and abstract for that feedback to be meaningful. As will be shown, Neville has not satisfyingly addressed this problem, evidenced by his reference to indeterminacy to deflect most criticisms of his work—the criticisms, being determinate, do not apply to his indeterminate God. Given his fallible method, the need to deal with such feedback is real. As will be argued in the next chapter, there are reasons native to Neville's thought to push vague categories like indeterminacy toward modifications in light of criticisms, rather than receiving criticism yet remaining indeterminate through and through.

Neville has the resources to put theological thinking in closer touch with the nitty gritty world, even if he often seems to hover above it.

The Indeterminate One and the Determinate Many

To summarize his grand metaphysical scheme before investigating its particulars, Neville argues that the universe of determinate harmonies cannot be understood apart from the affirmation of an indeterminate context beyond the determinate world. Determinacy is analyzed as the most basic feature of everything that exists. To be is to be determinate. Determinate entities are harmonies of essential and conditional features. Conditional features are how anything relates to anything else, the ways things condition one another. Essential features give each thing its unique identity by which it can relate to and be conditioned by other determinate things without losing that identity and being reduced to those relations.[7] Together, essential and conditional features explain the interrelatedness of reality while giving each existing thing a unique identity irreducible to mere relations. However, analyzing determinacy in terms of these features reveals a problem, according to Neville. To be is to be a harmony of essential and conditional features. Conditional relations are only possible because entities are already harmonies of essential features. Given that essential and conditional features cannot exist in isolation from one another, but must already be mutually related in each entity, their being must be grounded in something else accounting for such preexisting unity.

Neville argues that only an indeterminate ground can sufficiently function as a solution to this problem, which is his answer to the problem of the one and the many. If the ontological ground of essential and conditional features is determinate, it will also have conditional and essential features and will relate to other determinate entities through those features rather than grounding their already existing harmonies. As a determinate reality existing alongside them, God would require grounding as well. This is Neville's problem with theistic models of God, including process models such as Cobb's in which God is a being. He concludes there must be a purely indeterminate ground in contrast to the world of determinate entities for which it accounts. God is therefore "the creative act that is nothing without acting and which results in the world of determinate harmonies."[8] In short, nothing determinate can be the ontological one for itself and for others. Since the one must transcend determinations, it cannot be determinate. Besides classical substance theism, this also rules out process theology for Neville. "If it were to create out of its own potentialities instead of *ex nihilo*, then being-itself would have to be determinate, which it cannot be."[9] God is an indeterminate act, sheer making, accounting for the integration of essential and conditional features in determinate entities. The determinate world is the expression of God's creative act, and apart from that world the act cannot be known. For those unfamiliar with Neville's work, this argument can be difficult to grasp, so it should be unpacked in greater detail.

Everything determinate has essential and conditional features. "The essential feature of x is 'x' and the conditional features are '$not\text{-}y$,' '$not\text{-}z$,' and so forth. The conditional features come from the real distinctions that pertain between the determination and what it is determinate with respect to. It is necessary for any determination of being to have an essential feature *and* conditional ones."[10] Without conditional components, there would be no relations and we would be left with Leibniz's monads. Without essential components, there would only be conditional relations, except that would be impossible on such an account since there would be no different things to condition one another. Determinate reality falls away and we are left with absolute idealism. Therefore, the determinate world of both essential *and* conditional features is the context for asking the ontological question of the one and the many.

With the world understood in terms of his analysis of essential and conditional features of determinacy, Neville presents a proof for the radical contingency of the world that therefore needs to be explained by reference to God the creator. First, for real things to have relations and condition one another, they must have essential as well as conditional features. Second, essential components of one thing cannot be conditions for another without losing their identity. Third, the cosmological togetherness of essential components is seen but not explained, as conditional components function on this level. Thus, "the very possibility of a cosmological context of mutual relevance presupposes an ontological context of mutual relevance in which the essential components of different things are together in noncosmological ways."[11] This ontological context must be indeterminate, otherwise it would be in need of an ontological context for its determinate togetherness.

To be is to be a determinate harmony of essential and conditional features. Such a harmony is a contingent feature of reality requiring an explanation. The act of creation providing that explanation is not a onetime event in the distant past, but the immediate creation of every moment of determinate existence, an act not itself in time. The ontological creative act is infinite and eternal. In that act, God's character is given as creator, and the world's character is given as product. "The ontological creative act is a sheer making, with no potentials antecedent to the making. Any potentials would have to be determinate, at least in being something rather than nothing, and on this hypothesis all determinate things are created."[12] God is an indeterminate making without antecedent characteristics or thoughts. Neville's God is a wild one quite unlike a well-defined theistic being.

God is source, act, and product all at once in this view. It might seem natural to think of Neville's argument for God the creator as an equation with two parts, God apart from the act, apart from creation, and God with the act, with creation. However, God is not even indeterminate apart from creating the determinate world. There is no sense of taking about God *before* creation on Neville's account. God is an act accounting for everything determinate, and in the flash of creating that act is simultaneously established as the source and the world, defined in relation to the product of the act. There is a determinate world, God is connected to it as its creator, and apart from that relation there is no point of talking about God at all. There is no transcendent "thing" there. "The creator is *conditionally* transcendent in the sense that is has something to transcend only in virtue of its connection with the determinations."[13] Like any daily action we are familiar with, there is no act without what it produces, so there is no sense in talking about God existing before creation. But the conclusion to be drawn is not therefore that God is identified with the results of creation. Unlike describing an artist based on their art, God, being indeterminate, is not identifiable in certain respects as the sort of creator responsible for everything determinate. "The creator is *unconditionally* transcendent in the sense that, since it creates the determinations, its own being must be independent of them."[14] God cannot be essentially conditioned by something that depends entirely on God. You cannot read characteristics from the world back into God according to Neville's argument. If the reverse was true, God would depend on the world while at the same time the world would necessitate that God create it, a contradiction in terms. Without having already been created, determinations have no being to necessitate such a thing. Creation's three-part structure of source, act, and product is related asymmetrically. Beyond being identified with creativity, Neville's God remains entirely indeterminate. The divine act determines both the nature of the world and God in creating.

While he prefers to reference the ontological creative act in his writing, rather than God, Neville admits that the creative act can legitimately be referred to as God since God is traditionally singular, the most ultimate, and eternal. All these things are appropriate descriptions of the ontological creative act, even though determinate language does not literally apply to it. That is, and always will be, the sticking point in his work. God is a broken symbol. "The position taken in *Philosophical Theology* is that the term *God* is indeed legitimately used to refer to the ontological act of creating the world, bearing in mind the need to break the literal application of the model of the person in reference to the ontological act."[15] There is no intentionality apart from the creative act, no nature or moral evaluation of God apart from the act. There is no intentionality within God, which would require stages of creation and contemplation of options. God's nature is not something given by or deducible from the results of the creative act. There is too much chaos and discord to read perfect intentionality into creation. "The ontological creative act is a 'just making,' pure and simple, not an act of a willing intentional agent. So there is not much ground for saying that God is a person because of the character of the created world."[16] Indeterminacy is a concept with privileged explanatory power over determinate concepts. Determinacy always breaks on indeterminacy.

Divine Wildness over Goodness

Neville describes his argument for an indeterminate creator as placing his work on the side of Descartes against Leibniz on the priority of God's will and intellect, on the question of whether the structures of intelligibility are created.[17] Descartes prioritized God's will over God's intellect. God must have a totally indifferent and free will. What counts as good and understanding in God is a consequent result from whatever the divine will decides. God is perfect and can have no limitations on that perfection.[18] Leibniz, on the other hand, prioritized the divine intellect. To him, the claim that God's existence depends on God's will makes God both posterior and anterior to Godself. Besides, Leibniz would argue, some things like the rules of logic do not depend on God's will.[19] If God told everyone to believe A and ~A at the same time because God decided this, nobody would believe God. Descartes would counter that God creates whatever logic God wants.

The disagreement between Descartes and Leibniz is on the priority of God's will and intellect in creating the world. In creation, God is at one moment immanent and in another transcendent to creation. In the moment that God is immanent, God is known as the creator of the world, but as soon as God is so recognized, God is known as the transcendent creator on which the world depends. There is an order of ontological dependence implied. Descartes focuses on the moment of transcendence. God cannot depend on any understanding of creation when deciding to create or creation would be as basic and irreducible as God. Rather, creation is internal to God as wholly dependent on God. God's choice in creating must be completely indifferent. Anything bounding such a free choice is a limitation on God's absolute perfection. God must create freely and, in a sense, arbitrarily. Leibniz focuses on the moment of immanence. God must conceive a completed plan prior to choosing to create. In other words, God is conditioned by what the divine intellect chooses to create. If God's will is primary, as for Descartes, God's decision determines the structures of intelligibility. Creation will ground the structures of possibility. To even speak of infinite possibilities within God, which are known before creating and then selectively chosen in creating the world in a certain way, limits the divine will, which chooses from nothing.

This debate has consequences morally and theologically for the way differences between Cobb and Neville are to be understood. By siding with Descartes, Neville is asserting that God's ways are not our ways. "The ontological creative act is not intelligible as the actualization of antecedent potentials because all determination is the result of the act."[20] When the divine will is absolute and arbitrary, from our perspective, the responsibility is on us to figure out God's ways. We are responsible for knowing the world, one another, and God as carefully and as best we can. We don't have windows into God's mind. We have to work out our understanding of God. We cannot model ourselves after a blueprint in the divine intellect.

Leibniz, on the other hand, has a God who created the best possible world. God surveyed all possibilities in the intellect prior to creating and chose the best one. God is a being with a perfect intellect that chose what to create based on the understanding of that intellect. Siding with Descartes on this specific debate leads Neville to a wild understanding of God. "The history of the evolution of our Earthly animal species is red in tooth and claw. The more accomplished villains are at doing evil, the more evil they do. In contrast to the religious claim attractive to some that God is benign, the better summary judgment is that the ontological creative act is simply wild, and that the harmonies, all of which have value, are often in conflict."[21] Our standards of morality do not apply to God. In creating, God gives rise to the world in which such standards apply. Prior to creating, they do not exist. Prior to creating there is just the arbitrary wild will of God.

Transcendence *and* Immanence?

Neville clearly wants to distinguish God from the world, as their relationship of dependence is entirely asymmetrical, but he seems to equivocate when he addresses God's transcendence *and* immanence. On the one hand, he denies God is contingent upon the world, as the world comes entirely from God in the divine creative act. On the other hand, he does claim that divine act is present in the world.

> It is present in the sense that its creative act or productive power constitutes the determinations and gives them their being. The determinations are termini of the creative act. The creator transcends the determinations in the sense that its being in itself is something over and above the determinations, independent of them. Instead of the creator's transcending in the sense of starting in the determinations and extending out, the direction of the transcendence is reversed, as it were; the creator starts outside and comes in. But its coming in to the determinations and its creating of them are the same.[22]

Statements like this should not be read in terms of process theology. Essential and conditional or primordial and consequent features in God are misleading for Neville. "With respect to the creator, we cannot say whether its essential nature has many features or one, what the features are or not. The creator is essentially indeterminate and transcendent of the domain where such determinate considerations apply."[23] Determinate things have conditional features because they always exist together with other determinate things. God the creator is needed to explain how this togetherness could be the case. So, unlike all determinate things created by God, God creates the determinations with respect to which God is determinate.

Determinate things necessarily have conditional features. This is not so for Neville's God. "Since the creator is essentially indeterminate, there is no need at all for it to have conditional features. Why the creator creates and gives itself the conditional features is a question that cannot be answered."[24] Neville's indeterminate creator God is the most ultimate ontological structure explaining the basic features of reality. This God is in tension with many aspects of actual religious communities, insofar as they wish to employ immanent and personally meaningful religious imagery rather than always deferring to God's otherness. Neville's ontology and human anthropology butt heads, and however much he tries to hold them together, the ontological structure wins. God as conditioned in creating the world, the God who conceivably might be known in some respects as creator, is negated by the indeterminate God. This can be seen in Neville's attempts to affirm that God is both common to and independent of everything created.

On the one hand, God the creator is present to everything created due to being their creator: "First, the creator is the common ground of the determinations in the sense that it creates all of them together. It is the ground because it creates them, and it is common because it is the creator of them all, each and every one and all together."[25] This makes God immanent in the world as the common ground of everything. On the other hand, Neville can only affirm such universal presence of God in the world due to the act of creation, which involves a movement from indeterminacy to determinacy. The asymmetrical order of dependence in that act negates the seemingly symmetrical relation of creator being known in the world in which it is present as creator.

> To say that the creator must be independent in itself of the created determinations is not to say that it is a creator apart from them; the creator is a creator only insofar as it creates, and insofar as it creates it is connected with the determinations. But it is the case that, in order for the creator to create, it must have a reality in itself that is independent of the created determinations. The creator makes itself creator when and as it creates; in order to do this, it must be independent, in itself, of the products it creates and even of its own role of being creator. The role of creator is the nature the creator has in virtue of its connection with the created determinations.[26]

The sense in which God has more than an indeterminate character as a result of creating the determinate world is just a *sense,* not a reality. Neville grants that as creator of this world God has definite characteristics, characteristics one could plausibly call personal. However, this "person" is more like David Hume's impressions and ideas. God's personality is presented in the concept of creation, as an idea constantly connected with that concept. God's personal characteristics, being determinate, must be part of what is created. They are a phenomenon connected to creation, but nothing more than a phenomenon. God the creator is not really personal.

Normally we distinguish between a person and the expressions of character that give content to their personality. There is a person, with their private inner life, and their personality is expressed in a medium via certain characteristics. This is not the case for God the creator, however. God is only a person for Neville in the sense that God "is the one whose creation exhibits personality.... Of course, when the person of God is separated from his expressed personality, the term 'person' attributes nothing determinate to God. But this would make 'person' a useless term; so we should not separate it from personality in application to God. Our conclusion is to say that God is a person is the same as saying that he creates with personality."[27] For an indeterminate God that creates everything determinate, there is nothing that can be known of the person, what God has kept private, apart from the expression of creating. There are no private ideas in God not realized in the world. "Between the idea of the object of intention and the completed fact, there is no shadow; God's thoughts are the same as his creations: his ideas are real things."[28] Given that anything determinate can only insufficiently express God, finite/infinite contrasts and broken symbols dominate Neville's work.

True Engagement, Broken Symbols

From Neville's distinction of indeterminate creator and determinate creation comes his concept of finite/infinite contrasts. Though he is clear that no determinate statements, being determinate, can be univocally true of God, language can nonetheless raise awareness to the contrast between finite determinate things and their indeterminate creator. The more religious symbols can downplay their finite character and point toward their transcendent source, the more they can aid the task of realizing the distinction between God and the world. On his account, all talk of God is really talk about more and less adequate ways of raising awareness to the finite/infinite or indeterminate/determinate contrast. Another way of stating this is that all religious symbols, to be true rather than idolatrous, must be understood as broken.

The religious referents of the broken symbols that point to finite/infinite contrasts are five ultimates, one ontological and four cosmological. God is the ontological ultimate and points to the contingency of the world that depends on the creative act. Cosmological ultimates are the transcendental traits of determinate things: forms, components formed, location in an existential field, and the value that comes from having components formed in such a way in such a place.[29] It is to these features that religious symbols should point if they are to be taken as true by interpreters. Symbols should therefore relate to coming to terms with existence itself, the value of choosing between different forms, proper comportment and how we behave (our components), and how we act toward others (in our existential field—which includes institutions as well as people).

Neville argues that the truth of religious symbols pointing to these ultimates is not about correspondence with reality, that symbols depict reality just as it really is, but a matter of engagement. "Interpretation is the act of taking a sign to stand for an object in a certain respect. An interpretive act engages the object by means of the sign."[30] Epistemology in religious matters is not about mirroring the subject matter for Neville. He moves past this view to focus on proper relations, without denying that those relations are about reality. As with Peirce, there can be focus on human constructions without abandoning realism. The truth of our constructed religious symbols, however, no matter how much they are intended to be about God, will always be contextual, depending on societal and personal factors.

Any sign, religious or otherwise, can resist some attempts at semiotic engagement. This means doctrines alone are not true or false. That is a potential they only carry when asserted as an interpretation of some reality. Because religious symbols are true only as they are able to engage their interpreter with the reality they are meant to carry across, they face the danger of inauthentic engagement. Doctrines true in one context can, and may necessarily, be false in another. It can be a revelation that symbols are revelatory, so to speak, of the reality we mean them to engage. They are a free gift of the creative act used to great effect by intuitive insights of religious geniuses. "Our lives are nothing but God's grace, to use the monotheistic symbols. Thus, even our theological existence as symbolically engaged with ultimacy is the product of free, unmotivated grace."[31] Sacred canopies, while constructions, are our only means of engaging the otherwise indeterminate God. However, those canopies, rather than being inevitable, can break down. Rather than seeing this as negative or threatening, their problematic aspects are a clue to understanding Neville's view of truth in theology.

Neville's point about broken symbols is taken in part from Tillich, who argues that religious symbols reference the infinite, but are themselves finite. This is a problem for Tillich because the symbols must participate in the power of the infinite God to be true on his account. They are meant to transcend the present moment and conditions of the world, but necessarily include those elements in their constitution. As a result, religious symbols must be both affirmed and negated. This yes/but character is what makes them symbolic, as opposed to literal statements.[32] Neville expounds upon this basic point through the notion of contrasts established by the difference between indeterminacy and determinacy and the pragmatic semiotics of Peirce reinterpreted for religious purposes given such contrasts.

Neville employs the notion of finite/infinite contrasts that he developed in *The Truth of Broken Symbols* to make this point about broken symbols. He takes the notion of contrasts from Whitehead.[33] A contrast is not a third thing in addition to what is contrasted, just an expression of how the things contrasted are or are not held together. Neville argues that in religion the finite side employs materials from the world as used in sacred rites and rituals, and the infinite side both recognizes the need to use finite things while demarcating them as the boundary that rubs against the infinite. The problem for Neville is "the infinite part of the referents of religious symbols is precisely what finite things in the world cannot stand for."[34] They are means of addressing problems with what concerns us ultimately, though they perform this function while using resources that are limited and not ultimate. Peirce's semiotics is therefore reinterpreted by Neville in light of finite/infinite contrasts.

Since God can only be identified using determinate signs, the truth of religious symbols cannot be about their material content. Rather, truth in religious matters is about the carry-over from realities that are engaged according to the context of those engaging religious symbols.[35] Neville uses Peirce's taxonomy of icons, indices, and symbols to make this point, and creatively extends them beyond Peirce's usage to do so. While Peirce's philosophy deals with iconic, indexical, and symbolic signification, Neville notes that all signs involve arbitrary contextual elements. They are, in part, human constructions. If constructed well, they are even more meaningful. Thus, rather than icon, index, and symbol, Neville writes about iconic, indexical, and conventional symbols.

Iconic references are supposed to be similar to the objects they represent, but they make it possible to confuse images with that which they are meant to refer. If theological symbols are taken to have nothing but iconic reference, the lurking danger would be idolatry, assuming God is exactly as depicted in religious symbols—something that is not even possible if God is indeterminate. Neville's preferred alternative indexical approach is one in which "treating the object as the image depicts can cause the interpreter to pick up on what is valuable or important in the object."[36] Indexical symbols are closely related to conventional symbols, which are cultural constructions meant to engage reality as it exists in semiotic systems where those constructions have public meaning. The theological importance is when indexical symbols in a certain semiotic system raise awareness to something of ultimate concern, again echoing Tillich. "Without signs of the right sorts, realities cannot be discriminately interpreted in experience. Things can bump us, but they cannot be discriminated in response unless we have appropriate signs."[37] The potential danger is thinking that conventional symbols that point to that ultimate reality, traditional anthropomorphic models of God, are the object being engaged rather than the symbols engaging the object.

The difference between everyday sign usage on Peirce's account and engaging God with signs is that the need for materiality in interpretation is not as obvious in the latter situation. However, for an indeterminate God to be engaged, materiality is paradoxically necessary. Since it is necessary, but uses finite determinate signification, necessary signs must also be understood as broken. "A broken symbol is one whose iconic reference is known to be only metaphorical, with a need for the limits of the metaphor to be spelled out. A broken symbol *might* be true, but not necessarily."[38] Neville's theology is not just metaphysical. It involves an understanding of how to engage with what is determined as ultimate in the metaphysics. That engagement is performed in highly selective ways, bringing an object of interpretation into the foreground against a background of culture and history in which what is being given attention finds its meaning. Context matters in this process. Interpretation takes place within the context of worldviews. This means individual signs are never true or false on their own, their interpretations are true or false, and interpretations are always selected for a certain purpose (e.g., scientific reductionism is true for certain purposes but not exhaustive) and in a specific context (e.g., reductionism may not shed much light on a complex human emotion being discussed with a loved one or in a therapist's office). In an unexpected twist for a theological system so centered on preserving God's indeterminacy, extreme contextuality is viewed as a strength of religious symbols given that it is necessary to represent God in some manner in a semiotic system. "Like addressing a person, the singular ontological act of creation must be intended in order to be thought."[39] Indexical religious symbols do this, directing attention to the correct thing. Breaking is part of this proper intention, so that the indices themselves are not an obstacle to proper reference. When they break, it is the indeterminate God rather than determinate symbols that is intended by religious symbols. Living religious symbols allow people to see through them to God, while dead or dying symbols make it hard to see anything but their constructed finite character.

In this framework of broken symbols Jesus is a friend in our imagination, an aid in interpretation. The historical Jesus did not know anyone alive today. Jesus is not a conscious subject engaging people now. But we have imaginations capable of being shaped by what we know of Jesus, and that Jesus with us now in the imagination can help us engage God truly.[40] It does not matter how Jesus died, if Jesus was everything he claimed to be, or what his death means about God's relation to sinners. We need symbols to engage God in the determinate world with ultimate perspective. Jesus can be one of those symbols as our intimate companion, but in the sense that he exists in the imagination as our helpful aid in symbolically engaging God. Since Neville prefers to speak of engagement over reference, it is not a slight against Jesus to say he is in our imagination. It is among the highest honors one can have in Neville's system, an honor Jesus shares alongside Confucius, Buddha, and others. Jesus is one of many broken symbols for engaging God.

Unlike symbols that only point to God's eternity, Jesus also affects comportment. Being kind, generous, sympathetic, and courteous are ways of engaging God when we interact with others. Rather than giving up on eschatology and the idea of a coming Kingdom of God or expecting a literal divine kingdom to replace this one in the future, Neville claims Jesus offers us an "eschatologically judged way of life."[41] The imaginative power of Jesus and the ongoing work of the Holy Spirit is in judging an existential situation, marking better and worse ways of being in community with one another. Neville intends this symbolic approach to navigate between forcing literal supernatural beliefs on people and giving up all traditional theological beliefs in favor of simply performing Christian ethics. Attempting this balancing act means some supernatural symbols can mesh with a nonsupernatural metaphysical system. For example, during a personal or nationwide crisis, it may be appropriate to speak of God as our rock or sing the hymn "A Mighty Fortress Is Our God." These sorts of symbolic counterfactuals may be the ultimately true ways to continue existing in the face of tragedy, to affirm that the power of our being comes from elsewhere, and to live with courage in the face of despair in light of that gift. Of course, the truth of this view comes from not believing God is an enduring object like a rock or any sort of literal fortress.

The swastika is also a symbol that can engage the world truly or falsely. The word comes from the Sanskrit *svastika*, meaning good fortune or well-being.[42] It is still a live symbol in Buddhism and Hinduism. I saw it with some frequency while teaching in India in 2011. The swastika can be interpreted as an object in motion representing progress. Progress toward the good is a valuable symbol. However, after the Holocaust and Nazi use of the symbol one has to question whether the symbol can function to engage people with that truth or if it is more likely to work demonically by oppressing others and denying their lives. The same question can be asked of how Christian communities engage with the cross of Christ, sometimes yielding it as a weapon against minority communities, especially LGBTQ+ individuals.[43] For questions such as these context matters. Countries were touched differently by World War II and the Nazi regime. Perhaps the swastika can and should still be a living symbol in India today.

The extension of a symbol within a culture affects its intention, how it is taken to stand for its object. Context and the respects with which a sign is interpreted make all the difference. According to Neville, the death of Jesus, and the symbolic ritual of eating and drinking his "body" and "blood" in communion, indicates our blood guilt and taking on our punishment so we can move on to live better. Through no conscious fault of our own, our existence and use of resources means the livelihoods of others are reduced. We should accept that guilt and, like Jesus, die to ourselves and live better for others. In another context, communion could easily be understood and rejected as cannibalism.[44] Whether the swastika can stand for well-being and moving toward its realization or is more likely to be associated with the Nazis is similarly a contextual issue. Neville's point about extension and intention is that Christians should use symbols of Jesus to meaningfully engage with truths about their lives, without making the mistake of believing Jesus is literally God, a living dead person, or someone whose death altered the metaphysical scheme of the universe.

Challenges from and Challenges to Science

Neville's argument is that religious symbols engage us with what is ultimately meaningful, but they do so in constructed ways. In a sense, Neville's theology could incorporate any scientific finding and any scientific explanation of religion. Those studying the biological bases for religion could reduce it to nothing but human psychology and Neville might even agree with them. He notes that at their worst, religious symbols are nothing but human constructions. The necessarily fallible and changing character of engaging God with religious symbols can even awaken us to the fact that "our quotidian lives are most truly religionless religion."[45] Symbols are broken. Some scientists realize this and argue that societies should get rid of all religions, whether due to the origin of religious beliefs in our biology or their supposed falsehood established by incoherence with what we know about causality in the universe. Richard Dawkins is happy to make this point, arguing that religion is like a virus and that it is immoral to introduce children to it.[46] Neville, on the other hand, understands these "defects" in religion that popular atheists like to point out as precisely how religious symbols work. The difference is that the atheists only understand religious claims iconically, and thus dispense with them. Neville understands them indexically and uses them to engage God truly. His only squabble with scientists comes down to value, perhaps revealed in cases of scientist atheists like Dawkins only considering religious beliefs at the literal iconic level.

If scientists connect the metaphysical denial that value is part of reality with their scientific work, since it cannot be studied like other scientific facts, then Neville disagrees with science. If the natural is taken to be identical with the material, only capable of being studied in physics and biology, Neville rejects scientific naturalism and Cobb would stand by his side in support. But that is not how Neville understands naturalism.[47] Such atheist scientists take a specific abstract enterprise as exhaustive of reality, and our understanding of reality is greatly distorted when that is done. This is similar to Cobb's point of contention with scientists. Value involves intentionality. True engagement is done for a purpose, not by chance. To affirm value, intentionality is necessary, and intentionality may require subjectivity, as Neville notes. "Models of mind based on analogies with computers, with strictly 'forward causation,' might have some utility in explaining some things. But they cannot explain the kind of thinking that goes into explanation, understanding, inquiry, and other forms of truth seeking."[48] Take Neville's reaction to evolutionary biologists who explain religion as belief in supernatural agents, a belief that may have conferred adaptive benefit on our early human ancestors.[49] "Suppose this is a correct theory for explaining certain experiential properties. Nevertheless, this theory does not understand them, for understanding them would have to include showing how intentionality is involved in taking something to be an agent, how that act of 'taking' is a complex sign in a larger symbolic engagement with the thing so construed, related to contexts, purposes, and the like. For the elements of religion to be understood in terms of their roles in religion, most of them must be construed intentionally."[50] Neville is not against reductive explanations in science. He just argues they are a method chosen for specific purposes rather than exhaustive explanations of reality. His much more startling conclusion is about the potential challenge science brings to his philosophical theology.

Having settled the ontological question of the one and the many, clarified finite/infinite contrasts established by the indeterminate answer to that question, and the truth of broken symbols within such contrasts, Neville offers his definition of religion. "Religion is human engagement of ultimacy expressed in cognitive articulations, existential responses to ultimacy that give ultimate definition to the individual and community, and patterns of life and ritual in the face of ultimacy."[51] Neville, systematic thinker that he is, knows fully the implications of his philosophical theology. In his understanding, religion lives on a razor's thin edge at the cusp of negation. "Real religion kicks in when religion breaks down."[52] His system concludes with raising the possibility of being religious when religion ends.

Broken symbols are sacred canopies, constructed symbols that are nonetheless engaging and relevant for the conduct of life. They provide a worldview, and worldviews need plausibility. Plausibility comes from sufficient consistency with knowledge of the world. A sacred *world*view cannot be held if it is obviously not about the world. It requires consistency to achieve sustainability. It also needs to aid people seeking to remedy problems in their situation, to be a means to fulfillment not otherwise possible. Finally, and crucially for Neville, it needs to maintain tension in its symbols, tension between the utter transcendence of indeterminacy and the intimate determinacy of religious symbols.

Regarding consistency, many religious worldviews are insufficiently modern to avoid running afoul of science. In terms of appropriateness, all but the most isolated individuals live in a global society. My issues are not yours, and neither are my solutions. A global society with many fragmented and very different sacred worldviews reveals the false pretensions of those worldviews. In-group versus out-group sacred worldviews don't make much sense in a pluralistic context. Maybe everyone could convert to one view, or become so spiritually adept as to embrace them all, but nobody should hold their breath waiting for that to happen. The vast and largely empty universe revealed by science has also devastated the intimate religious symbols of everyday religious practice that are tied up with value. There is much more chaos and random destruction in reality than cases of tender lover and care, which are even rare on this planet. The result, Neville claims, is that symbols must be pushed toward transcendence. "To develop transcendent symbols of the ultimate in ways compatible with the blind wildness of the cosmos is quite possible. The symbols of an ultimate ontological act of creation giving rise to the determinate things with the ultimate traits of form, components, existential location, and value-identity are examples of a sacred canopy that is compatible with the scientific world picture."[53] The universe and Neville's God are wild, and sometimes awful in the full sense of invoking awe at what is terrifying and unknown.

Neville argues that this leaves religion, all religions, in a precarious position. "For most late-modern people, the best sacred worldviews available have difficulty with their plausibility, are under reconstruction, and offer little orientation about what to do other than to commend the process of inquiry in this precarious situation of imploded or potentially imploding sacred worldviews."[54] One possible solution Neville suggests is to end the struggle, to cease trying to fix traditional religious beliefs and start accepting their end. "The deepest ontological remedy for the brokenness of the human condition in its ultimate predicaments is to abandon the search for salvation in the sense that turns on prioritizing life in any ultimately important way. Most of the great religions have recognized this paradoxical situation. If one is struggling to attain salvation, one has not found it, and the concern for salvation is itself part of the problem."[55] His suggestion is to affirm "ontological faith" rather than seeking to resolve cosmological problems.[56] It is a suggestion that echoes Tillich's "courage to be." Ontological faith is about accepting cosmological limits, accepting with courage and terror that there be creation, forms, and so forth at all and that we may never be able to name them adequately.

This seems like a bleak conclusion. What does one do in such a situation? There seems to be a thin line between affirming we can do or say nothing meaningful in the face of the infinite and affirming existential meaninglessness. It is perhaps even more troubling that the lessons Neville draws from the life of Jesus are strikingly on point. "Yet those he healed often did not reciprocate with gratitude. His disciples were particularly dense about understanding his message, especially according to Mark's account. His critical revitalization of Second Temple Judaism was nipped in the bud, he was arrested on charges irrelevant to his own purposes, and he was executed at a young age."[57] Whether these are positive statements to be embraced or whether they are like singing "Always Look on the Bright Side of Life" while being crucified remains an open question. Neville is certainly correct that it takes ontological faith to live a life of value and love everyone, even one's enemies, when so many natural and social forces seem to reject that sort of life. However, if that is the only situation with which we are left, it is not clear if religionless religion is a positive affirmation or merely tilting at windmills.

Live your religion, even though it lacks objective reference, is a hard sell—like a scientist with the adaptation hypothesis arguing that religion should stick around for its potential social benefits rather than agreeing with Dawkins that we should dispense with the whole endeavor. If affirming religionless religion takes ontological faith, if it is an example of Tillich's courage to be, then an even more honest position might be to gather up a little more courage and do away with thoughts of an indeterminate God altogether. That is the very step LeRon Shults, former theist turned atheist, has taken partly under the influence of Neville's work. On Shults's account, the biological sciences have advanced in studying religion to the point of revealing that we are the *sole* source of ideas about God. God is nothing but a construction, and humans gave birth to that God. But it is a stillbirth, and theologians need to move past it and stop pretending God is alive, or so Shults claims. The only task this leaves for theologians is "the construction and critique of hypotheses about the existential conditions for axiological engagement."[58] If God is nothing but a construction, yet something about religious symbols is still important for living a valuable and ethical life, still engaging in Neville's sense, then it seems to be either a lack of nerve or imagination to abandon religion and reform secular systems so as to serve those functions. Altizer revealed to Cobb how the supernatural substance God of naïve realism is dead. Shults displays how a God supported by nothing but constructivism is a God that should be done without. A third option is available.

Steps toward a More Complete Model of God the Creator

Neville's theology has been so intricately worked out over a long and fruitful career that he opens the first volume of his systematic philosophical theology by reiterating the argument of his first book in just three sentences, then immediately retreats from the second half of the argument for God the creator he just put forward. "The ontological creative act is a making and its only nature comes in the determinate character of what it makes. Apart from creating the world, the ontological creative act is indeterminate, that is, nothing, not something rather than nothing nor something rather than something else. Without creating, the act is not an act."[59] Apart from creation, the divine act is nothing, since there would be no act in such a case. But there is creation, so nothing is not the end of the story. He continues: "Making cannot be modeled except in what it makes, which of course prescinds from the making itself."[60] The fact that he is one-sided in dealing with his model of God can be displayed more strikingly by listing several statements he makes in service of his argument for an indeterminate God. Many of these statements border on affirming the transcendence and immanence of God, but retreat to indeterminacy and away from immanence, denying God is fully in the world, impacted by it, or even known in some definite respects as the sort of God who created this sort of reality. For example:

> What is determinate about the act is not the whole of the act itself, only the nature of the act which is itself the product of the creating. Therefore, no determinate symbol can be applied literally to the act itself.[61]
>
> The conditional features constitute the nature of God in relation to the world. This, in fact, is the only sense in which God has a "nature," where "nature" has the connotation of determinate features. Except as creator, in connection with the world he creates, God is not determinate even in terms of a divine life.[62]
>
> We know the indeterminateness, the absolute transcendence, the independence, the aseity, of God in himself only insofar as it gets incarnated in the created determination of being creator.[63]

Neville's model for God is one-sided. God is nothing apart from creating. However, there is creation. We live in the determinate world, so there is no God apart from creating, only God in creating. The divine act is real, giving God the character of being creator of this reality. Nonetheless, Neville's thinking remains solely on the indeterminate side of creation. Attempts to model God the creator will inevitably use what is created, which is different than the act of creation. All symbols of God are therefore true only if broken.

Neville admits the tension being highlighted but does not solve it. "Roughly, ontological ultimates are realities on their own, whereas anthropological ultimates are human projects of ultimate importance."[64] This tension between what is truly ultimate and what people take as ultimately meaningful for their lives comes from Tillich's *Systematic Theology* and is one that he could not solve in examining the ontological and cosmological approaches to God. Both Tillich and Neville distinguish ultimate and proximate concerns. The problem is that the proximate material is necessarily taken up in matters of ultimate concern. To resolve the tension, Neville claims true religious symbols are always broken. This feels like giving up. However, Clayton has made a very pragmatic point by correctly noting that we now know all language is symbolic, meaning that pointing out the literal flaws in religious language can no longer be the distinctive marker of that language. Clayton also correctly notes that rather traditional theists can now call themselves critical realists and not leave behind many traditional affirmations about God as Tillich and Neville would like.[65] However, there are resources in pragmatism that Neville has left unexplored, resources that can bring the transcendent and immanent sides of his thought closer together than finite/infinite contrasts. Abduction is a means of working back from what exists to what might have been the case for it to exist, a pragmatic move at the heart of Peirce's philosophy that is open to bold theological probing. Signification of realities so hypothesized brings interpreters closer to them, into real relation, rather than pushing interpreters farther apart from the realities they interpret. As part of that real relation, interpretive activity can further develop the realities so signified and interpreted, including ultimate realities.

7 | Reinvigorating the Cobb-Neville Dialogue

A clash of doctrines is not a disaster—it is an opportunity....
Religion will not regain its old power until it can face change in
the same spirit as does science.—ALFRED NORTH WHITEHEAD,
Science and the Modern World

THE PURPOSE IN ARGUING FOR PCR is to reignite a conversation between two major figures of modern theology. John Cobb and Robert Neville, besides having a shared interest in Whitehead's philosophy, have spent considerable time directly debating each other. Their main point of disagreement is their different models of God, a conversation initiated by Neville's *Creativity and God*, which challenged the separation of God and creativity in process theology. That argument was followed by a series of back-and-forth debates in journals and book chapters. Despite basically agreeing on Whitehead's philosophy, the two always speak past each other when it comes to God. Cobb expresses this perfectly: "Even when we agree in our interpretation of Whitehead, we disagree in our evaluation."[1] A disagreement about ontology and cosmology overrides the entire conversation. Before moving on to show how this disagreement can be transformed when employing PCR rather than Whitehead's philosophy, it should be understood how they have disagreed up to this point. The debate between Cobb and Neville will be reviewed to prepare the way for reinvigorating that conversation in a more constructive fashion.

Criticisms and Defenses of God the Container

Neville applies the argument present in *God the Creator* to a criticism of process theology in Neville's *Creativity and God,* in which he argues God should be identified with creativity rather than understood in the throes of it along with the world. His problem is not necessarily with Whitehead's cosmology, but that it is only cosmology. Neville affirms an ontological creativity process thinkers do not. "What I call cosmological creativity, the only sort Whitehead acknowledges, is a descriptive generalization of the character of events; the reality of the events is accounted for with the ontological creativity of God the Creator."[2] This statement is merely making explicit that his argument in *God the Creator* disagrees with process theology on God. Two consequences Neville deems problematic flow from the separation of God and creativity made by process theologians. The first is God being subject to the same metaphysical structures as all occasions. This means that God is not an answer to the question of the one and the many, a nonstarter for Neville. The second problem flows from the first. For process theologians, everything is actual and in process, going against views of God as eternal.[3] Neville is sloppy with his language at times to heighten the polemical thrust of his argument, this being one of those cases. Unlike events in the world, Whitehead and Cobb have a God that is eternal, a never-ending process in which there is no perishing.[4] However, Neville is correct that this God is not unchanging or eternal in the sense of existing outside time and history. Neville has admitted to exaggerating to liven the debate in the preface of the new edition of *Creativity and God,*[5] so it is not worth reviewing such points again. More interesting than exaggerations that lead to obvious disagreement is that Neville argues that his conception of God better exemplifies the supposed virtues of the process God.

Regarding creaturely freedom, Neville rejects the claim that the process God leaves all creatures free to make themselves through their own decisions. Instead, he argues that the process God, as something among the initial data given to each occasion, is an external limit on all occasions. "Whereas finite occasions determine themselves, God is rather like a smother-mother, structuring all possibilities and continually insisting on values of her own arbitrary choice."[6] He acknowledges process theologians do not intend this limitation to be negative, to limit freedom, but as a necessary limitation for there to be any concrete value. However, Neville asserts that this understanding of God still limits freedom. "Insofar as God determines that value through the subjective aim in the initial data, the occasion's own choice is depleted."[7] The process God has already prepared all possibilities, leaving us only with the choice to ratify or reject that decision by God. Neville's alternative view is that God's contribution is identical with the free choice of occasions. For God to create value is just for something to determine value in one and the same act, a wondrous and mysterious gift of the ontological creative act. Furthermore, against the process notion that God's lures always relate to love and goodness, Neville notes that God is depicted in the Bible as free to perform terrifying acts: "The contemporary experience of God as Good is just a projection of human altruism. Without the terror it is not experienced as a real God. The genuine experience of the lure of goodness need not be projected onto an imagined fellow sufferer but can be grasped as God's creative deciding of our ownmost possibilities and the divine grace that wells up spontaneously each moment to give us an absolutely real and fresh start, ever again."[8] Regarding evil, Neville strikes at perhaps the heart of Cobb's theology, the claim that God is loving and good.

Neville argues that Whitehead's philosophy only eliminates the argument that God is evil. It does not prove God is good. "And the price of this move is to make the actual course of events *irrelevant* to God's moral character; this goes counter to the religious feeling that God's moral character is *revealed* in events, for better or worse."[9] Of course, Neville does not literally mean better or worse. His God is wild. Our standards of morality do not apply to the indeterminate creator, who is responsible for a world of natural beauty and destructive earthquakes, for the being of Mahatma Gandhi as well as of Adolf Hitler, and whose divine contribution is identical with such diametrically opposed free choices.

Regarding the basic principles of Whitehead's scheme, which Cobb shares, Neville argues that a reason must be given for their existence, for creativity, God, and the world existing together. If they are arbitrary, a mere surd, then there is no reason everything must be subject to them. An adequate account would amount to a solution to the problem of the one and the many, a push to ontological principles rather than cosmological principles. Whitehead and Cobb do not push that far. They only record the situation, rather than providing an explanation for it.

Neville suggests two adjustments to Whitehead's philosophy in light of his alternative theory of ontological creativity. First, ontological and cosmological creativity must be kept distinct. Entities must be cosmologically creative in themselves as well as the product of ontological creation, together with other entities. Cosmologically, everything is entirely free, but ontologically, all is entirely dependent on God. Second, God as an actual entity alongside the world will need to be abandoned for God as ontological creator. In response, Cobb simply grants Neville's point, noting it is not his concern. "Those who live and think by this intuition and need for unity will certainly not be satisfied with Whitehead's philosophy."[10] The real difference between ontological and cosmological concerns is admitted by both sides but left at an impasse.

Cobb's model of God is intended to be the one revealed in Jesus. God, like Jesus, is found in creative transformation of the world, not creativity apart from the world or merely creative of the world's existence. Having made his choice on being-itself and beings, Cobb suggests Neville should change his model of God or admit that he is speaking about the "Godhead" being-itself and not the God of the Bible.[11] It is interesting, in this context, that Neville argues that process theologians should do the same and admit the God of the Bible is wild and affirm his indeterminate God rather than settling for cosmological ultimates. Neville takes from Anselm the conviction that worshipfulness is the basic criterion for God, and that worshipfulness has to do with that than which nothing greater can be conceived. "The responses we make to the personalities of people may be those of hate or love, respect or disregard, admiration or disapproval, gratitude or disavowal. But we do not *worship* persons, even in a derivative sense. Worship is based on taking God's determinate characteristics as signs of his supremacy, transcendence, and abysmal independence of us and our claims, and this is what makes it awesome."[12] Neville also simply embraces the problem of evil, enveloping the process critique into his understanding of God. "God creating out of the divine aseity is awesome, terrible, glorious, and wild, not domesticated to take pains with the human scale of things."[13] This, echoing Cobb's insistence to be more biblical is a very biblical theme. Neville stands with Job in admitting the human standpoint cannot judge God's character.

Cobb grants that the concept of a transcendent creator God can evoke awe and wonder, a point on which Neville insists, though Cobb understands awe to be in tension with seeing dignity in ourselves. "This approach to God suggests that men are powerless in his hands, since they depend upon him for all that they are. It evokes the response of awe, obeisance, self-abnegation, and resignation. It is thus in tension with the view that men have dignity in themselves."[14] A God determining all is lawgiver and judge. We may have our own desires and thoughts, but they are nothing before God who has already set all standards. Invoking the positive lesson of the death of God movement, Cobb asserts this God is indeed dead to the modern world. Modern people do not need an all-determining God to find a sense of personal dignity. Scientists and philosophers can make progress without thinking the order they find is the result of God's creative decision. "Only when we have realized intellectually as well as in the depths of our sensibility both the impossibility of the continued reign of the Almighty father in the contemporary vision of reality and that the rejection of that reign is of the essence of Christian faith, can we authentically claim the future for Christ or, as I prefer, the God revealed in Jesus."[15] Thus, Cobb learned to see his crisis of faith, the death of the God he sought to defend when entering the University of Chicago, as a window into an authentic Christianity with a more adequate model of God.

Cobb argues that Whitehead's model of God configuring all possibilities is more worthy of worship than God the creator. Cobb even notes that he could grant Neville's argument for an indeterminate ground but go on devoting himself to his process understanding of God. "I am willing to grant that in some sense 'creativity' is more 'profound' than what I call 'God,' but not that it is more 'divine.' My own weighting is the reverse. For me, righteousness and love contribute more to 'divinity' than does power or metaphysical ultimacy."[16] Furthermore, Cobb interprets ground-of-being theologians like Neville as putting themselves in a bind. In their scheme, God is not experienced as some ultimate supreme being, but in and through ordinary experience as that which gives rise to those experiences. "God is the being of all the things that are, and God is experienced to whatever extent we experience the being of things in distinction from the particular forms of their existence."[17] The transcendent God is more immanent than we are to ourselves. This position is in tension with itself, according to Cobb.

It is not clear to Cobb how the God identified with being can be present and effective in the world. "If God is Being, and if the Logos is expressive Being, then the Logos is present and effective in the world to whatever extent the world has being. The efforts of theologians who think of God in this way to speak of his purposes and agency display the inherent tension of their thought of the God beyond the God of Biblical faith with the Biblical understanding of God as historically and personally alive."[18] Cobb simply encourages theologians to realize that any philosophically ultimate ground of being is not the same as the biblical God of Christianity. It is possible to speak of the utter transcendence of being-itself and it is possible to speak of intimacy with beings, but not both at the same time. In a sense, both Cobb and Neville have identified something real, one of those somethings is just not God, on Cobb's account. Neville has identified something else. God the creator is really "Gob" or the ground of being, not the God of Christianity.

Neville is not the only one guilty of exaggeration or misunderstanding in this back and forth. Hartshorne counters Neville's criticism of evil and creaturely freedom by making a point Neville could not have made better himself. "I take Whitehead and Peirce, preceded by Cournot and Boutroux, to have come closer to giving us a viable concept of divine creating than anyone had in the time of the writing of Job. God makes possible, but does not determine, the decisions of creatures. God does decide the kind of laws that are to obtain in a cosmic epoch. Not the Primordial but the Consequent Nature does this, for the laws are contingent and noneternal."[19] Neville has made the same point, albeit without affirming God's consequent nature. "There is serious divine interference on the views that God provides either subjective aim in initial data or the prefigured possibilities, but God on my view does neither. Rather, God on my view creates the spontaneous features within a person's decisions; the decisions are the person created, and since they are the person's resolving of indefiniteness, they are that person's responsibility. No other agent is responsible except the decision-maker."[20] Neville's God the creator is the source of everything, including the existence of free choices by humans and natural laws, while at the same time those choices are really free and laws are not manipulated by God. We make free choices, but for choices to be determinate existing things they must also be grounded in God. Similarly, natural laws are the results of nature's own powers. God does not force a structure on the determinate world. What unity exists in the world is an empirical question on the cosmological level, but God the creator is still the ontological explanation. "The question of the *one* for the many is not the same as the question of the *unity* of the many," a unity that Neville argues is left up to determinate things to make for themselves.[21] The loss of creaturely freedom would be a problem only if God was a being over and against things in the world. God the creator is not a being. God creates the structures of existence that allow there to be features admitting free choices, good and evil actions in history. But God is not an independent being to which responsibility can be ascribed.

Regarding ontology and cosmology, Neville's indeterminate answer for the determinate world, Hartshorne asserts the contrary: the most abstract understanding of definiteness is simply necessary, with contingency being the ability of creativity to produce something else instead. This creativity is not created, but just simply is the case. "God, the eternal abstractor, necessarily and always envisages it as an aspect of any and every concrete actuality. It has not been determined in the sense of having been made but is the identity of making as such."[22] He continues: "Universals express similarities of concrete realities, but they are also entertained as ideas or ideals. Over and above all the actualities, with their qualities, purposes, and ideas, there need be nothing further."[23] The process relationship between God and the world is one prehending the other, back and forth, forever. One need not be placed over and against the other.

In the end, Neville understands the difference between his wild God and Cobb's loving God as differing intuitions. He simply cannot share Cobb's God, viewing it as projection and wish fulfillment, whereas a God that is good and terrible is both biblical and reflective of a messy world, and therefore not obviously the projection of a desire for a cleaner, better world. Cobb's response would be that God's loving persuasion is also wild, insofar as it takes great risks. All God's lures for the world are adventurous, since God never knows what the result will be ahead of time. We do with the lures whatever we wish. In this sense, God has nothing to do with the specifics of order in our world. God's envisioning eternal objects is also the source of novelty, and thus unrest, in the universe. God's primordial nature is the push toward novelty in the universe. Order, societies, and a great nexus are required for enjoyment and the heights of civilization, but they can also get stale and inhibit enjoyment. As Whitehead says, it is a matter of "the contrast between order as the condition for excellence, and order as stifling the freshness of living."[24] Still, at the end of the day, the process God's life is adventurous in that the promotion of ideals among God's creatures depends on the decisions made by creatures, and those decisions are the material necessary for God's own enjoyment.

Cobb's response to Neville also comes to the same conclusion, that the two theologians are working based on differing intuitions, different Peircean habits as the point has been presented. "For me the recognition that no extant process formulation is free from difficulties calls for continued reflection within the tradition of process theism. For Neville it supports a position which has other roots."[25] This response relates to Cobb's highly contextual and always partially constructed way of thinking about any subject. From ideas about particles, evolution, and economics, to God, there are inconsistencies that have not been reasons to give up on physics, biology, or economic systems. Inconsistencies just provide reasons to keep doing better from within that framework. "The question about process theism for me, then, is not whether it is problem free but whether it is sufficiently cogent and fruitful to warrant continuing work within this tradition."[26] On what is worthy of being called God, they simply disagree, with seemingly no hope for reconciliation.

Neville claims the ultimate cause of all is the only thing worthy of worship, while Cobb focuses on what is good and loving, even if something that is philosophically more ultimate can be affirmed. Cobb is clear on where he has placed his stake. "I belong to the group who cannot worship that reality whose moral character is even partially revealed in the Holocaust or in torturing a single innocent child."[27] Cobb's God is the loving lure of possibilities for the world, not the creative source of everything in it. God is present when entities instantiate those possibilities and contribute to the creative transformation of reality. Neville simply grants this point, but names God as the creative source. "I agree with Cobb that the category of the ultimate, or 'creativity' taken as shorthand for that, expresses the most basic 'what is' of things. But according to the ontological principle, that 'what is,' being complex, must be the result of some decision. The decision is not another being, and it has no determinate character other than what it decides; but following the ontological tradition in the West and my own religious experience I still can call it divine."[28] To avoid this conclusion, one must ignore the ontological principle when it comes to ultimate matters, which Neville notes Whitehead and Cobb are happy to do. For him, this is arbitrary and a nonstarter for conversation. The ontological question of the one and the many is the overriding concern of his Peircean theological habit, but not for Cobb's.

Criticisms and Defenses of God the Creator

A fairly standard critique of classical substance theism given by process theologians relates to creation ex nihilo. For instance, Cobb's acceptance of Whitehead's understanding of God leads him to reject creation ex nihilo, a God that makes and determines everything. While Neville's theory of indeterminate creation ex nihilo is a novel advance on that theory, it is also certainly a God that makes everything in the divine act of creation. More interesting is that part of Cobb's criticism involves his claim that his process God is actually more powerful than the God who creates ex nihilo. This is not an obvious intuitive claim. It would seem a God creating and determining absolutely everything, a God that depends on nothing but the divine reality for doing said creating, would be the most powerful reality imaginable. However, Cobb locates an unexpected insight in the fact that the process God is not culpable for evil in the world because all occasions make themselves by their own choices.

The insight is that a God unable to control self-creative entities is more powerful than one that can control them. With no genuine competing powers, God's determining of everything from nothing is not very impressive, Cobb claims. "The power required to lead an army of tin soldiers is given to every child, since the soldiers have so little power to resist, but the power required to lead men is incomparably greater precisely because those who are led retain power of their own."[29] His elaborations of this point are striking: "The power that counts is the power to influence the exercise of power by others.... The only power capable of any worthwhile result is the power of persuasion.... Compulsion can be exercised on others only in proportion to their powerlessness. Persuasion is the means of exercising power upon the powerful."[30] Omnipotence in God has a more important meaning than the ability to fully control anything and everything. "It means instead that he exercises the optimum persuasive power in relation to whatever is."[31] The ability to tenderly lure the world forward with love is far more impressive for Cobb than the ability to create by fiat.

Regarding this divine lure, the power of persuasion, Cobb prefers other words to avoid misunderstanding. Persuasion can shade into bribery, promising a reward if something is done or withholding something if it is not. Parents might do this with children to get them to eat vegetables, for instance. To avoid such confusion, Cobb prefers "empowering power and liberating power."[32] If a way of thinking is offered that someone did not previously consider, and they accept it, that is a case of liberation and empowerment. In light of this way of thinking, Cobb criticizes Neville in a way that process theologians typically criticize creation ex nihilo theories. By determining everything, a God who creates from nothing eliminates the freedom of everything created. Neville anticipated this critique and already had a response to it in *God the Creator*. Determinate things can depend entirely on God for their *determinate* being and still be completely free to make their own decisions about who and what they are. "There is nothing more to the being of a determination than its being as determinate. It is its own being, different from the being of other determinations, just insofar as it is what it is. Being-itself is not a stuff to be carved up into portions, nor is it a universal property instantiated in many instances. Rather, it is the creator in which all determinations participate through being created."[33] Neville goes further than merely defending creaturely freedom in his position. He goes on to argue that his theory of creation ex nihilo gives creatures more freedom than a process model of God. "The attempt to give non-divine beings an integrity over against God by giving them a being independent of him only to be influenced by him necessarily fails, so long as God's will wins out by necessity in the long run. There is, on this view, no possibility of really thwarting God; yet that possibility should follow if one is to have integrity. Nor is there the possibility of damning oneself; one can only play a less-than-capacity role in bringing about God's will in the end."[34] Of course, this is not an accurate description of Cobb's God, which makes the best of a bad situation, so to speak. All beings could deny God and God would still envisage the maximum harmony possible for the next moment, though it would not be the same harmony had the previous divine lure succeeded in the world with the assurance Neville ascribes to it.

David Griffin has given a slightly more sustained critique of Neville, devoting a chapter to his theology in *Whitehead's Radically Different Postmodern Philosophy*, in which Griffin attempts to use Neville's position against itself. He throws Neville's criticisms of process theology back in his face, claiming it is Neville's theory of God the creator that is "incoherent, superfluous, and unworthy of worship."[35] On the ontological issue of the one and the many, Griffin brings up Neville's use of Peirce, who argues chaos needs no explanation. Only order needs explanation. In shifting the ontological question to one about order, rather than unity of diversity, Griffin can rightly claim Whitehead's God accounts for order. However, his use of Peirce to make this argument is misleading. Peirce notes that randomness does not call out for an explanation. To return to the example given already, finding random fallen trees in a forest does not violate any expectation, and therefore does not make existing habits problematic. Surprises calls for explanation. In this regard, order itself does not necessarily need explanation. There are pockets of order and disorder, and this is not surprising for Peirce. What is surprising for him is that order grows, becomes communicable, and takes on the character of self-control and lawlike behavior. Here is how Peirce stated his position: "Accordingly, the pragmaticist does not make the *summum bonum* to consist in action, but makes it to consist in that process of evolution whereby the existence comes more and more to embody those generals which were just now said to be *destined,* which is what we strive to express in calling them *reasonable*."[36] Order itself does not need explanation. The fact that it grows and is communicable does. Griffin cannot use this point to shift focus from Neville's God to Whitehead's. If anything, Whitehead makes the decisions of actual occasions, not God's work, account for enduring orders and laws, since such things are the results of the self-creativity of occasions. Despite this deceptive shift in focus, Griffin rightly names the sticking point of worshipfulness tied up with the ontological question.

Griffin, like Cobb, grants Neville's point that the category of the ultimate, creativity, does not answer the ontological question. It does not create through force. Actual entities create themselves. "Whitehead's God is not worthy of worship, Neville holds, because this God is finite, not the infinite source of everything determinate."[37] With Griffin's invocation of Peirce missing the mark, he also concludes, just as Neville and Cobb did, that the conversation seems to be at an impasse. "Thus phrased, the difference between the two views on the ontological question seems to be relativized to a standoff between two confessional stances."[38] Both sides think they are more adequately rational and empirical than the other, viewing the other's model of God as incoherent and the opposing method as leaving questions unresolved. Ontological causation is never a distinction Whitehead makes. Coherence forbids it. Griffin thinks Neville's argument that something formless and indeterminate can give rise to that which is formed and determinate is incoherent. Furthermore, Griffin denies the need to ask the question. God, creativity, and the world are features of reality that necessarily exist. The ontological principle that seeks explanations only applies to contingent things. As Whitehead states the point: "Metaphysics requires that the relationships of God to the World should lie beyond the accidents of will and that they be founded upon the necessities of the nature of God and the nature of the World."[39] In a sense Whitehead does answer the ontological question, or, more accurately, undercuts it by eliminating the argument for contingency that Neville makes. Why are there creative actual entities? They exist simply because they exist necessarily rather than contingently. Neville, of course, will not allow this escape route.

Neville argues it is impossible to avoid the question of the one and the many. Whitehead's attempt to undercut Neville's argument for contingency by asserting the necessity of the basic cosmological principles is not enough to avoid the ontological question. Neville counters that it does not matter if some principles are necessary and eternal, because "if they are determinate, the ground of their being lies in being created together."[40] The only thing eternal that does not require further explanation is his God the creator. In a sense, Neville agrees that Whitehead was correct about creativity—it is the making of something novel. "To put my point in Whiteheadian language, God the eternal creator is like an actual occasion but with all novelty and no prehensions."[41] Whitehead was simply wrong to not identify God and creativity, according to Neville's account. If that identification had been accepted, the entire divine nature would come from the divine creative act, no determinate prehensions necessary.

An Explanation of Different Peircean Habits

It might seem as if we have reached an impasse with Neville and Cobb. Both theologians, as well as Hartshorne and Griffin, have basically said as much. Despite agreeing on many defining features of good theology, that it is metaphysical rather than just narrative, fallible rather than foundational, consistent with other knowledge of the world, and pluralistic rather than imperialistic, their models of God are so different as to appear incommensurable. This might be the case if philosophy and theology must be about crafting final proofs and employing them to defeat all critics, but Robert Nozick offers a different way of viewing things. He presents philosophy not as the endeavor to create proofs, to create airtight arguments others must accept, but as the crafting and improving of explanations.

Criticism of arguments rarely, if ever, results in those being criticized adopting the position of their critic. Philosophy has a long history, and despite philosophers being trained in finding flaws in the great thinkers from that history, a myriad of positions flourish to this day. Attempts at philosophical coercion fail. Opponents will always make counter points or develop supplementary premises to support their preferred conclusion.[42] If you are not convinced, go back and reread the first two chapters of this book. It appears Nozick is correct that this is the case. Take Cobb and Neville, for another example. Despite years of creating and delivering clear and direct criticisms of each other's arguments for God, both have continued to develop and hone their different positions as if the criticisms never existed. The criticisms may be interesting in that they name differences between the two theologians, but they do not bring about actual change in conclusions. People are not easily forced into a position they do not want to accept by pointing out that certain premises are invalid or that a conclusion other than the one they want follows from their premises.

Explanations, as Nozick presents them, function differently than arguments, however. Explanations, roughly speaking, move from some given phenomena to asking how it is possible, and then offering an explanation that would answer that question. This flies in the face of critics who do not think an answer can be given to a given problem or doubt a certain answer is sufficiently proven. Proof is not the goal of explanations, though. The goal is to ask whether vexing problem q could be explained by p and, if the answer is yes, to develop an understanding of p with as much precision and clarity as possible.[43] Explanation is license for careful plausible exploration. Understood in this way, it would be expected that Cobb and Neville's theological habits continue along their separate tracks. Neville seeks an ontological answer to the question of the one and the many, while Cobb is content to develop a theology based on Whitehead's basic cosmological principles. Neville and Cobb are explaining different phenomena, in a sense, divine transcendence and immanence, respectively. However, explanations allow for more than understanding such differences. Very different explanations can be brought together intimately in ways that are not possible when they are viewed as exclusive either/or arguments.

Explanations allow for viewing the different positions of others as potential resources for deepening one's own position rather than as opponents to be defeated. Opposition between positions may not be logical, but a matter of tension. Explanation, by leaving behind absolute foundations, allows for risk taking, according to Nozick. "The question of how p is possible may cut so deeply that the only answers which suffice are implausible, as least as one judges before investigating how p is possible."[44] Rather than beginning with premises about which one is already convinced, an explanatory hypothesis can be introduced even if it is wild, unexpected, and not obvious. Starting from different highly specific standpoints, rather than supposedly neutral foundations from which one delivers proofs, means different positions may go places impossible for another. This also means there is value in tracking alternatives rather than supposedly defeating and rejecting them.

The way Nozick describes his ideal pluralistic situation for philosophy is a laudable goal for theology. "I stand on my position keeping track of the others, while you stand on yours. The position I occupy is modified somewhat by my broader knowledge, but I do not imagine that all the different positions so modified by knowledge of the others will converge."[45] There is value in theologians clustering around and further developing more or less plausible positions that are in dialogue with their more or less plausible alternatives, rather than affirming one position as a refutation of all others. However, what are deemed to be completely implausible alternatives will be left behind, as Cobb and Neville have done with supernatural substance theism. Better yet, plausible alternatives, which Cobb and Neville represent, will develop more fruitfully in dialogue with alternatives at their side than if they are isolated and alternatives are viewed only as worthy of defeat. In the case of Cobb and Neville, each is concerned with the transcendence and immanence of God, but each has focused most of their attention on only one of those aspects. Neville has focused on transcendent indeterminacy, and Cobb on immanent creative transformation. Both could better address the entirety of their concerns by thinking their position through the other.

Rather than choosing Cobb or Neville, a third mediating position should be developed. Still, the positions in dialogue are not meant to be entirely transcended or negated in favor of the new synthesis. They are encouraged to think about their own positions better through the other, transform, and enter dialogue again.

In terms of transcendence, being-itself is more ultimate, ontologically. Neville has a stronger model of God's transcendence than does Cobb. An indeterminate creator may even be more transcendent than classical substance theism. Even traditional attributes like omniscience and omnipotence do not apply to that God. The structures of intelligibility are among the determinate things created. Everything determinate breaks on indeterminacy. When it comes to immanence, there is also no comparison. Cobb's God provides initial aims for every occasion, receives whatever is done with those aims, reassesses, and provides new aims for new occasions. God is intimately tied to the creative transformation of the world. Left with Whitehead's philosophy, these are mutually exclusive options. Within Whitehead's philosophy a model of God that is more transcendent than the primordial nature of God will not be able to interact with actual occasions. Neville's theory of broken symbols makes this much clear. However, as excellent as it is, Whitehead's philosophy is not the only one available for negotiating these issues.

A strongly transcendent ontological ultimate and a fully immanent cosmological ultimate are both living options in a pragmatic philosophy like PCR. As already discussed, the two major interpretations of Peirce's philosophy of religion put him roughly on either side of this debate. Donna Orange argues that Peirce held something like traditional theism, with leanings toward process theology. This is seemingly what Peirce himself believed.[46] However, Michael Raposa argues that Peirce's metaphysical categories are open to pondering a creator of those categories that lies deeper than the cosmic nothingness of Firstness, interpreting Peirce as being closer to ground-of-being theology. Raposa's interpretation is a real option in Peirce's thought, an option congenial to Neville's God the creator. The difference between Whitehead and PCR is that ontological transcendence and cosmological immanence are not mutually exclusive in the latter. In the philosophical framework of PCR, which Rosenthal emphasizes is marked by the theme of emergence, it is possible to affirm both transcendence and immanence without exclusion. They would be inseparable from one another while remaining distinct and irreducible to one another, just like Firstness and Thirdness, because continuity is a defining feature of this philosophy. PCR is open to a transcendent God beyond Firstness and an immanent

God manifest in Thirdness, with connections between them developed in its emergent framework.

Different Names for the Same Concern

The differences between the methods of Cobb and Neville are striking, at least initially. Neville aims to present a philosophical theology that can be applied to any and all religious traditions. Cobb offers a natural theology while admitting up front that it is shaped by Christian commitments rather than supposedly pure rationality. Cobb claims he is postmodern while Neville claims to take the high road around modernity. Cobb accepts science and all the advances in knowledge made in the modern world but wants to transcend problematic aspects of its worldview. He adopts postmodern philosophy for the sake of his Christian identity. By moving through modernity to postmodernity, by accepting modernity's achievements and rejecting its problems, a new form of Christian existence is enabled. Neville also wants to avoid the pitfalls of modernity, but thinks religious problems are situated in late modernity, not in postmodernity.[47] Cobb speaks of contexts and *Christian* natural theology. Neville speaks of contexts only when it comes to symbolic engagement and provides a philosophical theology relevant to all world religions. However, both are simply seeking realism in religion against deconstruction, relativism, and nihilism. Both accept the achievements of modern science, construct philosophical cosmologies that are not welcome in postmodern circles, and aim to avoid the reductive, hierarchical, and exclusive tendencies associated with modern philosophical system-building. Others have also noticed that the concerns at the heart of the work of Cobb and Neville are closer together than labels would suggest.

David Tracy has challenged the relativistic aspects of Cobb's work, his qualification of natural theology, that it can only be approved once the contextual *Christian* preconfiguration of such work is admitted. He argues that Cobb's Whiteheadian worldview is not *just* useful for articulating Christian beliefs. In affirming it as a worthy worldview over alternatives, it is a critique of those alternatives. It is presented as a *true* and better option. It is not simply a different worldview. If this is the way Cobb views things, Tracy states, "then the theological use of philosophy for a natural theology should find itself committed to only and solely philosophical evidence. In short, the phrase 'a *Christian* natural theology' is a misnomer."[48] Cobb should just drop the Christian moniker and refer to his work as natural theology. If this is true, Cobb's Christian context, his Peircean habit of personal theism, would be cracked open to alternative metaphysical schemes and would need to be judged alongside them, whether they are deemed to be sufficiently biblical and Christian by Cobb or not. That result would be an opening to Neville's stronger concept of transcendence.

From a different angle Traugott Koch has shown how structures of existence being pregiven, having to deal with highly specific beliefs, can have disastrous consequences for those structures. He employs Tillich's treatment of myth in religion to make his point. All highly specific religious contexts contain myths, and myths always deal with origins in one way or another. Critics of these myths, especially since the explosion of the biocultural study of religion, will argue that the gods of the myths are just projections. God's origin is in us, and God is dead. Cobb, rather than accepting a given religious situation as the starting point of inquiry, must deal with origins and large-scale philosophical questions.[49] He needs to explain and reject alternative theories of the origins of religion for his conception of theology to survive. Again, this opens the door to Neville's favorite topic, asking the ontological question.

The relativism issue between Cobb and Neville is something of a verbal dispute because the heart of each project is in the same place, whether it be called late modern, postmodern, or relative. Neville has said as much to Griffin, noting that it is perfectly modern to criticize and experiment while still having a strong concept of reality.[50] Griffin opposes individualism, neoliberal capitalism, scientism, and yet he affirms God, purpose, meaning, and a real world. These are appropriate modern concerns, and Griffin should stop insisting on the "postmodern" label for process theology. Neville also understands valuation as crucial to any judgment, argues that those judgments get at reality, and that the sense of stability resulting from these grasps of reality are always hypothetical and fallible.[51] Lewis Ford lends support to this argument that there is a similarity of intent amid different labels. He notes that *Founders of Constructive Postmodern Philosophy*, of which Cobb is a coauthor, should be compared to Neville's *The Highroad around Modernism* in that, whether using Peirce or Whitehead, both share the agenda of avoiding deconstructive philosophy whether it is labeled postmodern or not.[52] Cobb and Neville reject materialism, if that means the deterministic position that all is made of matter that cannot act on its own. Cobb's actual entities make their own decisions before becoming objective fact. Neville affirms essential and conditional features, the essential being a guard against such deterministic materialism. For both, entities are affected by the environment and influence it in turn. PCR also takes postmodern critiques seriously, but places them back in a framework informed by all the achievements of modernism. It also rejects metaphysics as some aloof view from nowhere, but accepts it as an experimental tool formed like all other results of human inquiry. When it comes down to it, the different labels may be more a hindrance than a help if Cobb's postmodernism and Neville's late modernism aim to accept the achievements of the modern world without falling into its naïve traps.

Two Valid Guesses at the Riddle

In Peirce's terms, Cobb and Neville offer different retroductions and abductions. Cobb's work is a retroduction of classical biblical theism, reworking it in significant ways to preserve the insight of a divine loving being who is intimately connected to the world. Neville's work is a novel theological abduction, perhaps the first genuinely novel advance in the creation ex nihilo theory in over 1,500 years.[53] Retroduction introduces novel elements, but in an attempt to salvage as much as possible of an abduction that has become problematic. If it reaches its limit, if it is unable to salvage any aspects of a theory, another abduction must come in to keep inquiry going. Abductions infer from observations to possibly hidden antecedents, and for pragmatists this is not merely an act of the imagination. Ideas of God are not necessarily fictitious human creations. They are attempts to probe *reality*. Of course, imagination can either hinder or aid attempts to probe the depths of reality, so we can adjust accordingly based on the results. There are therefore tests, feedback from the independent world of Secondness, even for imaginative constructions.

The tests of these imaginative hypotheses are the standard ones for scientific theories: (1) empirical adequacy in accounting for the data; (2) fertility or long-term success that stimulates further inquiry; (3) the unifying power to show that things once thought to be separate are compatible; (4) correlation that makes them consistent with other established theories. Cobb fares better on the first and third tests. Neville fares better on the second and fourth tests. Both Cobb and Neville offer novel hypotheses moving from what is observed to what will explain it. In Neville's case, God explains the togetherness of determinate things. For Cobb, God explains the experience of novelty amid structured orders and subjective choices in the world.

Cobb's cosmological solution to the problem of the one and the many is not unlike that given by Neville's teacher, Paul Weiss, but rejected by the student. For Weiss, the modes of being unify the ways they are together with each other. Each mode is one for the others, without a singular unity grounding the many. Instead, many ones perform that role.[54] Neville's critique of his teacher would apply equally to the argument that God's primordial nature provides initial aims for the world as the many become one and then increase the many by one. "The one for the ontological many must not only unify the ways in which the presence of the many modifies it; it must also account for the unity of the being of the others. This is in inexpungeable insight in the view that being-itself must be common to the many in order to unify them."[55] On the other hand, the process of becoming is always transcending itself, indeterminate in constantly transcending given determinations. Cobb's process theology is therefore awash with indeterminacy. While this is the case, it is not what Neville means by indeterminacy.

Indeterminacy is something different than self-transcending spirit for Neville. While Cobb may emphasize that the determinate world is awash with indeterminacy, always fluctuating back and forth between indeterminate options and objective decisions of occasions, Neville means something more radical by the word. A determination can be determinate with respect to something and indeterminate with respect to something else. This is only to say that A is not-B and does not even have any acknowledgement of C. Obliviousness is not as deep as the sort of indeterminacy Neville affirms. "The indeterminateness of a *determination* is that it lacks a determinate real distinction from some other determination. But being-itself must be indeterminate with respect to *all* determinations."[56] The difference between Neville and Cobb boils down to cosmology and cosmogony. Cosmological explanations of ontology stop when they find an understanding of principles that explain everything else. Unity comes from the principles being interconnected. Cosmogony understands those principles as needing explanation. That they might be necessary principles presupposed by the rest of the system is not an explanation of those principles themselves.

Neville argues that his theory of God the creator provides stronger notions of both transcendence and immanence than focusing on just one, as in classical theism or pantheism. God creates all determinations, including God's character, and is thus infinitely transcendent. Since creation is not a moment in time in the past, God is always infinitely close to everything determinate as that responsible for their being. Not only is the union of being and God the basis of this view but also the union of God and creativity—all culminating in the ultimate ground that answers the question of the one and the many. In response to Cobb's criticisms Neville could respond it is a good thing his God is essentially indistinguishable from nothing apart from the act of creation. If God and creation are conflated, that is fine, even a biblical theme, as there is no concept of the divine apart from creation.[57] But if indeterminacy and the world presuppose or need one another, in the sense that Neville makes them both necessary for understanding either (i.e., without creation, no creator; without act, no awareness of the indeterminate God but only sheer nothingness), then they are on the same level. Indeterminacy is not more primal or ultimate, but always in need of the world to make sense of it as creative act. Rather than referencing everything—the existence of determinate things, the togetherness of our lives, religious symbols, and so forth—back to the indeterminate God, *indeterminacy and the world* should be implicated in explanations. That this is not Neville's position raises questions.

If we are so close to God as part of the termini of the creative act, and God creates God's own nature in that act, why is it that we as created things cannot better understand God? Why must all true symbols be broken? Adopting a more open stance toward constructed symbols, as opposed to broken ones, seems a more natural thing to do. Symbols, as determinate things, are part of God's nature that comes from creating. Furthermore, Neville admits speculative philosophy must not be so abstracted that it cannot be open to criticism from experience and spends the final third of *God the Creator* attempting to do just that, illustrating indeterminacy in the facts of daily religious life.[58] But his theory of God's indeterminacy seems immune precisely in the way he wishes to avoid. Unfalsifiable theories of God provide no means of critically sorting competing claims, of making progress in theology. However, Neville's theory could gain some concrete traction if instead of finite/infinite contrasts and broken symbols, it is pushed in the direction of finite/infinite growth.

In a sense, Neville's God the creator has essential and conditional features. "God in his aseity is that which creates the determinations of being, including his determinative character as creator; God moves out of his aseity by creating and, having moved out, is creator."[59] Neville will not allow questions about what God was before being determined as creator, which is fine. However, it does make sense to ask more about that determination that occurs in creating. Neville's wild God chooses to be an indeterminate creator, but the product, the world, is also part of the understanding of that creator. Neville has not sufficiently explored how that world, the world of determinacy, also determines God as creator. It extends God beyond sheer indeterminacy without erasing that transcendent aspect of God. Neville would balk at these suggestions. Instead, all determinations become, at best, broken symbols of

God given that everything breaks on the altar of indeterminacy. The God known through creation is determinate and intelligible, but the essential nature of God is indeterminate and free from determinations. It seems like Neville only ever paid lip service to the act of creation actually *determining* both God as creator and the world as product of that creation.

Whereas Neville retreats from this line of thinking to always affirm indeterminacy over determinacy, the next chapter will encourage him to step boldly into the determinate world. His God is indistinguishable from nothing, *except as being creator of the reality that happens to exist*. God has no predetermined will or nature prior to creation and is completely indeterminate. The present argument is in agreement on these points. However, in creating a determinate universe, one for which PCR has been defended as providing a good understanding, God is the sort of creator marked by Peirce's categories and semiotic activity. The indeterminate God, in creating, gave the divine self the character of growing concrete reasonableness—that is the sort of universe the wild divine will created, after all. If the only character God has is that given in creating, in relating to the world, nothing is more relational than Thirdness. Neville's indeterminate God needs to enter that world.

Neville has spent his career on the austere apophatic side of his work, clarifying the indeterminate ground needed for a determinate world. Whenever he gets close to affirming a robust sense in which God and the world mutually determine one another, Neville withdraws to finite/infinite contrasts and broken symbols. Cobb's criticism of analogy in Aquinas is relevant to this way Neville always refers back to the indeterminate side of his argument. Cobb's problem with Aquinas is that he initially establishes God as first cause. Once this is done, nothing further can be said about this nonfinite God from our position as finite beings, a position not unlike Neville's. Rather, God must be known as creator through God's effects. Cobb notes that this creates a problem when applying "cause" and "existence" to God. If they are not applied univocally, the entire basis of the theory of analogy is an equivocation. There is then tension with any religiously meaningful language about God and the affirmation of that very God.[60] Cobb suggests moving beyond this framework. If cause and existence mean birth and death, they must be meant analogically for God. But if they mean the capacity to selectively respond, making one's own decisions, then then there is no reason to not at least consider whether they can apply univocally to God as well. Applying Cobb's critique of Aquinas to Neville, absolute indeterminacy is eliminated. God cannot be only indeterminate if the determinate world is part of determining God as creator. In an emergent framework like PCR, indeterminacy can be saved, but not absolutely. Something like emerging or creeping determinacy in God would have to apply to preserve any sense of indeterminacy in the creator. It is not possible to talk about one without the other. If God is defined as creator by acting, creator and product are co-dependent. In order to fully affirm *both* the transcendence and immanence of God the creator, God must also be understood to be determined by the world resulting from the divine act. God the creator is also created by the world. To show that this is the case is the task of the next chapter.

8 | A Pragmatic Constructive
Realist Model of God

BEFORE MOVING ON TO the constructive results of engaging the theologies of Cobb and Neville through PCR, a powerful argument relying on Peirce that has been recently developed should be mentioned. Andrew Robinson and Christopher Southgate apply Peirce to the emerging field of biosemiotics, spelling out the implications they believe that field has for theology.[1] Robinson has also produced a lengthy book using Peirce almost exclusively to develop a semiotic model of the Christian Trinity.[2] To state differences between their work and the present argument up front, PCR directs questions about God and the world to Peirce's categories rather than his semiotics, which is embedded in the categories. From that perspective, Robinson and Southgate are playing something like a language game in mapping Christian doctrines onto the taxonomy of signs. Cobb and Neville can be understood as performing inquiry to discover and defend a model of God, whereas Robinson and Southgate merely assume and attempt to strengthen a model of God with Peirce's help. Cobb and Neville have different theological habits, but nonetheless share a method in offering novel theological hypotheses, a move never made in mapping rather classical theism onto Peirce's signs.

Pragmatic Constructive Realism:
A New Name for a New Way of Thinking

According to biosemiotics, there could be a universe without humans but not one without the use of signs. From intelligent animals to single-cell organisms, all engage in semiosis by converting physical signs into conventional information. Signification is basic to the emergence of life. "The result is that the nature/culture boundary, long cherished by humans as that which distinguishes humanity from mere animals or mechanical nature, erodes. Evolution emerges as a process whose intrinsic tendency is to generate coherent wholes with meaning."[3] Viewing signs as crucial to the evolution of life, Robinson and Southgate ask to what they owe their intentional nature. Their answer is God. Semiotic processes that are fundamental to life, human behavior, and cognition may be understood as "vestiges of the Trinity in creation."[4] They use biosemiotics to argue purpose is part of the natural world. Not only is purpose not metaphysically ruled out, they argue that a theological account of purpose is more satisfying than naturalistic ones.

Naturally evolving semiotic activity creates spaces in which novel varieties of signification grow. Jesper Hoffmeyer, a leading figure in biosemiotics, defines such spaces in terms of freedom. "The most pronounced feature of organic evolution is not the creation of a multiplicity of amazing morphological structures, but the general expansion of 'semiotic freedom,' that is to say the increase in richness or 'depth' of meaning that can be communicated: From pheromones to birdsong and from antibodies to Japanese ceremonies of welcome."[5] Semiotic freedom opens the possibility of religious signification. Meaning-making activity is open to theological questioning. For Robinson and Southgate, God is the condition of the possibility of all such meaning-making, in addition to being the goal of an emerging ability in the universe to use signs.[6] Just as Peirce's categories of Firstness, Secondness, and Thirdness are needed to make sense of signification in the universe, Robinson and Southgate claim the unbegotten nature of the Origin, the distinction of the Word from its Origin, and the mediating work of the Spirit can be affirmed by Christians as the ground of a semiotic universe. An implication of this position is that individuals can participate in the divine life in the sense that signs carry divine content over to interpreters.

A problem with their argument is that it never moves past the cosmological level of Peirce's categories, despite using them as support for a rather orthodox form of Trinitarian theism. Robinson finds precedent for treating God as Firstness in Plotinus whose reality of "the One" was like a category upon which further development depends.[7] It seems Robinson is content to allow his acceptance of Christian Trinitarian categories to prefigure the logical relation Peirce gave his categories where, in Robinson's words, "the logical priority of Firstness is nevertheless consistent with its ontological dependence upon the other two categories."[8] The problem is that Robinson's semiotic understanding of incarnation is mismatched with the pragmatic methodology he employs to reach that conclusion. Robinson's claim is that incarnation "may be understood as a recognition that Jesus' life as a whole was an 'iconic qualisign' of the being and presence of God."[9] To prepare the way for this claim, he presents an account of human evolution and anthropology in terms of semiotics. He argues that everything in the world, and especially humans within it, is moving toward transcendence. In particular, "the human capacity for self-transcendence may be thought of in terms of 'the gift of abduction': the possibility of acquiring knowledge beyond that which can be obtained deductively or inductively."[10] While he is correct that abduction is the only means of producing new knowledge, he does not take the bold step of doing that in theology.

Instead of asking what sort of ontological reality could lay deeper than Peirce's categories, Robinson is content to present abduction as drawing support for the Trinity through the categories. This may be "new" knowledge in that it affirms a divine being not accepted by everyone as real, but it is an impoverished understanding of abduction. Expressing God the Father as Firstness, the Son as Secondness, and the Holy Spirit as Thirdness is not actually the advancing of a new hypothesis. Rather, it is simply borrowing an established body of work that is now experiencing a resurgence, Peirce's philosophy, and claiming it implied God's Trinitarian nature all along, whether people knew it or not.

Others have also questioned whether Robinson's work is sufficiently pragmatic. In his review of *God and the World of Signs,* Gary Slater argues that this "categories-as-Trinities" approach verges on being very unpragmatic by blocking the way of inquiry, which Robinson seeks to avoid.[11] Rather than offering an abductive hypothesis for God and supporting it by displaying its consistency with the categories, Robinson claims that the categories are vestiges of the Trinity. This makes him more like Barth than Tillich, in terms of prioritizing narrative over truth in theology. Slater agrees, noting that "Robinson's thesis, if accepted in full, risks seeming less like an effort to find a mediating piece between science and religion and more like an effort to ground Peirce's categories in qualities intrinsic to religious belief.... Robinson's argument that his thesis is to be accepted on aesthetic grounds will likely be meaningful only to those already possessed of Christian faith."[12] Furthermore, Robinson's claim that Jesus is an iconic qualisign of the being and presence of God is problematic.

Peirce defines the qualisign along with the sinsign and legisign, dealing with qualities, existents, and laws, respectively. The perceptive reader will have already noted they also have to do with Firstness, Secondness, and Thirdness. Qualisigns deal with qualities in themselves, which do nothing unless embodied in something actual. Sinsigns are existing things that are signs, "sin" meaning "being only once."[13] Legisigns are laws and conventional signs, general types of signification. Presumably, Robinson wants the presence of God to be available for more people than just Jesus. For that to be the case, it would need to be communicable, involving Thirdness, and would therefore need to be a legisign involving more than iconicity. Presumably he also wants what was present in Jesus to be the *reality* of God, not the mere sensation of being full of God that could be nothing but an illusion. For that to be the case, a sinsign, involving Secondness, would need to be involved. Affirming nothing but an iconic qualisign in Jesus leaves Robinson with an understanding of God as nothing but an unavoidable feeling. Neville might say Robinson, given the way he uses Peirce for theology, is confused about intentional reference within different signs. "A person's fantasy world is intentional reference with iconicity but no direct indexicality (the indirect index might be to the person's unconscious processes)."[14] Robinson is drawn to a very specific feeling of God's reality, but he has not defended God as actually real or shown how to communicate that feeling to others. If that is all Robinson thinks Peirce can provide theology, he might be more consistent by joining constructivists and doing without the reality of any of it.

The problem is not with the scientific proposals given by Robinson and Southgate. The further development of biosemiotics is exciting, a field that accords with Peirce's enthusiasm over extending semiosis to nonhuman animals and even nonliving entities. Biosemiotics also offers a corrective to Peirce's panpsychism. Without forcing self-conscious experience on everything, it can still be affirmed that purpose emerges naturally. The problem is not with biosemiotics, but with how Robinson and Southgate confuse the place of Peirce's semiotics within his metaphysical categories. Peirce analyzes signs within the categories of Firstness, Secondness, and Thirdness. The result of this combination is a theory of inquiry. Communities of inquirers discover an evolving universe marked by the three categories, and both they and the universe adjust to novel facts discovered in that process of inquiry through a similarly triadic interpretive process. Though signs are responses to brute fact, some will not survive the test of time, while general truths will emerge as the universe grows from Firstness to a reasonableness that inquirers gradually understand. Philip Clayton also notes this problem in his summation of the special series of *Zygon* issues devoted to this topic.

Robinson and Southgate put themselves in a bind, according to Clayton, by simply mapping the Trinity onto Peirce's categories. "But doesn't this amount to a new form of subordinationism, this time, however (nicely corresponding to the present Zeitgeist), one in which Origin and Word are stages on the way to Spirit as genuine Thirdness?"[15] Forget people such as Cobb and Neville interested in alternative theological projects such as process and ground-of-being theology. The proposals from Robinson and Southgate do not even satisfy some traditional Trinitarian questions. Furthermore, Peirce's categories are *stages* of human inquiry and real *markers* of how the world evolves, not entities themselves that are reflected in signs.[16] Secondness makes the possibilities of Firstness existent, and Thirdness grows as inquirers correct beliefs over time and learn control over brute facts. Robinson's equivocation of these categories with the Christian Trinity neglects that these categories are parts of inquiry in which realities are discovered, not realities themselves. He and Southgate think Peirce employs the categories to understand the use of signs. However, what Peirce really does is place sign usage within the universe of Firstness, Secondness, and Thirdness, which constrains and modifies the viable usage of signs.

Sign relations and their functions in biological processes drive development in nature. Living systems are sign systems, and in sign systems interaction is as important as causal determination of what is given. Rather than being passive to greater forces, living systems possess semiotic freedom to create *and respond* to signs.[17] This means religious symbols are not an imposition to be simply mapped onto reality, but grow out of and are continuous with it. And due to degrees of freedom not present in natural semiosis, religious symbols can play a crucial role in connecting to their deepest ground, God as the ground of semiosis, which in turn makes God the highest developed achievement of that semiosis.

The Unnecessary Nature of God the Container

Cobb's God is not the philosophical necessity it is presented as when the philosophy in place is PCR rather than Whitehead's. Possibilities, novel creative ideas, can be located in some other source—or not need any container at all. Cobb argues that God primordially envisages all possibilities, so possibilities not realized remain available for actualization. Possibilities must be in an actual entity for them to be prehended by others at all. God is the ground for novelty in the world as that containing all possibilities. However, the natural world fulfills this role. Cobb contrasts his position with creation ex nihilo theories in which God is the ground of order, a problem for Cobb because without God containing possibilities and providing initial aims, he sees no way to account for novelty.[18] In PCR God can be the ground of the world, while the world can account for the emergence of novelty without need of recourse to eternal objects and initial aims. With Peirce, Robert Corrington, and Dewey it can be argued that Cobb's God is not necessary as a container for possibilities accounting for novelty in the world.

Corrington presents his argument in *Deep Pantheism* as a mediating position between Neville and process theology and is therefore a helpful guide even though the present argument goes ontologically deeper than Corrington allows. He argues the potencies of *natura naturans*, nature naturing, are capable of accounting for *natura naturata*, nature natured. In short, according to this alternative to Whitehead's cosmology, nature has a depth dimension that can account for novelty without recourse to an independent realm of eternal objects. "Metaphorically, while process theologians look *up* to the primordial mind of god as the *summum bonum*, a deep pantheist will look *down* into the depths from whence all divinities emerge."[19] Nature itself contains infinite possibilities and no other container is necessary.

Nature naturing is nature creating itself out of nothing but itself. Nature natured are the countless orders of the world that result from this process. Within the one reality of the natural world there are ontological distinctions, not distinctions between nature and something else. Corrington, being a pantheist, admits no ontological ground; nature is its own ground. Within this framework, Corrington describes the achievements of art and individual genius as the development of possibilities within nature. Pessimism is the denial of such possibilities, understanding them as nothing but human projections.[20] In this sense, Cobb is actually a pessimist regarding the possibilities of nature given his negative assessment of Dewey on ideals covered in chapter 5. "The one who dedicates himself to ideals does so out of the correct judgment that these ideals have objectivity to him, that they lay a claim upon him. Yet he can hardly provide for himself an intelligible explanation of how this is so. If he rejects God as the ground of their claim, then he is driven toward describing them—with Dewey—as projections."[21] PCR denies the necessity of eternal objects contained in God, without reducing ideals to projections.

There are good reasons to speak of possibilities to account for the mix of novelty and order we experience, but they need not reside in an eternal realm—possibilities are simply a way of speaking about powerful instrumental traits that have some degree of general power in the world. This is Dewey's argument, contra Cobb's criticism, especially in his analysis of the achievement of art. "Form may then be defined as the operation of forces that carry the experience of an event, object, scene, and situation to its own integral fulfillment. The connection of form with substance is thus inherent, not imposed from without. It marks the matter of an experience that is carried to consummation."[22] Form is the instrument with which artists and scientists solve problems, problems that arise in the natural world. Apart from such actualities, even in God, there are no possibilities. Someone could possibly not get a disease and outlive someone who gets the disease. If that happens, a possibility simply becomes an actuality and its status is changed. Possibilities are given in nature and change and evolve where they are found.

Dewey distinguishes brute facts from our highest achievements, but entirely on natural terms. Similarly, Corrington argues that skilled individuals, especially artists, take the potentialities of nature and further develop them. He expresses Dewey's point in terms of Peirce's immediate object (nature) and the dynamic object (deep potentials of nature being gradually revealed). "As 'immediate' the beautiful work of art does not open up its dynamic dimension until it suddenly and unexpectedly cracks open to the sublime and is permeated by the potencies of nature naturing. In such a rare case, beauty transcends itself and becomes a clearing within which the infinitude and encompassing of the sublime can present themselves."[23] Despite seeking a mediating position, on this point Corrington is closer to Neville's wild God than Cobb's process God. "The 'ungodly' aspect of the sublime and, for some, of art in general, is that it reveals the abyss of nature that prevails prior to the split between good and evil—nature in its raw and untamed giving of itself."[24] The deep, potentially dark, mysterious potentialities of nature, of Firstness, are enough to fulfill the supposedly necessary role of God in Cobb's theology.

Corrington explicitly considers the process alternative of a container for possibilities, but finds it wanting. "Need one posit an available Absolute sign container/creator in order to explain the nature of the actual infinite of semiosis that envelopes [sic] the finite sign user? This rather extreme conclusion can be avoided if one accepts the idea that sign systems can have a kind of inertial momentum of their own that allows for sign linkages that occur naturally within the sign series even if an attending human consciousness is not involved."[25] Also, against Peirce and with PCR, he does not affirm panpsychism in which an internal mentality of all signs is guiding the development of possibilities. New signs developed in and through nature can join the infinite open-ended series of signification. "The actual infinite of signs (interpretants) is always actualizing, that is, it is always affecting and making semiotic space for itself by lighting up an ongoing series of interpretations of the object sphere under its purview."[26] This point about nature developing its own possibilities is supported by Hoffmeyer's discussion of semiotic freedom in biosemiosis.

One way that Hoffmeyer introduces the concept of semiotic freedom is by distinguishing genes from pseudogenes, areas of the genome unavailable for transcription. Mutations of pseudogenes do not have functional consequences. By not contributing to the success or failure of their organism, pseudogenes are free to undergo mutations without incurring selective consequences. However, those mutations form a resource base out of which functional genes may someday be taken.[27] Furthermore, cues from neighboring cells are picked up by receptors on cell membranes and translated into signals that interact with DNA transcription. This means such genes do not determine their own reading, as contextual factors play a crucial role.[28] Given that autonomous resources are involved in determining organisms and their features, the process can be accurately called interpretation. "The big advantage of this mechanism is that contrary to physically based interactions, semiotic interactions do not depend on any direct causal connection between the sign vehicle and the effect. Instead, the two events are connected through the intervention of an interpretative response. The point is that in semiotic interactions the causal machinery of the receptive system is itself in charge of producing the behavior, and it thus only needs to acquire a sensitivity towards the sign as an inducing factor."[29] Unconscious biosemiotic processes are constantly occurring underneath our conscious ones. Interpretive biological activity extends to the micro scale of eukaryotic cells and the membranes of their organelles.[30] Nature contains the freedom and interpretive ability to develop its own possibilities. While this means that the concepts of eternal objects and the primordial nature of God are unnecessary, Cobb's argument for creative transformation is at the heart of PCR.

Individuals and their decisions are not discrete building blocks in pragmatic philosophy as they are for Whitehead, but the creative pole of continuous communities. Rosenthal describes the relationship between community and individual as follows: "In the continual interplay of adjustment of attitudes, aspirations, and factual perceptions between the common perspective as the condition for the novel emergent individual perspective and this individual perspective as it conditions the common perspective the dynamic community is to be found."[31] Creativity and conformity are worked out as community develops its means of self-control. Rosenthal's point about identity developing and growing in this process could not have been put better by Cobb. "The development of the ability both to create and to respond constructively to the creation of novel perspectives, as well as to incorporate the perspective of the other, not as something totally alien but as something sympathetically understood, is at once the growth of the self."[32] A suddenly problematic situation is an opportunity to apply intelligence and grow. While the real world constrains us and thwarts invalid attempts to control it, we control our own intellectual development or stubbornly resist by applying the wrong methods, and are left to the whims of nature. In Corrington's terms, it is a matter of living within the interplay of nature naturing and nature natured. However, it should be noted that this way of thinking about possibilities and their development leads Corrington to reject the premises upon which Neville argues for God the creator.

Corrington denies the analysis of determinacy in terms of essential and conditional features. For him "nature is so complex and multi-layered that it simply does not have *an essential* trait found in each and every order."[33] Corrington's basic situation is more like William James's pluralistic universe. "There are many 'ones' each shaping a region of nature-natured, but no meta-one that houses and locates all of the many orders of the world."[34] In fact, Corrington argues that "nature" does not exist. There are simply countless orders with no collective character to be mapped by the term "nature" and therefore no need for an ontological ground accounting for *the* order. "There are only orders not *the* Order."[35] We create such metanarratives about order that are pragmatically useful, but they are not accurate depictions of reality. This leads Corrington to directly reject Neville on creation.

From nature naturing comes the experienced order in the world, nature natured. Between the two is where the God of Corrington's pantheism lives. God is deep, under the ordered realities we experience, but not ontologically different than the natural world. For this reason, he cannot go where Neville goes.

> Neville argues that god and the world both emerged from an indeterminate ontological creative act that shaped both the world and the divine. God, in this scheme, is absolutely unique and is the primary emergent from the "act" that makes the world possible. The current

perspective prefers to use the concept of the "event" in that it doesn't, contra Neville, suggest an agent who acts consciously to make the world but rather stresses the mysterious potency of self-othering to spawn the innumerable orders of nature.... From the ordinal perspective, god prevails in innumerable ways in innumerable orders but is not present in or with all natural complexes as per the definition of natural complexes as always being located in orders that eclipse it while participating in the innumerable sub-orders that also belong to the natural complex per se. There is no such thing as a trans-ordinal divine essence that sits in its own plenitude outside of the dramas of all nature's creatures acting within "regular" time.[36]

The furthest Corrington will go toward Neville's ontological depths is admitting that God's revelation in this pantheistic in-between space is not foreign to Tillich's existentialism. "This 'new being,' to use Paul Tillich's phrase, is held to be a genuine opening onto the depth-dimensions of divinity and its 'agents.' These agents serve as modes of access to the divinity, which makes it more available to the finite human processes."[37] However, Corrington leaves the door open to probe further, deeper ontologically, than he allows. From nature naturing it is possible to move from the partly available to the conditions behind it, to offer an abductive hypothesis in Peirce's sense. This allows for positing something to be true about reality, not just as a convenient fiction, but as if it really is the case, which Corrington grants. For Peirce, the truth of things is gradually revealed through time. If there is a depth to that from which things emerge, its reality can be put forward in a novel abductive hypothesis. Corrington interprets this point as the incarnational core of Peirce's theology.

The three categories hunger for realization in the world of signs, and divine traces are left in the signs. Some traces are found in given signs, but those rooted in greater nothingness are found in "the between."[38] This is not Thirdness, but an element of the irrational in God. There is a manifest God of evolution (Thirdness and concrete reasonableness), but the depth of God is found in an irrational self-othering ground of nothingness. Corrington interprets this theme in Peirce pantheistically, everything rooted in the deep cosmic nothingness of Firstness, nature naturing, not in a God ontologically responsible for nature. The orders of nature interact in many ways without the governing of a separate divine being. There is also no separate realm of possibilities. Possibilities are what they are within their appropriate orders. Possibilities and actualities co-condition one another. The question still lingers, can God be found on both "sides" of this divide, ontologically more ultimate than cosmic possibilities and also manifest in them?

Recall that according to Michael Raposa, Peirce's God can be understood as the source of semiotic activity and the active reality bringing that semiotic activity in line with the divine plan.[39] The second half of that position is unnecessary. The potentials of the world are indeed created by God's free act of creation, as Neville argues, but there is semiotic freedom in the way those potentials are realized, from the natural world to cultural creations. The indeterminate ground of being accounts for the cosmic possibilities of Firstness. Creative transformation is the movement from Secondness to Thirdness. Whereas Peirce's panpsychism and strong teleology gives human beings a rather passive role in the inevitable march of God's plan, PCR, with Corrington, rejects panpsychism and evolutionary love. Divine creation remains real, but we have an active role in bringing created possibilities to completion. The connection between an indeterminate God and a God in process is the connection between Firsts and Thirds, in which we have an active role.

Concrete Determinations of God the Creator

Neville views leaving behind the question of being-itself and the one and the many as against the very spirit of philosophical and theological work. "That this move goes so counter to instinct, when properly understood, renders it initially implausible and suggests that it should be considered an alternative only in the last resort."[40] That this is Neville's *instinct* suggests, again, that Nozick has a point. But rather than leaving it at that, Neville and Cobb left to develop on their own, the present argument aims to make progress by learning through them and with them in order to reach a more balanced position affirming divine transcendence more strongly than Cobb and immanence more strongly than Neville. Neville lumps Peirce in with Whitehead as a cosmologist who was not concerned with the question of being-itself. Peirce left his three categories as unexplained basic principles.[41] This is a limitation in Peirce, despite his fragmented thoughts on God. In the same spirit as Neville, it is necessary to affirm an indeterminate creator of the categories. However, in PCR that creator is responsible for a world marked by Peirce's emergent metaphysics rather than Whitehead's metaphysics of discreteness. As Rosenthal has shown, Neville has not embraced the pragmatic insights on this theme, a fact that can be seen by the ways Neville comes to the cusp of saying the world determines God and gives God conditional features in some respects, but always retreats from making that assertion.

In Neville's theology, conditional features for God do nothing other than identify God as creator. "The created product *constitutes*, rather than *gives*, God's second conditional feature. Being the creator of the product constitutes God's first conditional feature. The power by which he is the creator and creates the product is the third. The features are *essential* to God's *creating*; but God's *creating* is conditional."[42] There is no God without creation. Talk of God as creator is meaningless without the world. But there is a world, which on Neville's account would seem to mean God is more than sheer indeterminacy and is determined by that world in some substantial way as its creator. To take the entire argument for God the creator seriously, there needs to be more determination of the creator by what is created than merely recognizing God as creator. Neville sometimes admits this necessary tension. "Just because God in himself is indeterminate and transcendent, all we know of him is his created manifestations. If God has a character, for example, is loving, or if he works miracles, for example, saves someone, this is indeed a contingent miracle, from free grace, not from necessity."[43] It therefore seems possible to know God determinately in the world; it is just a matter of what we find.

We cannot assume God has exactly the sort of character we wish, but maybe some character is real, a matter of empirical investigation to find just what sort of God created this world, an open abductive hypothesis. Clayton has made a similar point in discussing the struggles of modern thought to affirm a transcendent *and* immanent ultimate. "On the one side, postulating something that is unconditioned gives one a way of speaking of the contrast between this postulation and the (otherwise) conditioned character of human knowledge.... Approached from the other side, the apparent limits that we do discover tell us something about what the nature of an unconditioned ground (if such exists) would have to be, if it is both to transcend these epistemic limits and to 'condition' or account for them as their source."[44] In the picture painted by Clayton, we would know God's character as we come to know the character of the world. However, Neville recants from these implications: "God apart from determinate creation is indeterminate. But the paradox is that to be creator is to be something determinate. The resolution is to recognize that considering God as creator is indeed considering him in determinate connection with creation; part of the meaning of being creator is that God must also have reality apart from that determinate connection and that this other reality is prior to his reality as creator."[45] Earlier in his argument he cements the dividing line: "Since the creator gives itself conditional features as it creates the determinations of being, its conditional features must be among the determinations created."[46] Conditional features are not *really* conditional features. They are created determinate things and, like everything else determinate, are broken and do not truly apply to God. All of this is not quite right according to the framework of PCR.

Neville is correct that there is no creator without creating, no God apart from the world. God also needs to be indeterminate to be the creator of determinate things. That is not all God needs to be in relation to the world, however. An artist without art is not an artist. If God acquires conditional features from creating, once there is creation then the indeterminate free divine act has chosen to only be indeterminate in some respects. God is indeterminate as needed to ground the determinate world and conditioned by that determinate world in choosing to create it. Both determinations result from the same divine act. If this is not the case, God, being indeterminate, would be unknowable by anything determinate, even as creator. However, Clayton raises another possibility for God's relation to the world: "perhaps God's actions are fundamentally free and thus cannot be derived from rationality alone.... such a God would have to make himself known within the human agent."[47] Neville does claim that the ontological creative act is completely free, not even determined by a prior nature in God. Furthermore, what if God's conditional features, the determinate things created, are self-creative? In the pragmatic theme of continuous emergence, creators cannot be separated from what happens to their creation. Biosemiotics connects cultivated Thirdness to brute facts of nature's Secondness, which emerge from the possibilities of nature's Firstness, which are created by God. According to PCR, what emerges from something cannot be completely separated from that from which it emerged, meaning constructed religious symbols are real developments of the God from which they emerged in creation, without reducing the two to one another. God is transcendent and not the same as the world, but God is also intimately present and we can become symbols of God as part of the determinate creation identifying the creator. Creative transformations in the world take God the creator beyond the features self-given to God in the creative act, and such extension would be allowed by God in creating things with the freedom to evolve just as they have. Besides the contingent free act of divine creation, there is semiotic freedom for created things to play a role in determining creation through their interpretations. God is determined as creator by an emerging creation, not a static one. Neville has a response to this, but it does not hold.

Finite creators never give rise to the entire being of their products. They do not create ex nihilo like God creates. Finite creators use preexisting materials, so finite creations are not entirely conditional features of their creators. However, in the case of God and the world, Neville argues that the world does not give God conditional features. The reality of the situation works the other way around. If A is God and B is creation, Neville claims "as A gives rise to B, it gives itself these features. Its giving rise to B is a self-constituting with these features."[48] Finite creation involves relative nonbeing, the negation of something else. It is a feature of something that already exists. Neville's God, by contrast, creates from genuine nothingness, not even out of a preexisting divine nature. Neville also claims that the situation with God does not leave us with nonbeing, sheer nothingness. In his framework, God as nonbeing would be the contrast to determinate being. If the latter were not created, it would not exist and neither would absolute nonbeing. Neville's own formulation for God the creator is calling out for completion in these statements. There is a determinate world, there is creation, so God is more than nonbeing. In other words, an indeterminate God is more than nothing. If that is the case, it is not clear why he denies we can say anything of that God, as if God was nothing.

Any argument involving the concept of creation will involve the source, the act itself, and the product of that creation. In Neville's argument for God the creator all three elements arrive at once; acting itself is the relation of determination from indetermination. There is no reason the act itself cannot be an act of both indeterminacy and determinacy. Neville would be more consistent in drawing out the implications of his argument for God the creator if he argued that the act was an act of both. Indeterminacy can be justified as an abstraction, but it is qualified as soon as there is mention of action, doing something concrete.[49] That is, sheer indeterminacy is better understood as a pure abstraction of God from the world, but then it *would not be an act*. Acts do determinate things. Contrary to Neville's intent, an act presupposes the mutual determination of indeterminacy and determinacy. As soon as God is defined as an act of something determinate, God has freely chosen to define Godself in some determinate respects.

In an interesting way, Cobb agrees with Neville that God is nothing apart from creation, though for different reasons. Without the world, God would be a mere abstraction, a set of possibilities with nothing actualizing them. As Whitehead put it in one of his well-known phrases, "It is as true to say that God creates the World, as that the World creates God."[50] In a different sense than Neville, God is still nothing without the world, but this relation is symmetrical in process theology. For Neville, the relation is completely asymmetrical. What if there is another option? What if the act of creation is asymmetrical and what is created has the freedom to develop toward symmetry? The process cosmology of God and world always existing in mutual determination is not the only framework in which divine development is possible. Cobb's concept of creative transformation could transform Neville's God the creator. This point could be made with Pierce in the form of continuous emergence—that which emerges from something is different from, connected to, and impacts the understanding of that from which it emerges. Gary Dorrien, in summarizing the historical dialogue between Cobb and Neville, captures the direction in which this argument is pushing their work: "either there is more in becoming than in which becomes, or there is not. If there is more in becoming, process is the last word, and the Schleiermacher/Tillich/Gilkey model of conceiving divine transcendence is wrong. But if there is more in that which becomes, this 'more' must derive its being from that which does not become."[51] These are not exclusive options. An already existing set of possibilities is too determinate to function as the deeper ground of what becomes in the world. God is indeterminate and in creating determines even what is possible. However, in Peirce's philosophy a God deeper than Firstness will be connected to Thirdness due to the continuity of emergence. There is more in what becomes and, by realizing what was previously only a possibility, this "more" contributes to determining that God. This means stronger affirmations of God's transcendence and presence than are made by Cobb and Neville are possible within the framework of PCR.

Hermann Deuser has also noted that Peirce's thoughts on God were attempts to escape binary oppositions such as the one between Cobb and Neville. Thinking about theology after Kant, and before he embraced Peirce, Deuser saw only two theological options: Barth's insulation of theology from every sphere of knowledge, or the process approach of relativizing God. Once Deuser learned Peirce he realized God's reality can lie outside existence while being intimately connected to human concerns in the form of Thirdness, without being reducible to existence and Secondness as in pantheism.[52] For Peirce, the universe grows out of "pure possibility."[53] It is the First of a Third, as Deuser describes it, an infinitesimal no-thing that gradually shows itself as the possibility of concrete reasonableness, a Peircean emerging habit.[54] In Peirce's words, "when we gaze upon the multifariousness of nature we are looking straight into the face of a *living spontaneity*... the truth of God."[55] As has been covered, Peirce was so obsessed with the *living* aspect, with Thirdness, that he read life into matter and thought God must be a person. But on his own account, this was not necessary. Growth is the result of chance spontaneous developments that take hold in nature and develop into lawlike behavior. There can be an impersonal ground of personal processes.

Neville comes close to considering the possibility of growth in God but closes that route off as soon as its possibility arises. It is worth quoting his argument in its entirety.

> Some might think it possible to make the ontological creative act intelligible as symmetrical rather than asymmetrical by giving it an internal genetic process. That is, it might be possible to conceive the act as beginning with infinitesimal determinateness and then by stages, understood in symmetrical ways, unfolding to the complete definiteness of the world. This was Whitehead's ploy in attempting to explain creation of novelty within time. For him, an actual occasion within time as a "genetic" structure, as he called it, that begins with the past occasions as felt, proceeds through stages of sorting and integrating of these feelings of past actualities, and resulting in a completely definite actual entity. This genetic process is not itself temporal. It has stages of integration related as logically before and after, but not earlier and later. Whitehead said that this genetic process is not itself actual. What is actual is only the completed actual occasion that has some actual spatiotemporal thickness, joined with the spatiotemporal properties of environing actualities.... The concept of the ontological creative act, however, cannot appeal to past actual occasions so as to construct stages of concrescence or genesis. Everything in the ontological creative act is novel. It has no stages. Perhaps we can say that the ontological creative act is "immediate," although we should beware of the connotation that it takes place in an instantaneous now without duration. All "nows" are the end product of the ontological creative act. No temporal, albeit nondurational, medium exists within which the ontological creative act plays out. No proto-space exists within which the ontological creative act creates the world of spatial things; the act does not take place in any there—there is no "there" there until the act creates the world.[56]

This picture looks different if viewed through the philosophy of Peirce rather than Whitehead. Neville, in this passage, is focusing on what came prior to the emerging entities, Whitehead's actual occasions with objective immortality. Neville rules out meaningful talk in these terms since in his position there is nothing determinate prior to creation. But PCR shifts the focus. A more important question is what emerges out of something, and what that means about where it came from. There can be no prior reality, even sheer indeterminacy, that is not somehow impacted by what emerges out of its activity. Once there is determinant creation, the indeterminate God can no longer be the judge, jury, and executioner of all determinate symbols of God.

Emergence and Growth in God the Created

The work of Cobb and Neville is worthy of attention in the religion and science dialogue, philosophical theology, and any other theological approaches that seek consistency with knowledge of the world. Extending each theologian beyond their existing position is intended to more fully develop their keen insights. This mediating position seeks to be true to the goals of dialogue both have pursued in comparative theology throughout their careers, but have yet to apply to their intra-Christian dialogue with one another. Cobb is correct that any good dialogue must take participants beyond that dialogue.[57] In terms of this specific dialogue, Cobb affirms God's determinacy, *not* indeterminacy. Neville can claim to address God's determinacy, *but really* affirms indeterminacy. With PCR it is possible to affirm both indeterminacy *and* determinacy, transcendence *and* immanence. In the Whiteheadian framework that Cobb uses, when the many become one and, in turn, increase the many by one, all the actual entities involved are discrete units. They impact one another as causal influences, but as achievements they are all objective and discrete. With Cobb's model of God abandoned, Neville takes this cosmological scheme and sharply divides indeterminacy and determinacy. In the emergent framework of PCR, such an easy divide is, at best, an abstraction perhaps useful for some purposes. That is the lesson to be taken from the excursus into Rosenthal's pragmatism in chapter 4. God can be affirmed as the ontologically grounding creative act but cannot be separated from that which emerges from that divine act. God is indeterminate but, having created, is also connected to, revealed by, and growing determinately in what emerges from divine creation. The act of creating is an act of indetermination *and determination*. In creating, God self-determines as indeterminate in some respects and determinate in others. Cultivated religious symbols, rather than being necessarily broken in this alternative view, are related to the vague cosmic possibilities of Firstness and their deeper ontological ground. They are constructions that can repair fissures between God and the world left behind by Neville and never affirmed by Cobb. What this means can be further illustrated by comparison with Corrington's pantheistic position already mentioned.

The conclusion being drawn includes a God that is both ontologically more ultimate and more clearly realized cosmologically than Corrington allows. Nonetheless, there are informative analogies. As Corrington presents his pantheism in terms of Peirce's categories, God the creator is absolute Firstness. The terminus of that act, God fully revealed, is absolute Secondness. The universe at any point measured, humanity's cultivated reactions to that God found in the world's religious traditions, is Thirdness.[58] Both God and the world are growing toward something infinitely different than what they were in the past. The "goal" of the universe is to enact Thirdness through novelty and continuity. Still, Corrington's God is nothing but the cosmic possibilities of Firstness and their development. The present argument follows Neville here. God is the deepest ground of everything, being indeterminately deeper than the cosmic nothingness of Firstness. To Neville's position PCR adds that God immanently revealed is that toward which everything is developing. The two aspects of God can remain distinguishable as emergent and ground, but there cannot be an absolute break between God as indeterminate and determinate. However, because this indeterminate ground does not have the impetus for that development within it, does not have a primordial nature prehending and ordering possibilities so as to be relevant to the world, that ordered relevance and transformation of the world through novel possibilities becomes creation's contribution to God the creator.

Firstness is like nature naturing, the spontaneous release of nature's potencies. Thirdness, general encompassing laws, are products of nature natured, not spontaneous eruptions from nature. Hoffmeyer and biosemiotics supports this view. Hoffmeyer agrees with Peirce that nature is full of chance and indeterminacy. "The task for natural science is thus not so much to corral the slimy and messy diversity of life into the straightjacketed uniformity of natural law. The task is rather to explain how ordered structures emerge out of unordered, chaotic diversity."[59] As Peirce argues, uniformity and law need to be accounted for, not randomness.[60] Furthermore, Peirce's understanding of law, Thirdness, does not eliminate the reality of chance. As Hoffmeyer notes, they are intermingled: "Semiosis, sign action, is necessarily embedded in sensory material processes, and therefore has both a dynamic side, which allows a process of communications to take place, and a complementary logical, or mediating, side. The first of these sides stands under the force of efficient causality, and the second expresses the controlling agency of final causation."[61] As a consequence of developing deep potencies, we get developmental teleology; not one preordained by a divine mind or earned by claiming mind was always present in nature, but natural development of orders in the world. Against absolute chance and necessity, there are specific, limited, yet real developments. This position is nonteleological in the traditional sense because the development is not built in from the start by God. It is a contingent achievement. Chaos is at least as pervasive as order and creative transformations can go nowhere. There is growth, but it is contingent on our actions. Whatever develops just is what it is. Without a God containing all possibilities and ordering their relevance, there is no predetermined initial aim for all occasions. The push upward and onward is still in nature, not preconfigured in God though coming from God. The direction these developments take is partially up to our decisions and deliberate effort, and such effort, whatever it ends up being, is ultimately supported. The potentials in nature loosen existing structures and bring them to the edge of novelty. Like Tillich's description of courage, this ontological grounding in God breaks up the conservative impulse to protect things as they are and gives the impetus to step into the unknown and creatively transform the world. Unlike Tillich, such transformations also transform the God from which they emerged. They develop God's identity, extending it in the world. The potentials in nature need to be achieved. Though the potentialities are spontaneously given, their achievement is not. God's indeterminacy is a given condition for the world. God's determinacy is a precious achievement.

An analogy of how this can be understood comes from another example of how human signification is connected to signification in the rest of nature. Hoffmeyer has described how DNA and its digital codes are passive and need analogical signification. "As analogical codifications, organisms recognize and interact with each other in ecological space, whereas as digital codifications (genomes), they are passively carried forward in time from generation to generation (in sexually reproducing species, after recombination via meiosis and fertilization). Seen from this perspective, life must be understood as semiotic survival—survival via a fundamental code-duality."[62] The *play* between the two, the singularity of digital code and plurality of analog codes, makes evolution possible, as opposed to a static universe. Another example is the unicellular algae *Acetabularia acetabulum*, which consists of what looks like a root system, the *rhizoid* where the genome is located, a stalk, and a cap. If the stalk is cut in the middle, the rhizoid with the genome will regenerate an identical cap, but the upper part of the stalk will only live for weeks before dying—seemingly confirming that morphogenesis is exclusive to the genome, its digital code. However, if all three, rhizoid, stalk, and cap, are cut, then the stalk, not the rhizoid, will show the ability to produce a new cap. "The morphogenetic process is *not* the direct product of the genes alone, since, in the stalk, it continues to go on without the genes. The stalk, on the other hand, is dependent on gene *products* (proteins) that can only be produced when a nucleus is present (i.e., only in the rhizoid).... The *digital code,* thus, is necessary for the continuation of life, because it is needed for the formation of new proteins—but the *analog codes* in the cytoplasm of the stalk are responsible for the concrete execution of morphogenesis."[63] Self-organizing semiotics of the cytoplasm are required to explain the phenomenon. Digitally coded descriptions carry life forward through time, but do not control their own interpretations. *Living* analog codes are needed for that.

An example at an even simpler level of nature is "alarmones." These are signal compounds that accumulate in bacteria as signs of stress when cells are lacking glucose or amino acids, substrates for protein synthesis. They are a signal that protein cannot be made anymore, or that gene transcription would be a waste of metabolic energy. They are symbols in that they have no necessary physical relationship with the processes their signals control. Alarmones accumulate only when a cell is exposed to a certain environment. They disappear if conditions improve but have a domain of action in which they control metabolic processes when they are needed. Hoffmeyer notes this concentration of an alarmone as an index of glucose starvation is perhaps the most primitive example of digitizing analog codes.[64] There is semiotic freedom for bacteria to utilize molecules in ways different from their original biological functions. One alarmone can function as an icon confirming that enzymes can take a specific compound to be what it is, an index for increasing levels of that compound, and a symbol for glucose starvation. These concepts of digital and analog codes and natural symbols can be extended, though not literally, into thinking about God and the world to clarify the present argument.

Whatever about God's determination is "coded" in reality that determines God as the creator of that reality does not control its own interpretation. The divine act of creation is not self-interpreting. Living beings and intelligent beings are needed for that. We can become symbols of God by performing that needed interpretation. That phrase, which has now been used several times, that we can become symbols of God, should be unpacked in more detail.

You may balk at the notion that *we* can become symbols. Symbols are verbal statements and objects used in rituals, not human beings, after all. Not necessarily. Tillich made some moves that have also been made by Neville and in this argument. Tillich also dropped the concept of substance when thinking of God and replaced it with causality, as did Neville. However,

Tillich did not think that God and world were strongly separated as effects other than their causes. Recall the example of God instantiating a series from chapter 4. Tillich writes that cause and effect "include each other and form a series which is endless in both directions. What is cause at one point in the series is effect at another point and conversely. God as cause is drawn into this series, which drives even him beyond himself."[65] It is on this point that Neville is found wanting. The fact that God must be approached using structural elements of the series is not a weakness, according to Tillich. Just because symbols are determinate does not mean they must be broken, as Neville claims. They make God living, capable of being a matter of our ultimate concern, and give us assurance in our use of symbols, which *participate* in their divine ground.

Tillich claims that "every person and every thing participates in being-itself, that is, in the ground and meaning of being."[66] He refers to the manifestation of God not being automatically deterministically forced on us, but happening through creative mediation. Signs have no necessary relation with that to which they point, while symbols participate in the reality for which they stand. This leads him to raise Neville's question about broken symbols, but to provide a different answer to it. "Can a segment of finite reality become the basis for an assertion about that which is infinite? The answer is that it can, because that which is infinite is being-itself and because everything participates in being-itself."[67] Symbols can die when situations change and symbols that once provided meaning are now dead, but when symbols are revelatory of their divine ground they can be fully affirmed as participating in that ground. "[Religious symbols] force the infinite down to finitude and the finite up to infinity. They open the divine for the human and the human for the divine."[68] Such an interpretation of symbolism in religion is meant to preserve realism, to "consecrate" things like parent child relations or the power of words to a holy level—religious symbols affirm these things rather than negate them. In a biosemiotic world, our significations perform that mediation. We can become symbols of God in Tillich's sense that symbols participate in the reality that they symbolize. "A symbol participates in the reality it symbolizes; the knower participates in the known; the lover participates in the beloved; the existent participates in the essences that make it what it is, under the condition of existence; the individual participates in the destiny of separation and guilt; the Christian participates in the New Being as it is manifest in Jesus the Christ."[69] Given that nature is already full of meaningful signification rather than vacuous actualities bumping into one another, and God's character is determined by the act of creating that world, extensions of meaningful signification in complex organisms further determine God the creator.

Rather than barriers to an indeterminate God, active signification is a necessary part of the relation of God and world. Lewis Ford has correctly noted that religious symbols cannot be understood passively according to Tillich's account of participation just reviewed, with their finite medium performing no role other than getting out of the way and becoming transparent to God.[70] "If the finitude of the medium should be removed, nothing would remain. It has no infinite characteristics that would enable it to point beyond itself. What function then does the medium perform, if the divine revelation would appear even more completely in its total absence? It seems its function becomes purely negative."[71] To avoid this purely negative conclusion, symbols need to be understood as having some active role in uncovering their basis in the ground-of-being in which they are supposed to participate. In such a case, the medium of the symbols would not be passively transparent, but actively render something present. Attempting to live a fruitful religious life by becoming symbols of God ourselves is therefore one of the most natural things to do, regardless of how strange that may sound to those accustomed to associating religious symbols only with images in stained glass windows and elements of communal rituals. We are determinate beings, and our being, like that of everything determinate, is grounded in God's creative act. Just as structural constraints on organisms can be understood as precursors to semiotic activity, natural semiosis is something like a functional archetype preparing the way for us to signify God.

Again, such interpretive activity is continuous with the material world. Responding *selectively* makes all the difference, according to Hoffmeyer: "To say that living creatures harbor intentions is tantamount to saying that they can differentiate between phenomena in their surroundings and react to them selectively, as though some were better than others. Even an amoeba is capable of choosing to move in one direction rather than another. It will, for example, generally gravitate toward the richest source of nourishment."[72] In religious signification, being continuous with biosemiotics, what is selected in responses to God will make all the difference to that divine identity. While Tillich and Neville claim that the only nonsymbolic statement we can make about God is God is being-itself, or indeterminate creator, my position is that symbols of God become further determinations of God as creator. Robinson and Southgate think signification of God is literally iconically true. If that is the only affirmation of theological signs possible, Neville is correct that iconic signification should be understood as broken. But that conclusion can be avoided because semiotic freedom is real.⁷³ The relation between God and the world is awaiting our symbolic interpretations, which are crucially necessary rather than violations of the metaphysical scheme. How Tillich's assertion that religious symbols participate in that which they symbolize can be the case should now be clear. Not unlike the analog interpretations of digital codes, our interpretations of God give that ultimate reality a determinate identity it would be otherwise lacking.

If God is in any sense immanent in the world, then an essential aspect of any reception of that reality involves its interpretation making such reception possible. No interpretation, no immanent God. While the act of creation mutually determines God as indeterminate and determinate, there are not simple determinate statements about God's determinate character to be passively received, as if we could go for a walk and stumble upon them while admiring a sunset. Like the stalk is a symbol of mediation between the genome and the product of the cap in the algae *Acetabularia acetabulum*, we are symbols mediating between God and the world. God's revealed determinate nature is associated with Thirdness, the growth of concrete reasonableness. Symbols of God that are affirmed in all their materiality, as opposed to broken ones, do not eliminate God's indeterminacy in the same way that Thirdness does not eliminate Firstness from Peirce's philosophy. This is still a revelation, an "ontological shock" in Tillich's sense of when the truth of something else breaks in upon us.⁷⁴ Signification is a gift of God's creative act. It is a shock that our symbols reveal God in a way that would leave God hidden without symbolic engagement. In one and the same moment we are grasped by an understanding of God and creatively extend that understanding. To help clarify what this means, it is worth noting how this position goes beyond Corrington.

In Corrington's pantheism, God is revealed in Secondness. This is just sound pantheism. God and the facticity of the world are identified. Thirdness is identified with human responses to this revelation. This can happen in religions, but he looks to artists for inspiration. In the current argument, Thirdness is God's determinate revelation. On the one hand, this is a richer reading of Peirce's category of Thirdness. Laws of nature are examples of Thirdness, making certain traditional affirmations like God is in the world possible, but constructed means of communication are also examples of Thirdness. If God is determinately revealed in Thirdness, then God does not just create the world, the world also creates God, as do the results of intelligence in that world, once that ability emerges. The possibilities the indeterminate creator created are not ordered by that creator. Nature is enough to account for their reality, with the ordering coming from what living beings do with them. It is likely that nonhuman animals make important contributions when it comes to reacting to these possibilities, and anthropomorphic idolatry is to be avoided. Cosmic explosions, lost species, and cruel human cultures are also part of what determines the creator in creation. That point only heightens the importance of contributing what small amount of order and meaning we are capable of in our actions. The heights of human achievements and the depths of their failures also reveal and cover up God as we respond to the created possibilities.

Recall that Peirce calls the depth dimension of objects the "dynamic object" and the present aspect the "immediate object." The two grow toward convergence in the infinite long run. Unlike Kant's thing-in-itself, Peirce insists that inquiry can get us closer to the true dynamic object.[75] Against those like Neville who suggest that religious symbols point to God, but their materiality is always problematic, *our constructed beliefs about God can actually get us closer to that reality.* The deep nothingness that is the germ of the universe is connected to what evolves from that germ while still infinitely transcending it. God emerges from what is indistinguishable from nothingness, just like everything else marked by Secondness and Thirdness, while at the same time remaining the indeterminate creative ground distinguishable from those determinate achievements. If Peirce is right about continuity, which is supported by the continuity of signs in nature as explained in biosemiotics, there are already potentially signs of God all around us, just waiting for us to broaden our horizons enough to realize it. Signs would then be open-ended on both sides, open to affirming an indeterminate ground deeper than Firstness while also being open to evolving reasonableness.

In a sense, Peirce's failure is a theological opportunity according to PCR. For Peirce, history is the inevitable rational working out of ideas until they are finally realized. The process was so assured that he made it divinely preordained, but so much that happens is incomprehensible. Firstness and Secondness are real. Peirce sacrificed particularity in history by transforming everything into a preliminary realization of Thirdness. His panpsychism and evolutionary love leading to Thirdness run roughshod over history rather than being demonstrated by history. This same problem could be expressed in terms of the work of Cobb and Neville. Despite their omnipresence as initial aims, eternal objects don't seem to be realized much in the world. It is as much a mess as it is a beautiful order. This is less a problem for Neville's wild and chaotic God, in light of which Peirce's failure would be expected, but the world emerges from an indeterminacy that is not passive. Undifferentiated potentiality moves to the cosmic stock of potentials (Firstness) in the act of creation. Cosmic potentiality moves into existence (Secondness) and previously unpersonalized feelings give way to habits. Significations are natural by-products of transitioning from indeterminacy to experience. This means Neville's direction of symbolic intentionality moving from determinate existence to its ground should be reversed. Efficacy belongs to religious symbols expressing the ground of a growing universe coming to know itself as determined in creation, so to speak. Brokenness is maintained, though differently than for Neville. Infinitely many novel signs will express the divine in the future while many existing signs will become false.

That PCR is open to an ontological ground of Firstness opens it to Neville's indeterminate God. Firstness has to do with feeling, making it a route to that God mattering in the determinate world. Importantly, because Firstness is continuous with Secondness and Thirdness, it is a route to making God more than a feeling and capable of growth in the world. Thirdness reaches into Firstness and its indeterminate ground, just as Firstness and the indeterminate ground grow toward generality. This provides a stronger understanding of God's transcendence than Cobb allows, and it allows Neville to posit more than he does regarding God's immanence. Peirce allows flights of imagination as long as they have possible practical effects.[76] If the indeterminate God is so different from the determinate world so as to be indistinguishable from nothing, the difference it makes would also seemingly be nothing.[77] That is no longer the case. The only positive theological affirmation can no longer be that God is indeterminate.

Construed as a debate, Neville's main victory in this conclusion is that there is a deep indeterminate God. Cobb's main victory is that we nonetheless contribute to that God's growth; creative transformation is real for God and the world. They both lose in that they are being asked to think beyond themselves to improve themselves, but all sides really win. While Cobb and Neville both wish to affirm divine transcendence and immanence, their current efforts must be viewed as weighted toward one pole or the other. To balance that one-sidedness and think through the implications of transcendence and immanence for each other, Cobb and Neville need each other to push each other past their existing categories.

Is the God being affirmed with the aid of PCR in some sense terrible, beyond human standards of goodness like Neville's wild God? Certainly, but God is not *just* identified with nature in this argument. In pantheism, goodness and evil in God is simply an empirical matter. Create a measure for good and evil in the world, perform an exhaustive study, and create a ratio.

Religious traditions in such a scheme have little to do other than register the findings with an appropriate amount of shock and awe. It would be hard to read much personality into such a God, as the cosmos is overwhelmingly full of random chaos and destruction. However, God is not simply wild or terrible in the sense of just being indeterminate and incapable of being judged by the human standpoint. The God of Thirdness is not only found in nature. Human responses matter in the creative transformation from Secondness to Thirdness. Triadic activity, interpretation, is a cosmic sign of the God that lies deeper than the cosmic nothingness of Firstness and yet is more intimate than we are to ourselves. Our constructions are also part of God's reality participating in their ground of being.

In an ever violent and dogmatically partisan world, developing the right sort of constructive responses matters more than ever. Precisely because God is not just indeterminate nothingness, we are called to be symbols of God as best we can. While Neville is correct about an indeterminate creator, Cobb is also correct about the role of potentials for allowing novelty in the world. However, since Cobb's container God is rejected, the world does not create God by accepting or rejecting the divine lures and, in doing so, giving God things to which the divine mind can respond. Rather, the indeterminate God is drawn out, beyond Neville's breaking point, in our responses. If it seems shocking to say that God is created in religious responses to God, consider examples of dawning awareness when a wayward religious tradition finds itself by fully affirming LGBTQ+ individuals, and some within that tradition divorce themselves from it by creating a splinter group that will try and continue to hide God's grace from anyone not straight and cisgender. The United Methodist Church is currently on the verge of schism based on this issue, and it will be interesting to see whether they conclude their religious symbols entail a God for all or just some. Sometimes revelatory symbols are found in the *responsive work* of those who proclaim that Black lives matter in the face of unjust responses to police shootings.[78] Conversely, consider violence enacted in the name of God such as the Crusades, and the subsequent rejection of God by many people in response. People living in the Middle East should be angry with the West and Western Christianity given that George W. Bush claimed divine sanction for preemptively striking at Iraq and destroying so much. Every time a conservative Christian pastor endorsed Donald Trump as "God's candidate" in the 2016 and 2020 United States presidential elections, God was covered up a little bit. Rather than divine lures tailor-made for every situation, the divine gift of creation is a truly free one left up to us to develop or conceal. At their worst, the responses have been destructive of the world, and some people have been right to reject God and move on by themselves. At their best, the responses to God's creation improve the world so that it really looks like God's creation, because those responses truly have put God in it. We play a crucial role in making God wild, good, or a mixture of both.

This position technically amounts to an odd emergent sort of panentheism. God and world are not equal since God the creator is indeterminate while the created world is its determinate product. They can become more equal, contained in one another in some respects, though not all, as that determinate world further determines the character of its creator. The act of creation mutually determines both God as creator and world as created, and the determination of that created world is still ongoing as new orders of the world emerge. Symbols of an otherwise indeterminate God are parts of that God's determination. The world is not chipping away at God's indeterminacy as if to find the definite divine being within, but spelling out how the creator was, and is still, determined by the world in the mutually determining act of creation.

Despite his lifelong disdain for dogmatic authoritative theology, Peirce identified a future hope for an ideal community of inquiry with the heart of genuine religion. "The Gospel of Christ says that progress comes from every individual merging his individuality in sympathy with his neighbors."[79] There is hope that new communities will emerge as different individuals identify similar concerns in one another and seek to address them together in the creation of something new. The new community, as a community of interpretation, becomes related by shared interpretants, but such a community can become *too* coherent to the point that it resists all reform. Even as solutions, interpretations are transformational, never settled, which Peirce argues is just as true for religious achievements. "Man's highest developments are social; and religion, though it begins in a seminal individual inspiration, only comes to full flower in a great church coextensive with a civilization. This is true of every religion, but supremely so of the religion of love. Its ideal is that the whole world shall be united in the bond of a common love of God *accomplished by each man's loving his neighbor. Without a church, the religion of love can have but a rudimentary existence;* and a narrow, little exclusive church is almost worse than none. A great catholic church is wanted."[80] PCR stands with Peirce in anticipation of religion formed in light of his method.

Without the best of our responses, some possibilities are left to fade into oblivion. We really are created co-creators.[81] Violence cuts off possibilities for realization in the world. Saying no to destruction is to say yes to God, giving life the chance to flourish, which gives unrealized possibilities the chance to flourish, all of which gives God the chance to grow and flourish in the world. It was mentioned in chapter 3 that without the right method and the ability to consciously control hypotheses about novel developments, reality will leave a community of inquiry behind. It can now be said that without the right method and the ability to consciously control hypotheses about novel developments, God and God's interpreters will leave one another behind. Those responses, when at their best, become symbols of God in the world, not broken ones, just symbols of God. They are perhaps the highest achievement an otherwise indeterminate God could hope for.

Recall that PCR departs from Peirce's panpsychism. Not everything is marked by subjectivity. It is an emergent achievement. Even if all humans reject God and leave that reality behind, whatever character the world has would determine God's character as creator. However, what an impoverished character that would be. The emergence of ideas is where God *lives* in the world, as opposed to merely existing. They are where the cosmic possibilities created in Firstness come to fruition. As has been shown, Neville sides with Descartes over Leibniz in prioritizing God's will over God's nature. The same goes for finding God in the world in this conclusion. God as determined by the world is not a matter of a well-defined nature, but ideas that are enacted; from creation, to the natural world, to the biosemiotic emergence of life, and finally to the emergence of complex ideas. Ideals are real, and we play a constructive role in their formation and realization. Those ideals, our imaginative constructions, are not a barrier to the reality of this world or God. Rather, they are our only entry points. If we do this well, there is a sort of symmetry between us and our creator—we become symbols of God, at our heights—since Thirdness and concrete reasonableness are the most crowning achievements we can hope for, being far more important than any brute existing thing. We should also try to imitate God and grow in sympathy toward others. We should want to contribute to the divine life, to become symbols of God.

9 | Pragmatic Pluralism and Theological Progress

This is my song, O God of all the nations,
a song of peace for lands afar and mine.
This is my home, the country where my heart is;
here are my hopes, my dreams, my holy shrine;
but other hearts in other lands are beating
with hopes and dreams as true and high as mine.

My country's skies are bluer than the ocean,
and sunlight beams on cloverleaf and pine;
but other lands have sunlight too, and clover,
and skies are everywhere as blue as mine.
O hear my song, thou God of all the nations,
a song of peace for their land and for mine.[1]

IN HIS PULITZER PRIZE-WINNING BOOK, *The Metaphysical Club*, Louis Menand explores the role pragmatist thinking played in the development of the modern United States. He notes that a core similarity between the pragmatists is not in their conclusions on any topic, but their sharing a common idea about ideas. Ideas are nonfoundational, self-corrective, and developmental.[2] Pragmatists craft and apply tools for use in specific inquiries, success in which is a validation of the ideas being used as tools. No sign can have one exclusive object, because all signs require an interpretant, which is another sign. Signs allow multiple (potentially endless) interpretations that dyadic term-object relations do not. Rather than rejecting interpretations that are different from my own, they should be expected and welcomed, for they may highlight aspects of the object under investigation that familiar signs have not touched upon. Anyone sharing the pragmatic idea about ideas is embraced in the community of inquiry, even if their conclusions differ from mine. Pluralism is fundamental at the basic epistemic level of how human inquiry works, and arguments that exclude different understandings of an issue, rather than seeing them as chances for mutual growth, hinder the ability to know the truth about any issue. In a paradox required to be a pluralist, such exclusive positions should themselves be excluded for blocking the way of inquiry. This applies to religious ideas as much as scientific ones.

It is possible to affirm one's own religious identity and, in that very affirmation—the stronger the better—affirm the goodness, even ultimate truth, of those who do not share that identity. We can pray for ourselves and love our own tradition while loving and praying for the differences of others. With Cobb, this could be considered taking the Bible more seriously than those who would confine God to their small exclusive worldviews. Everyone should be engaging with other religious traditions not just to learn about them, but, as was Cobb's purpose for entering interreligious dialogue, to actively transform one's beliefs by engaging anyone and everyone who has thoughts on them. Neville's career in comparative theology displays the same traits. He is a Boston Confucian, after all. In this regard, consider Luke 6:37–42:

> "Do not judge, and you will not be judged; do not condemn, and you will not be condemned. Forgive, and you will be forgiven; give, and it will be given to you. A good measure, pressed down, shaken together, running over, will be put into your lap; for the measure you give will be the measure you get back."
>
> He also told them a parable: "Can a blind person guide a blind person? Will not both fall into a pit? A disciple is not above the teacher, but everyone who is fully qualified will be like the teacher. Why do you see the speck in your neighbor's eyes, but do not notice the log in your own eye? Or how can you say to your neighbor, 'Friend, let me take out the speck in your eye,' when you yourself do not see the log in your own eye? You hypocrite, first take the log out of your own eye, and then you will see clearly to take the speck out of your neighbor's eye."[3]

This passage is preceded by the Golden Rule, and on its face it simply indicates we should be nice and not judge others. But the message is deeper than that. It is pointing to similarity in difference. If you know yourself, you will know better what to expect in others—not perfection or full agreement with you, but fallible inquirers. Rather than eliminating supposed faults in another, they should be viewed as clues to one's own faults. Similarity in difference becomes an opportunity for growth. If I accept your difference and you accept mine, that acknowledgment becomes the basis for each of us learning more, doing better, and getting the specks out of both our eyes. It is possible to be a realist about one's own position while also being a pluralist.

Pragmatic pluralism is an alternative route around foundationalist and antifoundationalist debates, or the realist and constructivist debate with which this argument for PCR began. There can be both a real world and constructed meanings we bring to it and by which we make it intelligible. Experience may be interpreted and theory-laden, but concepts we employ in dealing with the world are not wholly our creations. They are what emerges from the interplay of our grasping and interpreting a real independent world. As such, knowledge advances by abductive leaps and bounds, meaning incommensurability is a very real possibility. Nonetheless, it is not necessary to entirely discard old theories. They will certainly need to be modified to meet the challenge of new and better standards. If they can, which is very possible given that retroductions can be made and many interpretants may be admissible for any subject matter, competing claims can exist side by side. Positively embracing and existing side by side with differences is exactly how Cobb presents the situation of Christianity and other religions.[4] Other religions like Buddhism are crucial resources for the creative transformation of Christianity, and without those differences Christianity would be in a worse position. It would have fewer resources with which to transform itself and grow toward the truth.

Cobb presents pluralism as intrinsic to the formation of Christian identity. "Christians must come to understand Christ in a world in which they deeply appreciate and respect those who do not find Christ to be what is supremely important to them."[5] We need to be brought together with others to work toward transformation, rather than excluding those who differ. New forms of Christianity affirm Christian history and continuity with that history precisely by differing from it and transforming it, not by returning to some earlier form. Christ stands against any claims of Christian exclusivity, as the principle of creative transformation overcoming any such claims to exclusion and superiority. The different structures of existence do not simply contain competing ideas, one set of which could possibly "win" and be adopted by every human being in the future. They really are different, and will remain so.

Cobb's vision of Jesus as creative transformation opens Christians up to a deeper and stronger conviction in the truth of their religious identity, while simultaneously opening them to embrace, rather than feel threatened by, those with different religious identities. Rather than ideological opponents, encouraging difference and learning from it is a crucial part of being Christian. Cobb suggests that is how Jesus lived his life, as far as we know. "In offering his insights to others he did not need, as we do, to glance to the side to see that they supported his self-image. Thus he could speak with a unique purity, simplicity, and directness."[6] This pluralistic mode of living stands in direct opposition to what was done with Jesus in creedal formations and the debates surrounding them.

The constant identifier of Christianity for Cobb is the spirit of self-transcendence, finding oneself by moving beyond given achievements. Other religions are not a rejection of this project, but entirely different projects altogether. Buddhism and Hinduism aim to establish selfhood beyond the world or annihilate selfhood. Spiritual existence will not fulfill this project, just as extinguishing the self with not fulfill the Christian project. They are side-by-side alternatives.[7] Christianity can legitimately not be a concern of others, even others with legitimate ultimate concern. This is reflected in the internal differences of Christianity, which is itself in the process of transformation. Cobb notes that Greek philosophy was once resisted by Christians before being embraced, and yet Christian theology was still Christian after the union. Theology was inwardly transformed by accepting the scientific method and its results, without ceasing to be Christian. The same transformation can be undergone by accepting the real and necessary differences between religions.[8] When Christ is identified as creative transformation, not only can transformations within Christianity be approved, changes brought about through interreligious dialogue can be fully approved by Christians without demanding religious conversion as a sign of correctness. When we truly know ourselves, we truly know others—that they may necessarily differ and this is a positive fact to be accepted rather than negated.

Due to the above considerations, Cobb ends up being a pluralist while at the same time rejecting pluralistic theologies of religions. The reason is that he understands such efforts as placing an abstract, often monistic, bow around all the religions. Cobb sees too much diversity to be so neatly tied up, and it is that diversity he wants to preserve. He does not want Christianity to claim superiority over all other religious traditions, but neither does he want to orchestrate all religions into one scheme. He opposes pluralistic theories that understand all religions as different ways to engage one ultimate reality "not for the sake of claiming that only in Christianity is the end of all religion realized, but for the sake of affirming a much more fundamental pluralism.... The issue, in my view, is not whether they all accomplish the same goal equally well—however the goal may be defined. It is first of all whether their diverse goals are equally well-realized."[9] In this regard, Cobb argues his position is more pluralistic than Neville's.

Neville only has one ontological ultimate, God the creator, while Cobb has three cosmological ultimates, creativity, God, and the world. Neville is a pluralist only in paths to God, while Cobb affirms multiple ultimates that can be understood as worthy of devotion without negating the others. Commenting on Neville's pluralism, Cobb claims Neville "allows other views only secondary status as ways of (mis)representing what he accurately describes."[10] However, it is a mischaracterization of Neville to claim he posits a position like John Hick's, an ultimate mystery behind all the different world religions.[11] In that sort of position, it is to some extent irrelevant to which religion one is devoted, since they all point to the same God (to put it positively) and fail to capture God in their numerous pictures of the ultimate (to put it negatively). For Neville, there is indeed one indeterminate reality engaged by determinate symbols, but those different specific religious symbols are needed to engage the ultimate. Contextual differences matter in that a symbol truly engaging for one person may be false for another.[12] In that sense, they are not arbitrary. Neville's difference from Hick is a matter of emphasis. It is not that religious symbols break on the indeterminate ultimate, and thus there is one mysterious God behind all the masks we put on God. Rather, there is no breaking of symbols, no engagement whatsoever with God, without specific religious symbols. Since meaningful interpretants of God will vary by context and culture, the "masks" different religions put on an otherwise indeterminate God are how that God is present in their lives here and now.[13] Without our preferred masks, there would be no God to engage.

PCR locates a pluralism at a more basic level than whether there is one ultimate with many ways to reach it or many different ultimates. Pluralism has to do with how knowledge is gained, and how that necessarily happens in many different ways. It also has to do with the goal of inquiry. It has to do with why it is crucial for process and ground-of-being theologians to think together instead of continually redrawing battle lines. To be true to the goal of always doing better, always moving toward what is true rather than what we wish, many different positions from which feedback can be obtained should always be present. Truth, real absolute truth, paradoxically requires that different perspectives on it always be present. PCR is modified Peircean pragmatism, after all, so it requires a community to make progress. Nobody should want to eliminate opportunities for growth toward truth, it is just necessary to make sure the community with which we grow is of the right sort.

When we encounter other worldviews and other interpretations that are viewed as necessary in their appropriate context, the effort to absolutize any interpretation is revealed as arbitrary. When unexpected Secondness of the world wrecks our understandings, impinges upon our previously comfortable ways of navigating reality and reveals their constructed nature, this is opportunity to either further growth with reality or resist change while trying to cling onto constructions. Peirce constantly pushes us to embrace higher and higher ideals, to be permeable to larger realities than we currently allow. Control is part of every person's and group's self-realization.[14] Control entails committing to ideals, comparing what is actually done and believed with what could have been. Obviously, chosen ideals can conflict, but at some point, to be true to reality rather than cling to only our personal wishes, it is necessary to surrender to higher ideals rather than constructing and choosing lesser ones. Larger and more generic structures of reality should be allowed to shape us more than our personal ideas and ideals.

Peirce makes philosophical pluralism the joy of meeting others, potential members of the community of inquiry. When Peirce writes about connected signs he is not simply abstractly discussing how interpretation works, but the people and conditions we encounter. If those others are met with an attitude of welcoming fallibility, there can be conversation instead of dictation. Such conversations can lead to increased understanding and widening the community of inquiry in the future, in growing Thirdness. We are rooted in rootlessness. Wherever we are, there we find our roots. These are not values alien to Christianity imposed by philosophy either. Why would Christians want to impose themselves on others when Jesus gave the example of learning and serving through creative transformation?[15] In a similar manner, Peirce argues that learning is more important than merely teaching.

Peirce makes this point while discussing academic institutions, arguing that they fail when they become centers of teaching instead of learning. A will to learn begins by being dissatisfied with a presented situation. Teaching requires that one is already fully confident about the importance and truth of what is being taught, with nothing to be done but empty those contents into students viewed as empty vessels. Learning demands being unsatisfied with the present condition of knowledge. As great as science is, and as much as we should prize being commensurate with the universe, it must be viewed for what it is, as Peirce wrote, "a child's collection of pebbles gathered upon the beach,—the vast ocean of Being lying there unsounded."[16] The same can be said of the world's religions. As great as they are, each is small in the vast universe. Rather than walling them off and being "defenders of the faith," being true to any one of them should propel learning from others without seeking to eliminate or convert them.

One way to stop inquiry is to maintain that any element is basic and necessary or inexplicable, not due to a lack of understanding, but because that is supposedly the way things are. Nothing justifies that claim except an explanation of the facts, and Peirce is clear that pronouncing something inexplicable prior to inquiry is not an explanation.[17] Such a conclusion must be reached by way of abduction and retroduction, putting it forth as a hypothesis. This way of thinking also applies to defects Neville and Cobb identify in each other. Neville can rightly criticize Cobb's process cosmology for refusing to ask whether a deeper ontological ground is possible. Neville affirms an ontological ultimate, but Cobb could nonetheless counter that Neville wrongly makes that ultimate's nature in the world inexplicable. If it is arbitrary to not ask the ontological question, it is equally arbitrary to not ask if God's identity as creator is growing as God's creation grows.

The correct position does not obliterate all alternatives. Rather, the correct position holds different positions in positive difference or contrast, thinking about itself through those others. Holding alternatives together rather than eliminating some of them is also how Whitehead described the correct way to approach contrasting positions. "A multiple contrast is [analyzable] into component and dual contrasts. It is one contrast, over and above its component contrasts. This doctrine that a multiple contrast cannot be conceived as a mere disjunction of dual contrasts is the basis of the doctrine of emergent evolution. It is the doctrine of real unities being more than a mere collective disjunction of component elements."[18] An unspoken rule simply needs to be added to this way of thinking. This kind of pluralism entails that positions that do try to obliterate all others, end all discussion, and eliminate all room for growth do not need to be included in the positive contrast. They should actually be actively excluded. Such exclusion is not a failure on the part of the one imagining the inclusive whole; it is not a failed attempt at pluralism. Rather, those holding exclusive positions have excluded themselves from possible inclusion by the way they define themselves.

The Paradox of Pluralism

Popper brings up Plato's "paradox of freedom" in the context of discussing how political institutions can be organized to minimize the damage of bad or incompetent rulers. In an eerily relevant example, Plato describes how the rise of tyrants is a problem for free democracies.[19] As Popper summarizes the issue, "Plato raises implicitly the following question: What if it is the will of the people that they should not rule, but a tyrant instead? The free man, Plato suggests, may exercise his absolute freedom, first by defying the laws and ultimately by defying freedom itself and by [clamoring] for a tyrant."[20] In the note to this passage Popper discusses Plato's paradoxes of freedom and democracy, adding his own paradox of tolerance to the list.

With regard to freedom, Plato claims freedom unchecked will exist on the precipice of its complete opposite. Unrestrained freedom, as in the rather popular usage of "freedom" in the United States, the notion that everyone in a free country should be allowed to do absolutely anything they want, leads to the powerful and cruel controlling their opposites. Freedom is a paradox because in order for it to be maintained restraints must be placed on it.[21] Democracy is a specific form of this paradox in which the free choices of people can lead to the selection of a tyrant that works against their interests, as happened in the 2016 United States presidential election. To Plato's list of paradoxes Popper adds the paradox of tolerance:

> Unlimited tolerance must lead to the disappearance of tolerance. If we extend unlimited tolerance even to those who are intolerant, if we are not prepared to defend a tolerant society against the onslaught of the intolerant, then the tolerant will be destroyed, and tolerance with them. In this formulation, I do not imply, for instance, that we should always suppress the utterance of intolerant philosophies; as long as we can counter them by rational argument and keep them in check by public opinion, suppression would certainly be most unwise. But we should claim the *right* to suppress them if necessary even by force.[22]

Intolerant people self-exclude themselves from tolerant conversations. If a person's position is that no other positions should be allowed, that person has defined themselves in a way that is incapable of rational debate and has excluded themselves from conversation. It is not intolerant for tolerant people to exclude such people from conversations, for the intolerant people have already excluded themselves. To this list we can add the paradox of pluralism, entered by way of Cobb.

In making Christ the opposite of closure and limitation, Cobb's Christology is meant to do justice to differences between religions and the way they are creatively transformed. Buddhists and Christians, when they view their differences positively rather than as features to be done away with, can be mutually transformed by that positive stance toward those who are different.[23] Stated in terms of Popper's concerns, pluralists are pluralists regarding those prepared to reciprocate. A religious pluralist does not need to bend over backwards to approve of young Earth creationists who deny all scientific evidence and think LGBTQ+ individuals are demonic just because that is technically a religious position. As Popper notes regarding political tolerance, "we should not try to answer the essentialist question: What is the state, what is its true nature, its real meaning? Nor should we try to answer the historicist question: How did the state originate, and what is the origin of political obligation? We should rather put our question in this way: What do we demand from a state? What do we propose to consider as the legitimate aim of state activity?"[24] Theologically, PCR demands pluralism, and that is compatible with putting up a sign that reads "exclusivists need not apply." They have excluded themselves from progressive, fallible, open-ended conversations, and such a sign just makes that fact explicit.

While alternative theologies are not to be obliterated, they must be open to dialogue. The argument to this point has been meant to show that the positions of Cobb and Neville can exemplify this, making their work and PCR a model for pluralism, with that pluralism being an ideal model for theological progress. However, if it is to be a true sign of such progress, such dialogue cannot be idle. If it occurs just for the sake of restating opposition over and over, rejecting one's opponent entirely and never growing or changing at all, then such a theological position shows no signs of progress. If I am Neville, I do not want Cobb's position to be eliminated because it helps me grow, and vice versa. What I want is for the position I am in conversation with to grow with me, and the lack of such growth would be evidence it lacks the supposed fruit identified in it. In short, different theologies must give evidence of being what Imre Lakatos calls progressive research programs.

The notion of research programs is Lakatos's replacement for Kuhn's scientific paradigms that were covered in chapter 1. These programs always include a hard core, fundamental claims without which it would be a different research program, and auxiliary hypotheses that are modified to protect the core against anomalous data.[25] Mention of hard cores and auxiliary hypotheses that function as a protective belt is a bit too foundational for someone embedded in Peirce's fallible way of thinking, and these concepts will not be defended here. What is interesting is Lakatos's understanding of progressive and degenerate research programs.[26] This way of thinking is amenable to PCR's focus on a plurality of novel hypotheses that exhibit explanatory power, as well as revising or abandoning them for alternatives when they no longer produce results. This should not give the impression that only one perspective, the successful one, is allowed. Rather, friendly competition and cooperation between progressive programs is the best way to accelerate their progress, in philosophical and theological debates as well as scientific ones. The right method and the right sort of dialogue partners are all that is needed.

Spelling out beliefs, critically testing them, and improving them, even throwing them away when necessary, cannot just amount to refining the internal standards of one worldview, however eloquently that view is described. Even for Peirce, there is underdetermination in inference to the best explanation. There are constraints in place, but not enough to force all opinion to converge on one explanation. But for progress and cross-fertilization between theories to occur, inquirers cannot be dogmatically set in their ways. They cannot follow the methods of tenacity, authority, or the a priori, in Peirce's sense of those terms.[27] PCR is not the only good way of thinking, though it has been defended as one. It is no coincidence that I am drawn to a conversation with Cobb and Neville, pluralistic dialogue partners and positions embraced for fruitful conversation and cross-fertilization because they are fallible, open to change, and have a method informed by science and capable of learning from other disciplines. Hopefully better than worse theories are adopted, but very different diametrically opposed theories could make sense now, with the better options only becoming clear in the long run.[28] Mono-cultural, mono-religious, mono-anything are not excluded from pluralistic perspectives; they are self-excluded by the way their own position is defined. They are doing the excluding, not pluralists, who are simply being consistent in pointing out that such positions are not part of pluralistic conversations. As Popper would argue, extending tolerance to the intolerant destroys tolerance. In Lakatos's terms, Cobb and Neville have both identified supernatural substance theism as a degenerating program. It does not have to remain so forever, but to change its status it would need to take better account of science and the historical consciousness of world religions. In short, it would need to perform something like the current argument, thinking about its static supernatural theology through other positions and transcending itself to a new position that is more adequate than its previous stance.

CONCLUSION

The argument in this book covered a lot of ground, spanning across historical periods and a diversity of topics. Epistemology was dealt with in both philosophy and theology. In both cases, a comparative analysis was made. In chapter 1 I surveyed debates between realists and antirealists in philosophy that echo the way Barth and Tillich debated each other's theological positions. That theological debate preconfigured the one between Cobb and Neville that was covered in chapters 5, 6, and 7. Whether dealing with purely philosophical problems or theological arguments, all that material informed the development of pragmatic constructive realism as a position that is needed in philosophy to navigate around endless debates and relevant in theology as a new perspective.

Postmodern constructivism is philosophically *en vogue*, but realism has yet to be definitively defeated. PCR is a position that avoids naïve forms of realism without giving up their intent and accepting that all knowledge claims are nothing but human constructions. As shown by the discussion of biosemiotics in chapter 8, human signification is actually continuous with and a novel development of unconscious signification and interpretation in nature. PCR similarly contributed an argument to the epistemology of religion, where the antirealists also currently have the upper hand, by indicating the strengths and weaknesses of *both* the epistemological realists and antirealists. The development of PCR as a means of escaping these binary debates occurred by way of a presentation of Peirce's philosophy and philosophical theology in chapter 2 followed by a modification of his work in chapter 3 that drove him deeper into his own general philosophical categories of Firstness, Secondness, and Thirdness. Chapter 4 highlighted how PCR, as a form of pragmatism, is an emergent way of thinking about possibility, novelty, and evolution, before putting that way of thinking into action by comparing Cobb and Neville on the way to an original theological conclusion.

All the philosophical discussion was not unrelated to theological concerns that dominated the latter portions of this book. Philosophy was needed and informs PCR as a method of inquiry and general program for theological work. The cluster of myself, Corrington, Popper, and Lakatos share important sensibilities while differing on specific positions. I share with Corrington the certainty that Peirce's work needs revisions, which also ended up being revisions of Cobb's theology. Panpsychism and agapism were rejected in chapter 3 as crucial steps in the development of PCR. I share the fallibilism of Popper and Lakatos. The result is a pluralistic form of inquiry that avoids relativism. Some positions should be discarded. Dogmatic fundamentalist attitudes block the way of inquiry in both philosophy and theology. While PCR is a new position, there are others besides the process and ground-of-being theologians that have been covered in these pages who are kindred spirits in affirming similar forms of inquiry as crucially needed in theology.[1] Reaching a novel theological position by comparing Cobb and Neville has also shown that this method of inquiry works.

Process theology and ground-of-being theology are two of the more live options in theology, especially for those convinced there are too many problems with supernatural theism for it to be salvaged. Just as with realism and constructivism, the insights of these live options can and should be synthesized. Others will surely have different ideas about how to achieve such a creative synthesis, with appropriately different conclusions, and I welcome such pushback just as Cobb and Neville were pushed beyond their existing positions through the application of PCR. As noted in chapter 9, this sort of pluralism in theology is crucial for its future prospects. Real progress in theology depends on pluralism, dialogue, and fallibilistic interchange. Theology has crossed the Rubicon from exclusivism to pluralism in terms of interreligious engagement in the form of comparative theology. However, theology itself has yet to move from exclusively presenting one's own position as a knockdown of all others, which at best might be deemed imperfect versions of the correct position, to a pluralism in which difference is understood as an opportunity for growth and creative transformation rather than something to be obliterated. The argument was not all methodological, though, as following PCR as a form of inquiry resulted in a model of God.

The model of God developed mostly in chapter 8 has features similar to panentheism, but the manner in which God is in and relates to the world is an emergent feature rather than antecedently given. The pragmatic constructive realist model of God is a unique emergent form of panentheism. God is both indeterminate *and* determinate. God's transcendence *and* immanence are affirmed. Just as it was shown that it is unnecessary to hold the position that philosophical concepts refer to nothing but constructions of the imagination, PCR was used to develop a concept of God to which human constructions are not obstacles. Perhaps even more decisively than in philosophy, human constructions play a crucial role in knowing that God rather than getting in the way. All this argumentation culminated with the perhaps startling claim that we can become symbols of God, that God is in part created and it is our imaginative constructions that do the creating. Due to its possibly surprising nature, this position should be described one more time to conclude.

The Courage to Continue Creating God

We cannot start inquiry with absolute doubt. Inquiry emerges out of a given stock of beliefs. In a sense, it is natural to be suspicious of alternative points of view that come from outside one's given community and that challenge that given stock. At worst, religious communities respond by trying to exert control through authority. Dogmatic conservative forms of religious communities have arguably been more successful in building walls than liberal ones have been in breaking them down or building bridges. Tillich knew the danger present in this situation. The autonomous self is always in danger of being suppressed by heteronomous forces from society that are vaster and stronger. Autonomous reason can be thwarted by institutional powers. Thus, Tillich introduces theonomy, a participatory understanding of self and world. "Theonomy does not mean acceptance of a divine law imposed on reason by a highest authority; it means autonomous reason united with its own depth."[2] We can hold onto our autonomy by rooting it in the sacred depths of the world, God as the ground of our being. With this more secure base, we can more confidently be ourselves without hiding behind institutional barriers. We can step out into the unknown by embracing novel interpretants of ourselves and our world. When the ultimate ground of that world is not antecedently known to be a well-defined being or reality with specific features, as is the case for Tillich's unconditional God or Neville's indeterminate creator, such courage to be is based on a groundless sort of ground. There is no "there" there. Tillich has a model of God that strikes some as obtuse, but his sermons and descriptions about the practical consequences of that God are moving.[3] The exact same is true of Neville.[4] Our ultimate grounding gives us the courage to resist, the courage to be rather than submit. This is the role of the Logos as identified by Cobb. "In short, the function of the Logos is to introduce tension between what has been and what might be and continuously to challenge and upset the established order for the sake of the new."[5] It is a judgment upon our desire to rest content with stability that simultaneously gives us the courage to upset those given structures. The judgment is one that is always for us, judging whatever prevents us from fuller achievements and demanding only what it gives us—creative transformation. Being grounded in an indeterminate creator that remains so apart from our actions means that learning more about God's features is not a matter of antecedently reading creation back into its creator, but looking to the future with courage. Indeterminate groundless grounds are an impetus to action.

Knowledge is demonstrated by the ability to construct something. Computers were not found in the woods as if left there by some advanced alien species and then replicated. They are learned about as they are created. We do not make advances by depending on that advance somehow already having been made. How does the understanding of God in relation to creation I have been developing in this book enact and sustain life-changing and world-changing work? In a short step, more a flash of awareness, the pragmatic way of thinking that I have named pragmatic constructive realism switches from metaphysics to ethics, from arguing for the God revealed as creator in creation to a process of inquiry in which we try to embody divine values and help them emerge in history. What is concrete reasonableness in religion when God is not a being with antecedent knowledge of and desires for the world? In summation, it is fallible inquiry, experimental theological ideas, and boldly seeing what happens. Like scientific truth found in a community, God's emergent determinate immanent identity is an ideal tied up with growth, and that growth is tied up with communal action. Without a God containing and preordering possibilities in terms of their relevance, there is no predetermined initial aim for all occasions. The push upward and onward is a struggle, not preconfigured in God though still coming from God. We can try to make sure the world reflects certain values and can do so with the confidence that our efforts have ontological support. God's indeterminate transcendence is a necessary condition for the world. God's determinacy is a precious achievement, an achievement to which we must contribute if it is to be achieved at all. That achievement is the seriousness of the religious call. God emerges determinately as we make our communities hateful or loving, and the direction is up to us. It is a project that ultimately matters, philosophically for the sake of God's ultimacy and existentially for the ultimate future of our fragile planet. Engaging in this project requires the courage to keep creating with the assurance that those creations, guided by the proper method, will be *the only way* to find *genuine truth* in the end.

NOTES

INTRODUCTION

1. Peirce, *Collected Papers*, 1.135 (hereafter CP, e.g., CP 1.135).
2. Center for Process Studies, "Cobb vs Neville: A Theological Dialogue," October 30, 2017, https://www.youtube.com/watch?v=bZ1qYtk7Jrk.
3. Peirce, *The Essential Peirce*, 1:115 (hereafter EP, e.g., EP 1:115).
4. Hume, *An Enquiry Concerning Human Understanding*, 12.3, 12.8.
5. Descartes, *Meditations on First Philosophy*.
6. Peirce, EP 1:1–10, 245–279.
7. Peirce, EP 2:75–114.
8. Peirce, EP 2:4–10.
9. Peirce, EP 1:312–333.
10. Peirce, EP 1:298–311.
11. Kuhn, *The Structure of Scientific Revolutions*.
12. Feyerabend, *Against Method*.
13. Peirce, EP 1:109–123.
14. Hoffmeyer, *Biosemiotics; Signs of Meaning in the Universe*.
15. Peirce, CP 6.24.
16. Peirce, EP 1:352–371.
17. Rosenthal, *Time, Continuity, and Indeterminacy*.
18. James, *The Principles of Psychology*, 462.
19. Cobb, *The Structure of Christian Existence*, 20–21; Dorrien, *The Making of American Liberal Theology*, 210.
20. Neville, *God the Creator; Ultimates*, 227–235.
21. Neville, *The Truth of Broken Symbols*.

CHAPTER ONE

1. See Alston, *A Realist Conception of Truth*, for a classic treatment of this issue.
2. Putnam, *Reason, Truth, and History*, is perhaps the most clear and direct statement as to why this issue endures.
3. See Carnap, *Meaning and Necessity*, for a classic argument that statements name nothing real, only logical relations with other statements.
4. In this context, Kant's *Critique of Pure Reason* is a landmark idealist argument.
5. Aristotle, *Metaphysics*, 1011b25, 201.
6. Aquinas, *Summa Theologica*, Q.16.
7. James, *Pragmatism*, 96.
8. Berkeley, *A Treatise Concerning the Principles of Human Knowledge*, §6.
9. Dummett, *Truth and Other Enigmas*, 146.
10. Devitt, "Dummett's Anti-Realism," 77 (emphasis in original).
11. McDowell, *Mind and World*, xi.
12. Wittgenstein, *Tractatus Logico-Philosophicus*.
13. Wittgenstein, *Philosophical Investigations*, 135.
14. Psillos, *Scientific Realism*, 105–108.
15. Votsis, "Is Structure Not Enough?"
16. French, *The Structure of the World*; Psillos, "Is Structural Realism Possible?"
17. Van Fraassen, *The Scientific Image*, 12.
18. Duhem, *The Aim and Structure of Physical Theory*, is widely credited for sowing the seeds of underdetermination.
19. Quine, *From a Logical Point of View*, 20–46.
20. Kuhn, *The Structure of Scientific Revolutions*, 23–34, 111–135.
21. Zammito, *A Nice Derangement of Epistemes*, 123–231.
22. Popper, *Conjectures and Refutations*, xi.
23. Feyerabend, *Realism, Rationalism, and Scientific Method*, 31; also see his "An Attempt at a Realistic Interpretation of Experience."
24. Feyerabend, *Realism, Rationalism, and Scientific Method*, ix.
25. Feyerabend, *Realism, Rationalism, and Scientific Method*, 3.
26. Feyerabend, *Realism, Rationalism, and Scientific Method*, 104–131, 176–202.
27. Feyerabend, *Realism, Rationalism, and Scientific Method*, 139–145, 247–297.
28. Kuhn, *The Structure of Scientific Revolutions*, 10–22.
29. See Van Fraassen, *The Scientific Image*.
30. Feyerabend, *Against Method*, 18–19.
31. Alston, *Perceiving God*.
32. Frei, *Types of Christian Theology*; Lindbeck, *The Nature of Doctrine*.

33. Alston, *Perceiving God*, 3.
34. Alston, "Externalist Theories of Perception," 73–97.
35. Alston, "Back to the Theory of Appearing," 193–194.
36. Alston, *Perceiving God*, 56.
37. Alston, *Perceiving God*, 28.
38. Alston, *Perceiving God*, 59–60.
39. Alston, *Perceiving God*, 65.
40. Alston, *Perceiving God*, 1.
41. Alston, *Perceiving God*, 63.
42. Barrett and Wildman, "Seeing Is Believing?," 72–73.
43. Alston, *Perceiving God*, 44.
44. Hardin, *Color for Philosophers*; Varela, Thompson, and Rosch, *The Embodied Mind*.
45. Dubin, *How the Brain Works*, 60–61.
46. Varela, Thompson, and Rosch, *The Embodied Mind*, 158–161.
47. Barrett and Wildman, "Seeing Is Believing?," 76–77 (emphasis in original).
48. Van Woudenberg, "Alston on Direct Perception and Interpretation," 120 (emphasis in original).
49. Grimes, "On the Failure to Detect Changes in Scenes across Saccades," 89–109.
50. Noë, *Action in Perception*, 66–67.
51. See also Frei, *The Eclipse of Biblical Narrative*.
52. Lindbeck, *The Nature of Doctrine*, 131 (emphasis mine).
53. Neville, *Realism in Religion*, 9–22.
54. Barth, *Church Dogmatics*, 1.1:1–3.
55. Barth, *Church Dogmatics*, 11–17.
56. Tillich, *Systematic Theology*, 1:100–105.
57. Tillich, *Systematic Theology*, 1:11–15.
58. Barth, *Church Dogmatics*, 1.1:82.
59. Barth, *Church Dogmatics*, 1.1:150–162.
60. Tillich, *Systematic Theology*, 1:1–11.
61. Tillich, *Systematic Theology*, 1:59–66.
62. Barth, *Church Dogmatics*, 1.1:79–97, 141.
63. Hempel, "On the Logical Positivists' Theory of Truth."
64. Thagard, "Coherence, Truth, and the Development of Scientific Knowledge," 29–30.

CHAPTER TWO

1. Descartes, *Discourse on Method*, pt. 6.
2. Peirce, CP 7.108.
3. Peirce, EP 1:115.

4. See Olsson, "Not Giving the Skeptic a Hearing," for a longer discussion of the resources Peirce has available for rejecting skepticism.
5. Peirce, EP 1:114 (emphasis in original).
6. Peirce, EP 2:88.
7. See Hookway, "Peirce and Skepticism," 316, for another defense of this point.
8. Peirce, EP 1:137.
9. Peirce, EP 1:115–123.
10. Peirce, CP 1.635.
11. Peirce, EP 1:120.
12. Peirce, EP 1:162–165, 212–214.
13. Peirce, EP 2:194.
14. Peirce, EP 1:132.
15. Peirce, CP 5.416–417.
16. Peirce, CP 8.208.
17. Peirce, CP 5.589.
18. Peirce, CP 2.166; CP 5.197.
19. Peirce, CP 2.137.
20. Peirce, EP 1:40–44, 226–228.
21. Peirce, CP 5.572.
22. Peirce, CP 5.569.
23. Peirce, *Writings of Charles S. Peirce*, 3:326.
24. Peirce, CP 5.189.
25. Peirce, EP 1:192.
26. Hoffmeyer, *Biosemiotics*.
27. Moore, "On the World as General," 91.
28. Ayala, "The Baldwin Effect," 194.
29. LaPorte, *Natural Kinds and Conceptual Change*; Wilson, *Species*.
30. Peirce, CP 8.12; EP 2:115–132.
31. Peirce, EP 2:67–68.
32. Peirce, EP 2:267–288.
33. Peirce, EP 2:154.
34. Peirce, EP 2:194.
35. Almeder, "Charles Peirce and the Existence of the External World."
36. Peirce, CP 3.527; 8.308; 1.23.
37. Peirce, EP 1:5.
38. Peirce, EP 1:278.
39. Peirce, EP 1:2 (emphasis in original).
40. For excellent commentary on this point, see Corrington, *An Introduction to C. S. Peirce*, 126–127, 133.
41. Fisch, *Peirce, Semeiotic, and Pragmatism*, 190.
42. Peirce, CP 8.216.
43. Corrington, *An Introduction to C. S. Peirce*, 143.

44. Peirce, EP 2:477, 480–483.
45. Corrington, *An Introduction to C. S. Peirce*, 143.
46. Peirce, CP 5.520.
47. Peirce, EP 1:293.
48. Peirce, EP 1:25.
49. The opposite interpretations of Peirce's philosophy of religion given by Donna Orange and Michael Raposa are dealt with in the next section.
50. Peirce, EP 2:434–450.
51. Corrington, *An Introduction to C. S. Peirce*, 71–72.
52. Peirce, CP 5.93.
53. Orange, *Peirce's Conception of God*, 32.
54. Orange, *Peirce's Conception of God*, 58.
55. Tillich, *Systematic Theology*, 1:207–208.
56. Raposa, *Peirce's Philosophy of Religion*, 40.
57. Peirce, CP 1.362.
58. Raposa, *Peirce's Philosophy of Religion*, 72.
59. Raposa, *Peirce's Philosophy of Religion*, 47.
60. Raposa, *Peirce's Philosophy of Religion*, 50.
61. Peirce, CP 6.45, 466, 508–510.
62. Raposa, *Peirce's Philosophy of Religion*, 91; "Peirce and Modern Religious Thought," 350.
63. Peirce, CP 6.452, 490, 508–510.
64. Raposa, "Peirce and Modern Religious Thought," 350.
65. Peirce, CP 1.362.
66. A similar argument has been made recently by Roger Ward. See Ward, *Peirce and Religion*.
67. Peirce, CP 6.217.

CHAPTER THREE

1. Brandom, *Making It Explicit; Between Saying and Doing*.
2. Sellars, *Empiricism and the Philosophy of Mind*.
3. Peirce, EP 1:30.
4. Brandom, *Perspectives on Pragmatism*, 149.
5. Bernstein, *The Pragmatic Turn*, 49–50.
6. Rorty, "Pragmatism, Categories, and Language," 197–198.
7. Weiss, "The Essence of Peirce's System," 262.
8. Rorty, *Consequences of Pragmatism*, 165.
9. Putnam, *Words and Life*, 152.
10. Putnam, *Pragmatism*, 11.
11. See Putnam, *Representation and Reality*, as well as *Realism with a Human Face*, for his lengthy treatment of these issues.

12. Putnam and Putnam, "The Real William James," 370.
13. Putnam, *Realism and Reason*, 246 (emphasis in original).
14. Putnam, *Realism with a Human Face*, 114–115.
15. Putnam, *Words and Life*, 201.
16. Putnam, *Renewing Philosophy*, 187 (emphasis in original).
17. Hildebrand, "Putnam, Pragmatism, and Dewey," 126.
18. Peirce, EP 1:25–27.
19. James, *A Pluralistic Universe*, 86–87, 111–117.
20. Dewey, *The Essential Dewey*, 1:115–120.
21. Dewey, *Experience and Nature*, 4; *The Essential Dewey*, 1: 385.
22. James, *Pragmatism*, 28–30.
23. Dewey, *The Essential Dewey*, 2:3–10.
24. Dewey, *The Essential Dewey*, 1:39–45, 380–390.
25. Dewey, *The Essential Dewey*, 1:3–13.
26. Peirce, EP 2:259.
27. Peirce, CP 8.284.
28. Peirce, CP 8.284.
29. Peirce, EP 1:120.
30. Peirce, EP 54.
31. Corrington, *An Introduction to C. S. Peirce*, 91.
32. James, "Does 'Consciousness' Exist?"
33. James, *Pragmatism*, 12.
34. James, *Pragmatism*, 32.
35. Brodsky, "Rorty's Interpretation of Pragmatism."
36. Hildebrand, *Beyond Realism and Antirealism*. Hildebrand interprets the point of pragmatism as moving beyond the realism and antirealism debates and simply working effectively for life, whereas the debates theorize but never really gain knowledge of any use.
37. Rosenthal, "Neville and Pragmatism," 64.
38. See Clayton, *Mind and Emergence*, for a strong defense of mind in philosophy that leads directly to the same defense in theology.
39. Cobb, *Back to Darwin*, 122.
40. Clayton, "The Emergence of Spirit," 15.
41. Peirce and process thinkers who affirm panexperientialism do not mean that rocks have *human* experiences, but that everything actual undergoes experience. Conscious human experience is just a refined development of this omnipresent experiential feature of reality, one in which present reactions to the past can introduce novel changes as opposed to entirely conforming to past experiences. However, affirming experience is an emergent feature that is not present in all reality is a position that requires fewer metaphysical assumptions, as well as a position that actually includes greater diversity and pluralism in its ontology.

42. Clayton, "Neuroscience, the Person, and God"; "The Emergence of Sprit."
43. Deacon, "The Hierarchic Logic of Emergence," 273–308.
44. Hoffmeyer, *Signs of Meaning in the Universe*, 32; *Biosemiotics*, 36–37, 114.
45. Peirce, EP 1:362–363.
46. Corrington, *An Introduction to C. S. Peirce*, 196, 212–217.
47. Murphey, "On Peirce's Metaphysics," 21–22.
48. Moore, "On the World as General," 97.
49. Peirce, CP 2.149.
50. Peirce, CP 7.471.
51. Short, "Peirce's Concept of Final Causation," 372.
52. Short, "Peirce's Concept of Final Causation," 374.
53. Hoffmeyer, *Signs of Meaning in the Universe*, 47–48.
54. Short, "Peirce's Concept of Final Causation," 376.
55. Corrington, *An Introduction to C. S. Peirce*, 201.
56. Peirce, EP 1:251.
57. Corrington, *An Introduction to C. S. Peirce*, 187.
58. Peirce, CP 5.412.
59. Peirce, EP 2:180.
60. Corrington, *An Introduction to C. S. Peirce*, 61.
61. Peirce, EP 2:331–397.

CHAPTER FOUR

1. See Cobb, *Back to Darwin*.
2. For his systematic approaches to synthesizing multiple traditions, see Neville, *Behind the Masks of God; Boston Confucianism; Ritual and Deference*. See Neville, *Ultimates*, 91–93, for a brief defense of the importance of engaging in such projects.
3. Cobb, *Jesus' Abba*, xii.
4. As will be covered in the next chapter, Cobb went through a personal intellectual crisis when he realized the personal responsive God he knew through church and devotional contexts was in conflict with modern knowledge he learned as part of his graduate school education.
5. Cobb, *Jesus' Abba*, xvii.
6. The major mistake Peirce supposedly made was affirming continuity, which led him to affirm too many categories. Of course, Hartshorne wrote many defenses of pieces of Peirce's philosophy, but those defenses almost always contain more fundamental disagreements as well. Hartshorne praised Peirce for developing an evolutionary rather than a static philosophy, and even compared his system favorably to those of Henri Bergson and Whitehead. See

Hartshorne, "Charles Sanders Peirce's Metaphysics of Evolution." Hartshorne thought his own focus on feeling was at home in Peirce's categories, and he also approved of uniting sense with feeling. See Hartshorne, *The Philosophy and Psychology of Sensation*, 37; *Beyond Humanism*, 185. However, Hartshorne criticized Peirce for not resting content with these points and for focusing too much on continuity among his categories. According to Hartshorne, all feeling results from the impact of Secondness and there are no genuine Firsts. Prehension comes first (Peirce's Secondness) and then feeling follows. See Hartshorne, *Creative Synthesis and Philosophic Method*, xvi; Hartshorne, "A Revision of Peirce's Categories"; Vitali, "The Peircean Influence on Hartshorne's Subjectivism." Peirce's defense of continuity is also rejected for being too abstract, not concrete. For Peirce, there is a continuum of the actual and possible. For Hartshorne, continuity is itself a member of abstract possibilities, and actuality requires breaking that continuity. Again, Secondness is primary for Hartshorne. See Hartshorne, *Creative Synthesis and Philosophic Method*, 122. However, this critique contains a philosophical flub. Hartshorne claims William James sided with him, but James clearly affirmed a continuous stream of experience out of which discrete experiences emerge. Such emergences do break continuity, but should not be confused with the more fundamental continuity of experience that comes first. Secondness is not primary for James. Hartshorne also appealed to quantum mechanics and the exclusion of possibilities in actuality, but science has advanced and Hartshorne never considered quantum states as parts of a more basic, continuous quantum field. See Hartshorne, "Charles Peirce and Quantum Mechanics." To summarize, Hartshorne and Peirce share a temporal understanding of possibilities emerging. Hartshorne departs from Peirce on the basic issues of feeling and continuity. The defense of Peirce on these points found in the opening chapters of this book is not the only one in existence. For Peircean rejections of Hartshorne's criticisms, see Sessions, "Charles Hartshorne and Thirdness," and Wells, "An Evaluation of Hartshorne's Critique of Peirce's Synechism."

7. Cobb, *The Structure of Christian Existence*, 20–21.
8. Neville, *Ultimates*, xvi.
9. Cobb, *God and the World*, 125.
10. See Heim, *Saved from Sacrifice*, for an excellent overview of problematic atonement models, as well as his own argument for a nonpenal alternative.
11. Neville, *Realism in Religion*, 17–21.
12. Tillich, "The Two Types of Philosophy of Religion," 289.
13. Tillich, "The Two Types of Philosophy of Religion," 292–294.
14. Tillich, *Systematic Theology*, 1:204–206.
15. Tillich, "The Philosophical Background of My Theology," 414.
16. Tillich, "The Two Types of Philosophy of Religion," 290 (emphasis in original).

17. Neville, *Ultimates*, 184–191
18. Tillich, "The Two Types of Philosophy of Religion," 297.
19. Tillich, "The Two Types of Philosophy of Religion," 296–298.
20. Tillich, *Systematic Theology*, 3: 119–120.
21. Tillich, "The Two Types of Philosophy of Religion," 298–299.
22. Tillich, *Systematic Theology*, 1: 235–236.
23. Tillich, "The Two Types of Philosophy of Religion," 299–300.
24. Tillich, *What Is Religion?*, 139.
25. Barrett, "On the Evolutionary Plausibility of Religion as Engagement with Ultimacy," 90.
26. Neville, *The Truth of Broken Symbols*.
27. Tillich, "The Religious Symbol/Symbol and Knowledge," 276.
28. Tillich, *What Is Religion?*, 140–141.
29. Neville, *God the Creator*, xvi.
30. Altizer, *The Gospel of Christian Atheism; The Self-Embodiment of God; History as Apocalypse*.
31. Whitehead, *Process and Reality*, 21, 343–351.
32. Peirce, CP 6.189–209.
33. There is a sense in which process thought is only partially divergent from Peirce on this matter. Whitehead, Hartshorne, and Cobb all affirm abstract possibilities as continuous. However, those possibilities are not concretely instantiated in reality apart from decisions by actual occasions. That concrete reality, impacted by the decisions that occasions make regarding possibility, is discontinuous. Individuals break up what is an otherwise continuous realm of possibilities when they make decisions about them with regard to this world. While process thinkers and Peirce therefore both have a concept of continuity, that continuity is not actualized in concrete reality in process thought. Peirce affirms a continuum of the possible and actual.
34. Rosenthal, *Time, Continuity, and Indeterminacy*, 9–30.
35. While it was just noted that process thinkers do affirm a continuity of possibilities, others have also noted that Whitehead and those like Hartshorne who follow his thinking should have actually gone further with Peirce. For an argument as to why Hartshorne needs Thirdness and concrete continuity, as opposed to the abstract continuity of possibilities, see Sessions, "Charles Hartshorne and Thirdness." While only an article and therefore not presented in as much detail as the current argument for PCR, Kelly Wells has noted that the temporal succession process thinkers point to in support of their theory of discreteness is present in Peirce in the form of pragmatic effects on future conduct. Therefore, against one of Neville's major criticisms of Rosenthal and Peirce on this point, an event ontology can be rejected while maintaining temporal succession. See Wells, "An Evaluation of Hartshorne's Critique of Peirce's Synechism."
36. Neville, "Responding to My Critics," 296–297; *The Highroad around Modernism*, 214–215.

37. Neville, *Metaphysics of Goodness*, xxviii–xxix.
38. Hartshorne, "Charles Peirce's 'One Contribution to Philosophy' and Most Serious Mistake"; "Continuity, the Form of Forms in Charles Peirce."
39. Rosenthal, "Neville and Pragmatism," 66.
40. Rosenthal, *Time, Continuity, and Indeterminacy*, 105.
41. Dubin, *How the Brain Works*, 41.
42. Rosenthal, *Time, Continuity, and Indeterminacy*, 123.
43. Rosenthal, "Neville and Pragmatism," 71.
44. Rosenthal, "Neville and Pragmatism," 72.
45. Rosenthal, "Continuity, Contingency, and Time," 543–544.
46. Whitehead, *Process and Reality*, 15, 18.
47. Leclerc, "Alfred North Whitehead."

CHAPTER FIVE

1. Dorrien, *The Making of American Liberal Theology*, 210.
2. Cobb, *The Structure of Christian Existence*, 20–21.
3. Cobb, "Intellectual Autobiography," 9–11.
4. Altizer, "Spiritual Existence as God-Transcending Existence," 56–57.
5. Cobb, *Christ in a Pluralistic Age*, 31–32.
6. Cobb, *Christ in a Pluralistic Age*, 33.
7. Cobb, *A Christian Natural Theology*, xiv.
8. Cobb, "Introduction," 6–7.
9. Cobb, *A Christian Natural Theology*, 2.
10. Whitehead, *Process and Reality*, 53.
11. Cobb, *Jesus' Abba*, 91.
12. Margulis, *Origin of Eukaryotic Cells*.
13. Cobb, *Jesus' Abba*, 94.
14. Whitehead, *Process and Reality*, 3, 7–9, 72–73.
15. Whitehead, *Process and Reality*, 23, 25.
16. Whitehead, *Process and Reality*, 53.
17. Whitehead, *Process and Reality*, 20, 25, 84, 116, 194–195.
18. As noted in chapter 3, even if subjectivity is negligible, its presence in every interaction seems like an assumption more than a proven fact. Alternative emergence theories in which subjectivity emerged from a reality in which it was once not present not only allow for greater novelty in their ontologies, but have scientific support in the form of biosemiotics, which will be covered in chapter 8. While Peirce affirmed panpsychism, his philosophy also had resources for an alternative view in which signs and their transformations are the basic ontological units of reality. Emergence theories and Peirce's alternative also do not require what I take to be the metaphysical liability of requiring Platonic forms, eternal objects in God's primordial nature, to account

for novelty in experience. For more on the way pragmatists relate to process thinkers on this point, see Wildman, *In Our Own Image*, 167, 174–177.

19. Whitehead, *Process and Reality*, 18–20, 85–87.
20. Whitehead, *Process and Reality*, 29.
21. Cobb and Griffin, *Process Theology*, 26.
22. Cobb and Griffin, *Process Theology*, 26.
23. Whitehead, *Adventures of Ideas*, 20–21.
24. Whitehead, *Adventures of Ideas*, 216.
25. Cobb, *Christ in a Pluralistic Age*, 56.
26. Cobb, "Is the Later Heidegger Relevant for Theology?," 189.
27. Cobb, *The Structure of Christian Existence*, 110–111.
28. Cobb, *Christ in a Pluralistic Age*, 45.
29. Cobb, *Christ in a Pluralistic Age*, 65.
30. Cobb, *Christ in a Pluralistic Age*, 66.
31. Cobb, *God and the World*, 168.
32. Cobb, *The Structure of Christian Existence*, 114–115.
33. Cobb, *God and the World*, 10.
34. Cobb, *God and the World*, 45 (emphasis in original).
35. Wieman, *The Source of Human Good*.
36. Wieman, *The Directive in History*, 16–18.
37. Wieman, *The Source of Human Good*, 224–225.
38. Wieman, *The Source of Human Good*, 42–43, 58–65, 269–270.
39. Cobb, *God and the World*, 51.
40. Cobb, *God and the World*, 57.
41. Whitehead, *Process and Reality*, 19.
42. Cobb, *God and the World*, 58.
43. Cobb, *God and the World*, 62.
44. Dewey, *A Common Faith*, 48–51.
45. Cobb, *God and the World*, 50.
46. Cobb, *Beyond Dialogue*, 135.
47. Cobb, *Christ in a Pluralistic Age*, 71.
48. Cobb, *Christ in a Pluralistic Age*, 71.
49. Whitehead, *Science and the Modern World*, 154–155.
50. Cobb, *Christ in a Pluralistic Age*, 74.
51. Cobb, *Christ in a Pluralistic Age*, 74.
52. Cobb, *Christ in a Pluralistic Age*, 75.
53. Whitehead, *Process and Reality*, 23, 32–34.
54. Cobb, "Alfred North Whitehead," 190.
55. Whitehead, *Process and Reality*, 345, 347.
56. Whitehead, *Religion in the Making*, 120.
57. Cobb, *A Christian Natural Theology*, 89–90, 104; Whitehead, *Religion in the Making*, 100, 104, 135–160.

58. Cobb, *Beyond Dialogue*, 112 (emphasis in original); see also his "Buddhist Emptiness and the Christian God."
59. Whitehead, *Process and Reality*, 7, 20, 88, 108.
60. Cobb, *Christ in a Pluralistic Age*, 77.
61. Whitehead, *Science and the Modern World*, 258.
62. Aquinas, *The Summa Theologica*, Q20, art1, obj1.
63. Anselm, *St. Anselm's Proslogion*, chap. 8.
64. Whitehead, *Process and Reality*, 340.
65. Cobb, *God and the World*, 80.
66. Cobb, *God and the World*, 82.
67. Cobb, *Christ in a Pluralistic Age*, 15.
68. Cobb, *Christ in a Pluralistic Age*, 21.
69. Cobb and Griffin, *Process Theology*, 101.
70. Cobb, *Christ in a Pluralistic Age*, 80.
71. Cobb, *A Christian Natural Theology*, 24.

CHAPTER SIX

1. Neville, *God the Creator*, 11.
2. See Weiss (*Modes of Being; Nature and Man; Beyond All Appearances*) for his alternative cosmological answer to that question.
3. Neville, *God the Creator*, 48.
4. The use of the word "ontological" should not be taken to indicate that Neville engages in a classical form of the ontological argument that is a priori, uses reason alone rather than observation, and deduces God's reality from necessary premises. He is not giving a mathematical proof. Instead, when Neville mentions ontology, he is usually contrasting cosmological understandings of creativity with ontological understandings, individual instances of causation in reality versus the creation of all reality. If this is unclear, consider that Neville agrees with Hartshorne that classical theism does not get a coherent concept of God out of the ontological argument. However, Neville does not follow Hartshorne in making God's being relative to that of the world. Neville moves beyond classical theism to affirm God is not a being. God is indeterminate creativity responsible for all that has being. Those different moves represent the difference between focusing on cosmological and ontological creativity, respectively.
5. Neville, *God the Creator*, 48 (emphasis in original).
6. Neville, *Ultimates*, xvi.
7. Neville, *God the Creator; Ultimates*, 173–191, 193–197, 211–244.
8. Neville, *Religion in Late Modernity*, 21.
9. Neville, *God the Creator*, 12.
10. Neville, *God the Creator*, 45.
11. Neville, *Ultimates*, 214.

12. Neville, *Ultimates*, 216–217.
13. Neville, *God the Creator*, 72 (emphasis in original).
14. Neville, *God the Creator*, 73 (emphasis in original).
15. Neville, *Ultimates*, 230 (emphasis in original). For Neville's complete treatment of this issue, see *The Truth of Broken Symbols*.
16. Neville, *Ultimates*, 281.
17. Neville, *Realism in Religion*, 203–212.
18. Descartes, *The Philosophical Works of Descartes*, 2:248.
19. Leibniz, *Philosophical Papers and Letters*, 1:586; *Discourse on Metaphysics*, 5.
20. Neville, *Ultimates*, 222.
21. Neville, *Ultimates*, 264.
22. Neville, *God the Creator*, 72.
23. Neville, *God the Creator*, 75.
24. Neville, *God the Creator*, 75.
25. Neville, *God the Creator*, 71.
26. Neville, *God the Creator*, 72.
27. Neville, *God the Creator*, 270.
28. Neville, *God the Creator*, 270.
29. Neville, *Ultimates*, 193–209.
30. Neville, *On the Scope and Truth of Theology*, 31.
31. Neville, *Ultimates*, 17.
32. Tillich made this same point about qualifying all positive religious assertions in *Systematic Theology*, 1:239.
33. Whitehead, *Process and Reality*, 24, 228–229.
34. Neville, *The Truth of Broken Symbols*, xvi.
35. Neville, *Boston Confucianism*, 70.
36. Neville, *On the Scope and Truth of Theology*, 69.
37. Neville, *Ultimates*, 65.
38. Neville, *Ultimates*, 76.
39. Neville, *Ultimates*, 298.
40. Neville, *Symbols of Jesus*, 206.
41. Neville, *Symbols of Jesus*, xxiv.
42. It can also simply mean crossed limbs, and the swastika can reasonably be interpreted as limbs in motion. That interpretation can function as a symbol of progress.
43. Giving up who you are in order to follow Christ, sacrificing your identity for God, is the sort of thinking being referenced. Interestingly, it is rare that straight cisgender white Christians are asked to sacrifice much by churches in order to bear the Christian moniker, while gay, lesbian, and transgender individuals are often asked to give up all they are if they wish to be Christian. That is wielding the cross as a weapon.

44. Neville, *Symbols of Jesus*, 79–84.

45. Neville, *Religion*, vi.

46. Dawkins, *The God Delusion*, 308.

47. See Neville, *Religion*, 30–33, 181–198, for a defense of naturalism that incorporates the reality of value.

48. Neville, *Religion*, 40.

49. See McNamara, *The Neuroscience of Religious Experience*, for a serious yet accessible account for philosophers and theologians of the state of this research.

50. Neville, *Religion*, 42.

51. Neville, *Ultimates*, 84.

52. Neville, *Religion*, 249.

53. Neville, *Religion*, 277.

54. Neville, *Religion*, 295.

55. Neville, *Religion*, 297.

56. Neville, *Religion*, 299–314.

57. Neville, *Religion*, 302.

58. Shults, *Theology after the Birth of God*, 12.

59. Neville, *Ultimates*, 1.

60. Neville, *Ultimates*, 1.

61. Neville, *Ultimates*, 228.

62. Neville, *God the Creator*, 98.

63. Neville, *God the Creator*, 167.

64. Neville, *Ultimates*, 105.

65. Clayton, *The Problem of God in Modern Thought*, 470. For an example of someone embracing traditional theism through critical realism, see Van Huyssteen, *Theology and the Justification of Faith*.

CHAPTER SEVEN

1. Hartshorne, Cobb, and Ford, "Three Responses to Neville's *Creativity and God*," 100.

2. Neville, *Creativity and God*, 8.

3. Neville, *Creativity and God*, 21.

4. Whitehead, *Process and Reality*, 345.

5. Neville, *Creativity and God*, x–xi.

6. Neville, *Creativity and God*, 9.

7. Neville, *Creativity and God*, 10.

8. Neville, "Concerning *Creativity and God*," 1–10, 7.

9. Neville, *God the Creator*, 11 (emphasis in original).

10. Hartshorne, Cobb, and Ford, "Three Responses to Neville's *Creativity and God*," 101.

11. Cobb, "A More Radical Pluralism," 317.

12. Neville, *God the Creator*, 265 (emphasis in original).
13. Neville, "A Letter of Grateful and Affectionate Response," 26.
14. Cobb, *God and the World*, 28.
15. Cobb, *God and the World*, 33.
16. Cobb, "A More Radical Pluralism," 322.
17. Cobb, *Christ in a Pluralistic Age*, 78.
18. Cobb, *Christ in a Pluralistic Age*, 78.
19. Hartshorne, Cobb, and Ford, "Three Responses to Neville's *Creativity and God*," 97.
20. Neville, "Concerning *Creativity and God*," 6–7.
21. Neville, *Ultimates*, 176 (emphasis in original).
22. Hartshorne, Cobb, and Ford, "Three Responses to Neville's *Creativity and God*," 95.
23. Hartshorne, Cobb, and Ford, "Three Responses to Neville's *Creativity and God*," 96.
24. Whitehead, *Process and Reality*, 338.
25. Hartshorne, Cobb, and Ford, "Three Responses to Neville's *Creativity and God*," 98.
26. Hartshorne, Cobb, and Ford, "Three Responses to Neville's *Creativity and God*," 98.
27. Hartshorne, Cobb, and Ford, "Three Responses to Neville's *Creativity and God*," 101.
28. Neville, "Concerning *Creativity and God*," 3–4.
29. Cobb, *God and the World*, 89.
30. Cobb, *God and the World*, 89–90.
31. Cobb, *God and the World*, 90.
32. Cobb, *Jesus' Abba*, 138.
33. Neville, *God the Creator*, 91.
34. Neville, *God the Creator*, 103.
35. Griffin, *Whitehead's Radically Different Postmodern Philosophy*, 187.
36. Peirce, EP 2:343 (emphasis in original).
37. Griffin, *Whitehead's Radically Different Postmodern Philosophy*, 188.
38. Griffin, *Whitehead's Radically Different Postmodern Philosophy*, 193.
39. Whitehead, *Adventures of Ideas*, 168.
40. Neville, "A Letter of Grateful and Affectionate Response," 14.
41. Neville, "A Letter of Grateful and Affectionate Response," 16.
42. Nozick, *Philosophical Explanations*, 3–4.
43. Nozick, *Philosophical Explanations*, 7–11.
44. Nozick, *Philosophical Explanations*, 12.
45. Nozick, *Philosophical Explanations*, 20.
46. See Ward, *Peirce and Religion*, for an even stronger defense of Peirce as something like an orthodox Christian theist, with Peirce's philosophy propping up that identity.

47. Cobb, "Alfred North Whitehead"; Neville, *The Highroad around Modernism; Religion in Late Modernity*.

48. Tracy, "John Cobb's Theological Method," 31 (emphasis in original).

49. Koch, "Some Critical Remarks about Cobb's *The Structure of Christian Existence*," 49.

50. Neville, *The Highroad around Modernism*, 11.

51. Neville, *Reconstruction of Thinking*, 5–32.

52. Ford, review of *Founders of Constructive Postmodern Philosophy*.

53. Wildman, "How to Resist Robert Neville's *Creatio Ex Nihilo* Argument," 56–57.

54. Weiss, *Modes of Being*.

55. Neville, *God the Creator*, 55.

56. Neville, *God the Creator*, 60 (emphasis in original).

57. Neville, "Responding to My Critics," 309–310.

58. Neville, *God the Creator*, 3, 183–304.

59. Neville, *God the Creator*, 163.

60. Cobb, *Living Options in Protestant Theology*, 53–56.

CHAPTER EIGHT

1. Robinson, "Continuity, Naturalism, and Contingency," is where the model was first proposed. Robinson and Southgate elaborated the proposal in a series of articles found in *Zygon* 45, no. 2 and no. 3. See Robinson and Southgate, "God and the World of Signs," "Introduction: Toward a Metaphysic of Meaning," and "Semiotics as a Metaphysical Framework for Christian Theology."

2. Robinson, *God and the World of Signs*.

3. Goodwin, "Bateson," 150.

4. Robinson, *God and the World of Signs*, 192; Robinson and Southgate, "Semiotics as a Metaphysical Framework for Christian Theology."

5. Hoffmeyer, *Signs of Meaning in the Universe*, 61.

6. Robinson and Southgate, "Introduction: Toward a Metaphysic of Meaning"; "God and the World of Signs"; "Semiotics as a Metaphysical Framework for Christian Theology."

7. Robinson, *God and the World of Signs*, 74.

8. Robinson, *God and the World of Signs*, 79.

9. Robinson, *God and the World of Signs*, 114.

10. Robinson, *God and the World of Signs*, 114–115.

11. Slater, review of *God and the World of Signs*, 88–89.

12. Slater, review of *God and the World of Signs*, 89.

13. Peirce, EP 2:291.

14. Neville, *Ultimates*, 72.

15. Clayton, "Critical Afterword," 768.
16. Peirce, EP 2:179.
17. Hoffmeyer, *Biosemiotics*, 265–313.
18. Cobb, *God and the World*, 28–37, 80–82, 89–90.
19. Corrington, *Deep Pantheism*, xi (emphasis in original).
20. Corrington, *Deep Pantheism*, xi.
21. Cobb, *God and the World*, 62.
22. Dewey, *Art as Experience*, 142.
23. Corrington, *Deep Pantheism*, 53.
24. Corrington, *Deep Pantheism*, 54.
25. Corrington, *Nature's Sublime*, 83–84.
26. Corrington, *Nature's Sublime*, 85.
27. Hoffmeyer, "Biology Is Immature Biosemiotics," 56.
28. Hoffmeyer, "Biology Is Immature Biosemiotics," 55–56.
29. Hoffmeyer, "Biology Is Immature Biosemiotics," 60–61.
30. Hoffmeyer, *Biosemiotics*, 25–28. Hoffmeyer summarizes the phenomenon as follows: "And across all these membranes there occurs constant biosemiotics activity whereby molecular messages are exchanged in order to bring the biochemical functions and the inside and the outside of these interior membranes into concordance. Thus, the meta-membrane that is the human skin is indeed a highly specialized manifestation of the very same interior interface principle whereby life processes are most generally built up." Hoffmeyer, *Biosemiotics*, 27.
31. Rosenthal, *Time, Continuity, and Indeterminacy*, 114.
32. Rosenthal, *Time, Continuity, and Indeterminacy*, 115.
33. Corrington, *Deep Pantheism*, 3.
34. Corrington, *Deep Pantheism*, 4.
35. Corrington, *Deep Pantheism*, xxii (emphasis in original).
36. Corrington, *Deep Pantheism*, 17.
37. Corrington, *Deep Pantheism*, 38.
38. Corrington, *An Introduction to C. S. Peirce*, 208.
39. Raposa, *Peirce's Philosophy of Religion*, 122.
40. Neville, *God the Creator*, 131.
41. Neville, *Ultimates*, 224–225.
42. Neville, *God the Creator*, 102 (emphasis in original).
43. Neville, *God the Creator*, 119.
44. Clayton, *The Problem of God in Modern Thought*, 373.
45. Neville, *God the Creator*, 99.
46. Neville, *God the Creator*, 77 (emphasis in original).
47. Clayton, *The Problem of God in Modern Thought*, 476.
48. Neville, *God the Creator*, 97.
49. See Clayton, *The Problem of God in Modern Thought*, 487, for a similar

point he makes in favor of his panentheistic position in contrast to both the pantheistic denial of a transcendent God and the classical theistic denial that the world determines God in any way.

50. Whitehead, *Process and Reality*, 348.
51. Dorrien, *The Making of American Liberal Theology*, 520.
52. Deuser, *Gott: Geist und Natur*, 28.
53. Peirce, CP 6.268.
54. Deuser, *Gott: Geist und Natur*, 73, 106–107.
55. Peirce, CP 6.613 (emphasis in original).
56. Neville, *Ultimates*, 223.
57. Cobb, *Beyond Dialogue*, 47.
58. Corrington, *Deep Pantheism*, 70.
59. Hoffmeyer, *Biosemiotics*, 63.
60. Peirce, CP 6.12–13.
61. Hoffmeyer, *Biosemiotics*, 68.
62. Hoffmeyer, *Biosemiotics*, 80.
63. Hoffmeyer, *Biosemiotics*, 114 (emphasis in original).
64. Hoffmeyer, *Biosemiotics*, 216–217.
65. Tillich, *Systematic Theology*, 1:238.
66. Tillich, *Systematic Theology*, 1:118.
67. Tillich, *Systematic Theology*, 1:239.
68. Tillich, *Systematic Theology*, 1:240.
69. Tillich, *Systematic Theology*, 1:177.
70. Ford, "The Three Strands of Tillich's Theory of Religious Symbols," 116.
71. Ford, "The Three Strands of Tillich's Theory of Religious Symbols," 115.
72. Hoffmeyer, *Signs of Meaning in the Universe*, 47–48.
73. Hoffmeyer, *Signs of Meaning in the Universe*, 61.
74. Tillich, *Systematic Theology*, 1:113.
75. Peirce, EP 2:407–408, 480–482.
76. Peirce, EP 2:440.
77. See Clayton, *The Problem of God in Modern Thought*, 154, for a similar critique of forms of apophatic theology that ultimately deny the meaning of all religious language.
78. West and Blackmon, "Clergy in Charlottesville Were Trapped by Torch-Wielding Nazis." While counterprotesting neo-Nazis and Ku Klux Klan members marching in Charlottesville, Virginia in 2017, Cornel West and Traci Blackmon were cornered by the angry mob. West credited anarchists and members of antifa for literally saving their lives. Such a direct confrontation with hatred is an excellent example of becoming a symbol of God.
79. Peirce, CP 6.924.
80. Peirce, CP 6.443 (emphasis mine).
81. Hefner, *The Human Factor*.

CHAPTER NINE

1. Stone and Harkess, "This Is My Song."
2. Menand, *The Metaphysical Club*, xi–xii.
3. Luke 6:37–42 (NRSV).
4. Cobb, *Beyond Dialogue*.
5. Cobb, *Christ in a Pluralistic Age*, 19.
6. Cobb, *Christ in a Pluralistic Age*, 144.
7. Cobb, *The Structure of Christian Existence*, 143–148.
8. See Cobb, *Christ in a Pluralistic Age*, for this sort of congenial placing of the religions beside one another as engaged in different legitimate projects, especially pages 204–205 for a wonderful summary of the project.
9. Cobb, "Beyond Pluralism," 84, 83.
10. Cobb, "A More Radical Pluralism," 315.
11. Hick, *An Interpretation of Religion*.
12. Neville, *Ultimates*, 298–300.
13. Neville, *Behind the Masks of God*.
14. See Colapietro, *Peirce's Approach to the Self*, for a detailed description of personal and group identity as consisting of developing the right method of control for opening oneself and one's communities to greater connections and ideals.
15. Cobb, *Christ in a Pluralistic Age*, 21.
16. Peirce, EP 2:50.
17. Peirce, EP 2:48.
18. Whitehead, *Process and Reality*, 229.
19. Plato, *Republic*, 565c.
20. Popper, *The Open Society and Its Enemies*, 117.
21. Plato, *Republic*, 564a.
22. Popper, *The Open Society and Its Enemies*, 581.
23. Cobb, *Christ in a Pluralistic Age*, 53–54; *Beyond Dialogue*.
24. Popper, *The Open Society and Its Enemies*, 104.
25. Lakatos, *The Methodology of Scientific Research Programmes*, 47–51.
26. Lakatos, *The Methodology of Scientific Research Programmes*, 31–47.
27. Peirce, EP 1:115–123; EP 2:25.
28. See De Regt, "Peirce's Pragmatism, Scientific Realism, and the Problem of Underdetermination," for a discussion of how embracing pluralism not only makes sense in science but is also a virtue.

CONCLUSION

1. See Wheeler, *Religion within the Limits of History Alone*, especially chapters 6 and 7; Ryder, *The Things in Heaven and Earth*; Wildman, *Religious*

Philosophy as Multidisciplinary Comparative Inquiry. While sharing methods of inquiry that generally agree with mine, Wheeler, Ryder, and Wildman all disagree with the model of God I have developed. However, as I have shown, that disagreement is fine given our shared methodology!

2. Tillich, *Systematic Theology*, 1:85.

3. Tillich, *The Shaking of the Foundations; The New Being; The Eternal Now.* See especially his sermon "You Are Accepted" in *The Shaking of the Foundations*, 153–163.

4. Neville, *The God Who Beckons; Preaching the Gospel without Easy Answers; Nurture in Time and Eternity; Seasons of the Christian Life.*

5. Cobb, *Christ in a Pluralistic Age*, 84.

BIBLIOGRAPHY

Almeder, Robert. "Charles Peirce and the Existence of the External World." *Transactions of the Charles S. Peirce Society* 4, no. 2 (Spring 1968): 63–79.
Alston, William P. "Back to the Theory of Appearing." *Philosophical Perspectives* 13 (January 1999): 181–203.
Alston, William P. "Externalist Theories of Perception." *Philosophy and Phenomenological Research* 50 (October 1990): 73–97.
Alston, William P. *Perceiving God: The Epistemology of Religious Experience.* Ithaca: Cornell University Press, 1991.
Alston, William P. *A Realist Conception of Truth.* Ithaca: Cornell University Press, 1996.
Altizer, Thomas J. J. *The Gospel of Christian Atheism.* Philadelphia: Westminster Press, 1966.
Altizer, Thomas J. J. *History as Apocalypse.* Albany: SUNY Press, 1985.
Altizer, Thomas J. J. *The Self-Embodiment of God.* New York: Harper & Row, 1977.
Altizer, Thomas J. J. "Spiritual Existence as God-Transcending Existence." In *John Cobb's Theology in Process,* edited by David Ray Griffin and Thomas J. J. Altizer, 54–66. Philadelphia: Westminster Press, 1977.
Anselm. *St. Anselm's Proslogion.* Translated by M. J. Charlesworth. Oxford: Clarendon Press, 1965.
Aquinas, Thomas. *The Summa Theologica of St. Thomas Aquinas.* 2nd ed., rev. ed. Translated by Fathers of the English Dominican Province. London: Burns Oates & Washbourne; New York; Cincinnati: Benziger, 1914.

Aristotle. *Metaphysics*. Vol. 1, *Books 1–9*. Translated by Hugh Tredennick. Cambridge, MA: Harvard University Press, 1933.

Ayala, Francisco J. "The Baldwin Effect." In *Back to Darwin: A Richer Account of Evolution*, edited by John B. Cobb, 193–195. Grand Rapids, MI: William B. Eerdmans, 2008.

Barrett, Nathaniel F. "On the Evolutionary Plausibility of Religion as Engagement with Ultimacy." *American Journal of Theology & Philosophy* 36, no. 1 (January 2015): 85–93.

Barrett, Nathaniel F., and Wesley J. Wildman. "Seeing Is Believing? How Reinterpreting Perception as Dynamic Engagement Alters the Justificatory Force of Religious Experience." *International Journal for the Philosophy of Religion* 66, no. 2 (October 2009): 71–86.

Barth, Karl. *Church Dogmatics*. Vol. 1, pt. 1, *The Doctrine of the Word of God*. Edited by Geoffrey W. Bromiley and Thomas F. Torrance. Translated by Geoffrey W. Bromiley. London: T & T Clark International, 2004.

Berkeley, George. *A Treatise Concerning the Principles of Human Knowledge*. Edited by Kenneth Winkler. Indianapolis: Hackett Publishing, 1982.

Bernstein, Richard J. *The Pragmatic Turn*. Cambridge: Polity Press, 2010.

Brandom, Robert. *Between Saying and Doing: Towards an Analytic Pragmatism*. Oxford: Oxford University Press, 2008.

Brandom, Robert. *Making It Explicit: Reasoning, Representing, and Discursive Commitment*. Cambridge, MA: Harvard University Press, 1994.

Brandom, Robert. *Perspectives on Pragmatism: Classical, Recent, and Contemporary*. Cambridge, MA: Harvard University Press, 2011.

Brodsky, Gary. "Rorty's Interpretation of Pragmatism." *Transactions of the Charles S. Peirce Society* 18, no. 2 (Fall 1982): 311–337.

Carnap, Rudolph. *Meaning and Necessity: A Study in Semantic and Modal Logic*. Chicago: University of Chicago Press, 1956.

Clayton, Philip. "Critical Afterword." *Zygon* 45, no. 3 (September 2010): 762–772.

Clayton, Philip. "The Emergence of Sprit." *CTNS Bulletin* (Fall 2000): 3–20.

Clayton, Philip. *Mind and Emergence: From Quantum to Consciousness*. Oxford: Oxford University Press, 2004.

Clayton, Philip. "Neuroscience, the Person, and God: An Emergentist Account." *Zygon* 35, no. 3 (September 2000): 613–652.

Clayton, Philip. *The Problem of God in Modern Thought*. Grand Rapids, MI: William B. Eerdmans, 2000.

Cobb, John B. "Alfred North Whitehead." In *Founders of Constructive Postmodern Philosophy: Peirce, James, Bergson, Whitehead, and Hartshorne*, edited by David Ray Griffin, John B. Cobb, Marcus Ford, Pete A. Y. Gunter, and Peter Ochs, 165–195. Albany: SUNY Press, 1993.

Cobb, John B., ed. *Back to Darwin: A Richer Account of Evolution*. Grand Rapids, MI: William B. Eerdmans, 2008.

Cobb, John B. *Beyond Dialogue: Toward a Mutual Transformation of Christianity and Buddhism*. Philadelphia: Fortress Press, 1982.
Cobb, John B. "Beyond Pluralism." In *Christian Uniqueness Reconsidered: The Myth of a Pluralistic Theology of Religions*, edited by Gavin D'Costa, 81–95. Maryknoll, NY: Orbis Books, 1990.
Cobb, John B. "Buddhist Emptiness and the Christian God." *Journal of the American Academy of Religion* 45, no. 1 (March 1977): 11–25.
Cobb, John B. *A Christian Natural Theology: Based on the Thought of Alfred North Whitehead*. 2nd ed. Louisville, KY: Westminster John Knox Press, 2007.
Cobb, John B. *Christ in a Pluralistic Age*. Philadelphia: Westminster Press, 1975.
Cobb, John B. *God and the World*. Philadelphia: Westminster Press, 1969.
Cobb, John B. "Intellectual Autobiography." *Religious Studies Review* 19, no. 1 (January 1993): 9–11.
Cobb, John B. "Introduction." In *Back to Darwin: A Richer Account of Evolution*, edited by John B. Cobb, 1–18. Grand Rapids, MI: William B. Eerdmans, 2008.
Cobb, John B. "Is the Later Heidegger Relevant for Theology?" In *The Later Heidegger and Theology*, edited by James M. Robinson and John B. Cobb, 177–197. New York: Harper & Row, 1963.
Cobb, John B. *Jesus' Abba: The God Who Has Not Failed*. Minneapolis: Fortress Press, 2015.
Cobb, John B. *Living Options in Protestant Theology: A Survey of Methods*. Philadelphia: Westminster Press, 1962.
Cobb, John B. "A More Radical Pluralism." In *Theology in Global Context: Essays in Honor of Robert Cummings Neville*, edited by Amos Yong and Peter Heltzel, 315–326. New York: T & T Clark International, 2004.
Cobb, John B. *The Structure of Christian Existence*. Philadelphia: Westminster Press, 1967.
Cobb, John B., and David Ray Griffin. *Process Theology: An Introductory Exposition*. Louisville, KY: Westminster John Knox Press, 1976.
Colapietro, Vincent. *Peirce's Approach to the Self: A Semiotic Perspective on Human Subjectivity*. Albany: SUNY Press, 1989.
Corrington, Robert S. *Deep Pantheism: Toward a New Transcendentalism*. Lanham, MD: Lexington Books, 2016.
Corrington, Robert S. *An Introduction to C. S. Peirce: Philosopher, Semiotician, and Ecstatic Naturalist*. Lanham, MD: Rowman & Littlefield, 1993.
Corrington, Robert S. *Nature's Sublime: An Essay in Aesthetic Naturalism*. Lanham, MD: Lexington Books, 2013.
Dawkins, Richard. *The God Delusion*. Boston: Houghton Mifflin, 2006.
Deacon, Terrence William. "The Hierarchic Logic of Emergence: Untangling the Interdependence of Evolution and Self-Organization." In *Evolution*

and *Learning: The Baldwin Effect Reconsidered*, edited by Bruce H. Weber and David J. Depew, 273–308. Cambridge, MA: MIT Press, 2003.

de Regt, Herman C. D. G. "Peirce's Pragmatism, Scientific Realism, and the Problem of Underdetermination." *Transactions of the Charles S. Peirce Society* 35, no. 2 (Spring 1999): 374–397.

Descartes, René. *Discourse on Method*. Translated by Donald A. Cress. Indianapolis: Hackett Publishing Company, 1980.

Descartes, René. *Meditations on First Philosophy*. Translated and edited by John Cottingham. Cambridge: Cambridge University Press, 1996.

Descartes, René. *The Philosophical Works of Descartes*. 2 vols. Translated by Elizabeth S. Haldane and G. R. T. Ross. New York: Dover Publications, 1955.

Deuser, Hermann. *Gott: Geist und Natur; Theologische Konsequenzen aus Charles S. Peirce's Religionsphilosophie*. Berlin: Walter de Gruyter, 1993.

Devitt, Michael. "Dummett's Anti-Realism." *Journal of Philosophy* 80, no. 2 (1983): 73–99.

Dewey, John. *Art as Experience*. 1934. Reprinted in *John Dewey: The Later Works, 1925–1953, Vol. 10*, edited by Jo Ann Boydston. Carbondale: Southern Illinois University Press, 1987.

Dewey, John. *A Common Faith*. New Haven, CT: Yale University Press, 1934.

Dewey, John. *The Essential Dewey*. Vol. 1, *Pragmatism, Education, Democracy*. Edited by Larry A. Hickman and Thomas M. Alexander. Bloomington: Indiana University Press, 1998.

Dewey, John. *The Essential Dewey*. Vol. 2, *Ethics, Logic, Psychology*. Edited by Larry A. Hickman and Thomas M. Alexander. Bloomington: Indiana University Press, 1998.

Dewey, John. *Experience and Nature*. London: Allen & Unwin, 1929.Dorrien, Gary. *The Making of American Liberal Theology: Crisis, Irony, and Postmodernity 1950–2005*. Louisville, KY: Westminster John Knox, 2006.

Dubin, Mark Wm. *How the Brain Works*. Abingdon, England: Blackwell Science, 2002.

Duhem, Pierre Maurice Marie. *The Aim and Structure of Physical Theory*. Princeton: Princeton University Press, 1954.

Dummett, Michael. *Truth and Other Enigmas*. Cambridge, MA: Harvard University Press, 1978.

Feyerabend, P. K. *Against Method*. 3rd ed. London: Verso, 1993.

Feyerabend, P. K. "An Attempt at a Realistic Interpretation of Experience." *Proceedings of the Aristotelian Society* 58 (January 1957): 143–170.

Feyerabend, P. K. *Realism, Rationalism, and Scientific Method. Philosophical Papers*, Vol. 1. Cambridge: Cambridge University Press, 1981.

Fisch, Max H. *Peirce, Semeiotic, and Pragmatism: Essays by Max H. Fisch*. Edited by Kenneth Laine Ketner and Christian J. W. Kloesel. Bloomington: Indiana University Press, 1986.

Ford, Lewis S. Review of *Founders of Constructive Postmodern Philosophy: Peirce, James, Bergson, Whitehead, and Hartshorne,* by David Ray Griffin, John B. Cobb, Marcus P. Ford, Pete A.Y. Gunter, and Peter Ochs. *Transactions of the Charles S. Peirce Society* 30, no. 1 (Winter 1994): 220–226.

Ford, Lewis S. "The Three Strands of Tillich's Theory of Religious Symbols." *Journal of Religion* 46, no. 1, pt. 2 (January 1966): 104–130.

Frei, Hans W. *The Eclipse of Biblical Narrative: A Study in Eighteenth and Nineteenth Century Hermeneutics.* New Haven, CT: Yale University Press, 1974.

Frei, Hans W. *Types of Christian Theology.* New Haven, CT: Yale University Press, 1992.

French, Steven. *The Structure of the World: Metaphysics and Representation.* Oxford: Oxford University Press, 2014.

Goodwin, Brian. "Bateson: Biology with Meaning." In *A Legacy for Living Systems: Gregory Bateson as Precursor to Biosemiotics,* edited by Jesper Hoffmeyer, 145–452. Dordrecht: Springer Netherlands, 2008.

Griffin, David Ray. *Whitehead's Radically Different Postmodern Philosophy: An Argument for Its Contemporary Relevance.* Albany: SUNY Press, 2007.

Grimes, John. "On the Failure to Detect Changes in Scenes across Saccades." In *Perception,* edited by Kathleen Atkins, 89–109. Oxford: Oxford University Press, 1996.

Hardin, C. L. *Color for Philosophers: Unweaving the Rainbow.* Indianapolis: Hackett Publishing, 1986.

Hartshorne, Charles. *Beyond Humanism: Essays in the Philosophy of Nature.* Chicago: Willet, Clarke and Company, 1937. Reprint, Lincoln: University of Nebraska Press, 1968.

Hartshorne, Charles. "Charles Peirce and Quantum Mechanics." *Transactions of the Charles S. Peirce Society* 9, no. 4 (Fall 1973): 191–201.

Hartshorne, Charles. "Charles Peirce's 'One Contribution to Philosophy' and Most Serious Mistake." In *Studies in the Philosophy of Charles Sanders Peirce,* 2nd series, edited by Edward C. Moore and Richard S. Robin, 455–474. Amherst: University of Massachusetts Press, 1964.

Hartshorne, Charles. "Charles Sanders Peirce's Metaphysics of Evolution." *New England Quarterly* 14, no. 1 (March 1941): 49–63.

Hartshorne, Charles. "Continuity, the Form of Forms in Charles Peirce." *Monist* 39, no. 4 (October 1929): 521–534.

Hartshorne, Charles. *Creative Synthesis and Philosophic Method.* London: SCM Press, 1970. Reprint, La Salle, IL: Open Court, 1970.

Hartshorne, Charles. *The Philosophy of Psychology and Sensation.* Chicago: University of Chicago Press, 1934. Reprint, Port Washington, NY: Kennikat Press, 1968.

Hartshorne, Charles. "A Revision of Peirce's Categories." *Monist* 63, no. 3 (July 1980): 277–289.

Hartshorne, Charles, John B. Cobb, and Lewis S. Ford. "Three Responses to Neville's *Creativity and God.*" *Process Studies* 10, nos. 3–4 (Fall/Winter 1980): 93–109.

Hefner, Philip J. *The Human Factor: Evolution, Culture, and Religion.* Minneapolis: Fortress Press, 1993.

Heim, S. Mark. *Saved from Sacrifice: A Theology of the Cross.* Grand Rapids, MI: William B. Eerdmans, 2006.

Hempel, Carl G. "On the Logical Positivists' Theory of Truth." *Analysis* 2, no. 4 (January 1935): 49–59.

Hick, John. *An Interpretation of Religion: Human Responses to the Transcendent.* New Haven, CT: Yale University Press, 1989.

Hildebrand, David L. *Beyond Realism and Antirealism: John Dewey and the Neopragmatists.* Nashville, TN: Vanderbilt University Press, 2003.

Hildebrand, David L. "Putnam, Pragmatism, and Dewey." *Transactions of the Charles S. Peirce Society* 36, no. 1 (Winter 2000): 109–132.

Hoffmeyer, Jesper. "Biology Is Immature Biosemiotics." In *Towards a Semiotic Biology: Life Is the Action of Signs,* edited by Claus Emmeche and Kalevi Kull, 43–65. London: Imperial College Press, 2011.

Hoffmeyer, Jesper. *Biosemiotics: An Examination into the Signs of Life and the Life of Signs.* Scranton, PA: University of Scranton Press, 2008.

Hoffmeyer, Jesper. *Signs of Meaning in the Universe.* Translated by Barbara J. Haveland. Bloomington: Indiana University Press, 1996.

Hookway, Christopher. "Peirce and Skepticism." In *The Oxford Handbook of Skepticism,* edited by John Greco, 310–329. Oxford: Oxford University Press, 2008.

Hume, David. *An Enquiry Concerning Human Understanding.* Edited by Stephen Buckle. Cambridge: Cambridge University Press, 2007.

James, William. "Does 'Consciousness' Exist?" In *Sciousness,* edited by Jonathan Bricklin, 112–141. Guilford, CT: Eirini Press, 2006.

James, William. *A Pluralistic Universe.* Cambridge, MA: Harvard University Press, 1977.

James, William. *Pragmatism: A New Name for Some Old Ways of Thinking; The Meaning of Truth: A Sequel to Pragmatism.* Cambridge, MA: Harvard University Press, 1978.

James, William. *The Principles of Psychology.* Cambridge, MA: Harvard University Press, 1981.

Kant, Immanuel. *Critique of Pure Reason.* Translated by Paul Guyer and Allen W. Wood. Cambridge: Cambridge University Press, 1998.

Koch, Traugott. "Some Critical Remarks about Cobb's *The Structure of Christian Existence.*" In *John Cobb's Theology in Process,* edited by David Ray Griffin and Thomas J. J. Altizer, 39–53. Philadelphia: Westminster Press, 1977.

Kuhn, Thomas S. *The Structure of Scientific Revolutions*. Chicago: University of Chicago Press, 1962.

Lakatos. *The Methodology of Scientific Research Programmes. Philosophical Papers*, vol. 1. Edited by John Worrall and Gregory Currie. Cambridge: Cambridge University Press, 1978.

LaPorte, Joseph. *Natural Kinds and Conceptual Change*. Cambridge: Cambridge University Press, 2004.

Leclerc, Ivor. "Alfred North Whitehead: His Philosophy." In *Process in Context: Essays in Post-Whiteheadian Perspectives*, edited by Ernest Wolf-Gazo, 25–44. Bern: Peter Lang Publishing, 1988.

Leibniz, Gottfried Wilhelm. *Discourse on Metaphysics*. Translated by George R. Montgomery. La Salle, IL: Open Court Publishing, 1968.

Leibniz, Gottfried Wilhelm. *Philosophical Papers and Letters*. 2 vols. Edited by Leroy E. Loemker. Chicago: University of Chicago Press, 1956.

Lindbeck, George A. *The Nature of Doctrine: Religion and Theology in a Postliberal Age*. Philadelphia: Westminster Press, 1984.

Margulis, Lynn. *Origin of Eukaryotic Cells: Evidence and Research Implications for a Theory of the Origin and Evolution of Microbial, Plant, and Animal Cells on the Precambrian Earth*. New Haven, CT: Yale University Press, 1970.

McDowell, John Henry. *Mind and World*. Cambridge, MA: Harvard University Press, 1994.

McNamara, Patrick. *The Neuroscience of Religious Experience*. Cambridge: Cambridge University Press, 2009.

Menand, Louis. *The Metaphysical Club: A Story of Ideas in America*. New York: Farrar, Straus and Giroux, 2001.

Moore, Edward C. "On the World as General." *Transactions of the Charles S. Peirce Society* 4, no. 2 (Spring 1968): 90–100.

Murphey, Murray. "On Peirce's Metaphysics." *Transactions of the Charles S. Peirce Society* 1, no. 1 (Spring 1965): 12–25.

Neville, Robert Cummings. *Behind the Masks of God: An Essay toward Comparative Theology*. Albany: SUNY Press, 1991.

Neville, Robert Cummings. *Boston Confucianism: Portable Tradition in the Late-Modern World*. Albany: SUNY Press, 2000.

Neville, Robert Cummings. "Concerning *Creativity and God*: A Response." *Process Studies* 11, no. 1 (Spring 1981): 1–10.

Neville, Robert Cummings. *Creativity and God: A Challenge to Process Theology*. New ed. Albany: SUNY Press, 1995.

Neville, Robert Cummings. *God the Creator: On the Transcendence and Presence of God*. Albany: SUNY Press, 1992.

Neville, Robert Cummings. *The God Who Beckons: Theology in the Form of Sermons*. Nashville, TN: Abingdon Press, 1999.

Neville, Robert Cummings. *The Highroad around Modernism.* Albany: SUNY Press, 1992.

Neville, Robert Cummings. "A Letter of Grateful and Affectionate Response to David Ray Griffin's *Whitehead's Radically Different Postmodern Philosophy: An Argument for Its Contemporary Relevance.*" Process Studies 37, no. 1 (January 2008): 7–38.

Neville, Robert Cummings. *Metaphysics of Goodness: Harmony and Form, Beauty and Art, Obligation and Personhood, Flourishing and Civilization.* Albany: SUNY Press, 2019.

Neville, Robert Cummings. *Nurture in Time and Eternity.* Eugene, OR: Cascade Books, 2016.

Neville, Robert Cummings. *On the Scope and Truth of Theology: Theology as Symbolic Engagement.* New York: T & T Clark, 2006.

Neville, Robert Cummings. *Preaching the Gospel without Easy Answers.* Nashville, TN: Abingdon Press, 2005.

Neville, Robert Cummings. *Realism in Religion: A Pragmatist's Perspective.* Albany: SUNY Press, 2010.

Neville, Robert Cummings. *Reconstruction of Thinking.* Albany: SUNY Press, 1981.

Neville, Robert Cummings. *Religion in Late Modernity.* Albany: SUNY Press, 2002.

Neville, Robert Cummings. *Religion: Philosophical Theology.* Vol. 3. Albany: SUNY Press, 2015.

Neville, Robert Cummings. "Responding to My Critics." In *Interpreting Neville,* edited by J. Harley Chapman and Nancy K. Frankenberry, 291–328. Albany: SUNY Press, 1999.

Neville, Robert Cummings. *Ritual and Deference: Extending Chinese Philosophy in a Comparative Context.* Albany: SUNY Press, 2008.

Neville, Robert Cummings. *Seasons of the Christian Life.* Eugene, OR: Cascade Books, 2016

Neville, Robert Cummings. *Symbols of Jesus: Christology as Symbolic Engagement.* Cambridge: Cambridge University Press, 2001.

Neville, Robert Cummings. *The Truth of Broken Symbols.* Albany: SUNY Press, 1996.

Neville, Robert Cummings. *Ultimates: Philosophical Theology.* Vol. 1. Albany: SUNY Press, 2013.

Noë, Alva. *Action in Perception.* Cambridge, MA: MIT Press, 2004.

Nozick, Robert. *Philosophical Explanations.* Oxford: Clarendon Press, 1981.

Olsson, Erik J. "Not Giving the Skeptic a Hearing: *Pragmatism and Radical Doubt.*" Philosophy and Phenomenological Research 70, no. 1 (2005): 98–126.

Orange, Donna M. *Peirce's Conception of God: A Developmental Study.* Lubbock, TX: Institute for Studies in Pragmaticism, 1984.

Peirce, Charles Sanders. *Collected Papers of Charles Sanders Peirce.* Vol. 1 and 2, *Principles of Philosophy and Elements of Logic.* Edited by Charles Hartshorne and Paul Weiss. Cambridge, MA: Harvard University Press, 1932.

Peirce, Charles Sanders. *Collected Papers of Charles Sanders Peirce.* Vol. 3 and 4, *Exact Logic (Published Papers) and The Simplest Mathematics.* Edited by Charles Hartshorne and Paul Weiss. Cambridge, MA: Harvard University Press, 1933.

Peirce, Charles Sanders. *Collected Papers of Charles Sanders Peirce.* Vol. 5 and 6, *Pragmatism and Pragmaticism and Scientific Metaphysics.* Edited by Charles Hartshorne and Paul Weiss. Cambridge, MA: Harvard University Press, 1935.

Peirce, Charles Sanders. *Collected Papers of Charles Sanders Peirce.* Vol. 7 and 8, *Science and Philosophy and Reviews, Correspondence and Bibliography.* Edited by Arthur W. Burks. Cambridge, MA: Harvard University Press, 1958.

Peirce, Charles Sanders. *The Essential Peirce: Selected Philosophical Writings.* Vol. 1, *1867–1893.* Edited by Nathan Houser and Christian Kloesel. Bloomington: Indiana University Press, 1992.

Peirce, Charles Sanders. *The Essential Peirce: Selected Philosophical Writings.* Vol. 2, *1893–1913.* Edited by the Peirce Edition Project. Bloomington: Indiana University Press, 1998.

Peirce, Charles Sanders. *Writings of Charles S. Peirce: A Chronological Edition.* Vol. 3, *1872–1878.* Edited by the Peirce Edition Project. Bloomington: Indiana University Press, 1986.

Plato. *Plato's Republic.* Translated by G. M. A. Grube. Indianapolis: Hackett Publishing Company, 1974.

Popper, Karl. *Conjectures and Refutations: The Growth of Scientific Knowledge.* London: Routledge Classics, 2002.

Popper, Karl. *The Open Society and Its Enemies.* Princeton: Princeton University Press, 2013.

Psillos, Stathis. "Is Structural Realism Possible?" *Philosophy of Science* 68, no. 3 (September 2001): S13-S24.

Psillos, Stathis. *Scientific Realism: How Science Tracks Truth.* London: Routledge, 1999.

Putnam, Hilary. *Pragmatism: An Open Question.* Oxford: Blackwell, 1995.

Putnam, Hilary. *Realism and Reason. Philosophical Papers,* Vol. 3. Cambridge: Cambridge University Press, 1983.

Putnam, Hilary. *Realism with a Human Face.* Edited by James Conant. Cambridge, MA: Harvard University Press, 1990.

Putnam, Hilary. *Reason, Truth, and History.* Cambridge: Cambridge University Press, 1981.Putnam, Hilary. *Renewing Philosophy.* Cambridge, MA: Harvard University Press, 1992.

Putnam, Hilary. *Representation and Reality*. Cambridge, MA: MIT Press, 1988.

Putnam, Hilary. *Words and Life*. Edited by James Conant. Cambridge, MA: Harvard University Press, 1994.

Putnam, Hilary, and Ruth Anna Putnam. "The Real William James: Response to Robert Myers." *Transactions of the Charles S. Peirce Society* 34, no. 2 (Spring 1998): 366–381.

Quine, W. V. *From a Logical Point of View: 9 Logico-Philosophical Essays*. 2nd ed., rev. ed. Cambridge, MA: Harvard University Press, 1961.

Raposa, Michael L. "Peirce and Modern Religious Thought." *Transactions of the Charles S. Peirce Society* 27, no. 3 (Summer 1991): 341–369.

Raposa, Michael L. *Peirce's Philosophy of Religion*. Bloomington: Indiana University Press, 1989.

Robinson, Andrew J. "Continuity, Naturalism, and Contingency: A Theology of Evolution Drawing on the Semiotics of C. S. Peirce and Trinitarian Thought." *Zygon* 39, no. 1 (March 2004):111–136.

Robinson, Andrew J. *God and the World of Signs: Trinity, Evolution, and the Metaphysical Semiotics of C. S. Peirce*. Leiden: Brill, 2010.

Robinson, Andrew, and Christopher Southgate. "God and the World of Signs: Introduction to Part 2." *Zygon* 45, no. 3 (September 2010): 685–688.

Robinson, Andrew, and Christopher Southgate. "Introduction: Toward a Metaphysic of Meaning." *Zygon* 45, no. 2 (June 2010): 339–344.

Robinson, Andrew, and Christopher Southgate. "Semiotics as a Metaphysical Framework for Christian Theology." *Zygon* 45, no. 3 (September 2010): 689–712.

Rorty, Richard. *Consequences of Pragmatism: Essays, 1972–1980*. Minneapolis: University of Minnesota Press, 1982.

Rorty, Richard. "Pragmatism, Categories, and Language." *Philosophical Review* 70, no. 2 (April 1961): 197–223.

Rosenthal, Sandra B. "Continuity, Contingency, and Time: The Divergent Intuitions of Whitehead and Pragmatism." *Transactions of the Charles S. Peirce Society* 32, no. 4 (Fall 1996): 542–567.

Rosenthal, Sandra B. "Neville and Pragmatism: Toward Ongoing Dialogue." In *Interpreting Neville*, edited by J. Harley Chapman and Nancy K. Frankenberry, 59–76. Albany: SUNY Press, 1999.

Rosenthal, Sandra B. *Time, Continuity, and Indeterminacy: A Pragmatic Engagement with Contemporary Perspectives*. Albany: SUNY Press, 2000.

Ryder, John. *The Things in Heaven and Earth: An Essay in Pragmatic Naturalism*. New York: Fordham University Press, 2013.

Sellars, Wilfrid. *Empiricism and the Philosophy of Mind*. Cambridge, MA: Harvard University Press, 1997.

Sessions, William Lad. "Charles Hartshorne and Thirdness." *Southern Journal of Philosophy* 12, no. 2 (1974): 239–252.

Short, T. L. "Peirce's Concept of Final Causation." *Transactions of the Charles S. Peirce Society* 17, no. 4 (Fall 1981): 369–382.

Shults, F. LeRon. *Theology after the Birth of God: Atheist Conceptions in Cognition and Culture*. New York: Palgrave Macmillan, 2014.

Slater, Gary. Review of *God and the World of Signs: Trinity, Evolution, and the Metaphysical Semiotics of C. S. Peirce*, by Andrew Robinson. *American Journal of Theology & Philosophy* 34, no. 1 (January 2013): 86–89.

Stone, Lloyd, and Georgia Harkess. "This Is My Song." In *The United Methodist Hymnal: Book of United Methodist Worship*, 437. Nashville, TN: United Methodist Publishing House, 1989.

Thagard, Paul. "Coherence, Truth, and the Development of Scientific Knowledge." *Philosophy of Science* 74, no. 1 (January 2007): 28–47.

Tillich, Paul. *The Eternal Now*. New York: Charles Scribner's Sons, 1963.

Tillich, Paul. *Main Works/Hauptwerke*. 6 vols. Edited by Carl Heinz Ratschow. Berlin: Walter de Gruyter, 1987–92.

Tillich, Paul. *The New Being*. New York: Charles Scribner's Sons, 1955.

Tillich, Paul. "The Philosophical Background of My Theology." In *Main Works*, vol. 1. *Philosophical Writings*, edited by Carl Heinz Ratschow. Berlin: Walter de Gruyter, 1989.

Tillich, Paul. "The Religious Symbol/Symbol and Knowledge." In *Main Works*, vol. 4. *Writings in the Philosophy of Religion*, edited by Carl Heinz Ratschow. Berlin: Walter de Gruyter, 1987.

Tillich, Paul. *The Shaking of the Foundations*. New York: Charles Scribner's Sons, 1948.

Tillich, Paul. *Systematic Theology*. Vol. 1, *Reason and Revelation; Being and God*. Chicago: University of Chicago Press, 1951.

Tillich, Paul. *Systematic Theology*. Vol. 2, *Existence and the Christ*. Chicago: University of Chicago Press, 1957.

Tillich, Paul. *Systematic Theology*. Vol. 3, *Life and the Spirit; History and the Kingdom of God*. Chicago: University of Chicago Press, 1963.

Tillich, Paul. "The Two Types of Philosophy of Religion" In *Main Works*, vol. 4, *Writings in the Philosophy of Religion*, edited by Carl Heinz Ratschow. Berlin: Walter de Gruyter, 1987.

Tillich, Paul. *What Is Religion?* Translated by James Luther Adams. New York: Harper & Row, 1973.

Tracy, David. "John Cobb's Theological Method: Interpretation and Reflections." In *John Cobb's Theology in Process*, edited by David Ray Griffin and Thomas J. J. Altizer, 25–38. Philadelphia: Westminster Press, 1977.

van Fraassen, Bas C. *The Scientific Image*. Oxford: Clarendon Press: Oxford University Press, 1980.

van Huyssteen, J. Wentzel. *Theology and the Justification of Faith: Constructing Theories in Systematic Theology*. Grand Rapids, MI: William B. Eerdmans, 1989.

van Woudenberg, René. "Alston on Direct Perception and Interpretation." Review of *Perceiving God: The Epistemology of Religious Experience*, by William P. Alston. *International Journal for Philosophy of Religion* 36, no. 2 (October 1994): 117–124.

Varela, Francisco J., Evan T. Thompson, and Eleanor Rosch. *The Embodied Mind: Cognitive Science and Human Experience*. Cambridge, MA: MIT Press, 1991.

Vitali, Theodore R. "The Peircean Influence on Hartshorne's Subjectivism." *Process Studies* 7, no. 4 (Winter 1997): 238–249.

Votsis, Ioannis. "Is Structure Not Enough?" *Philosophy of Science* 70, no. 5 (December 2003): 879–890.

Ward, Roger A. *Peirce and Religion: Knowledge, Transformation, and the Reality of God*. Lanham, MD: Lexington Books, 2018.

Weiss, Paul. *Beyond All Appearances*. Carbondale: Southern Illinois University Press, 1974.

Weiss, Paul. "The Essence of Peirce's System." *Journal of Philosophy* 37, no. 10 (May 1940): 253–264.

Weiss, Paul. *Modes of Being*. Carbondale: Southern Illinois University Press, 1958.

Weiss, Paul. *Nature and Man*. New York: H. Holt and Company, 1947.

Wells, Kelley J. "An Evaluation of Hartshorne's Critique of Peirce's Synechism." *Transactions of the Charles S. Peirce Society* 32, no. 2 (Spring 1996): 216–246.

West, Cornel, and Traci Blackmon. "Clergy in Charlottesville Were Trapped by Torch-Wielding Nazis." *Democracy Now*, August 14, 2017. https://www.democracynow.org/2017/8/14/ cornel_west_rev_toni_blackmon_clergy.

Wheeler, Demian. *Religion within the Limits of History Alone: Pragmatic Historicism and the Future of Theology*. Albany: SUNY Press, 2020.

Whitehead, Alfred North. *Adventures of Ideas*. New York: Free Press, 1967.

Whitehead, Alfred North. *Process and Reality: An Essay in Cosmology*. Corrected ed. Edited by David Ray Griffin and Donald W. Sherburne. New York: Free Press, 1978.

Whitehead, Alfred North. *Religion in the Making*. 2nd ed. New York: Fordham University Press, 1996.

Whitehead, Alfred North. *Science and the Modern World*. New York: Free Press, 1967.

Wieman, Henry Nelson. *The Directive in History*. Boston: Beacon Press, 1949.

Wieman, Henry Nelson. *The Source of Human Good*. Carbondale: Southern Illinois University Press, 1964.

Wildman, Wesley J. "How to Resist Robert Neville's *Creatio Ex Nihilo* Argument." *American Journal of Theology & Philosophy* 36, no. 1 (January 2015): 56–64.

Wildman, Wesley J. *In Our Own Image: Anthropomorphism, Apophaticism, and Ultimacy.* Oxford: Oxford University Press, 2017.

Wildman, Wesley J. *Religious Philosophy as Multidisciplinary Comparative Inquiry: Envisioning a Future for the Philosophy of Religion.* Albany: SUNY Press, 2010.

Wilson, Robert A., ed. *Species: New Interdisciplinary Essays.* Cambridge, MA: MIT Press, 1999.

Wittgenstein, Ludwig. *Philosophical Investigations.* Translated by G. E. M. Anscombe, P. M. S. Hacker, and Joachim Schulte. Malden, MA: Wiley-Blackwell, 2009.

Wittgenstein, Ludwig. *Tractatus Logico-Philosophicus.* Translated by D. F. Pears and B. F. McGuinnes. London: Routledge & Kegan Paul, 1961.

Zammito, John H. *A Nice Derangement of Epistemes: Post-Positivism in the Study of Science from Quine to Latour.* Chicago: University of Chicago Press, 2004.

INDEX

abduction, 149, 157, 185; deduction and, 3, 64–65, 86, 157; induction and, 3, 41–42, 51, 157; musement and, 51; perception and, 72
agapism, 6, 68, 194
"alarmones," 174. *See also* biosemiotics
algae, 173–74, 177
Alston, William, 20–26; critics of, 23–25, 39; Tillich and, 81, 82
Altizer, Thomas, 92, 129
altruism, 135
Amazon Corporation, 104
analog / digital codes, 173–74, 177
Anselm, Saint, 107, 111, 136
antifa, 216n78
Aquinas, Thomas, Saint, 12, 107, 111, 152
Aristotle, 12–13, 111
aseity, 130, 136, 151

Baldwin effect, 42–43
Barrett, Nathaniel, 23–25, 39, 84
Barth, Karl, 27–29, 72, 169; Cobb and, 78; Robinson and, 157
being-itself, 176; Cobb on, 136; Neville on, 114, 141, 146, 150, 165, 176; Tillich on, 175, 176

Bergson, Henri, 205n6
Berkeley, George, 13
Bernstein, Richard, 54
biosemiotics, 167, 172–76; evolution and, 5–6, 156–59, 162, 172–73; Hoffmeyer on, 156, 162, 172–74, 176, 215n30; Peirce and, 155, 158, 165, 172. *See also* semiotics
Black Lives Matter, 180
Blackmon, Traci, 216n78
blank slate (*tabula rasa*), 2, 34
Boutroux, Émile, 138
Brandom, Robert, 54
Buddhism, 20, 124, 185, 186, 191
Bush, George W., 180

"call forward," 100
Carnap, Rudolf, 200n3
chaos, 142, 173
Clayton, Philip, x–xii, 65–66, 130, 159, 166
Cobb, John, x–xii, 65, 75, 91–109; Aquinas and, 152; Barth and, 78; Christology of, 77, 91, 95, 98–103, 108–9, 186, 191; on creation ex nihilo, 140–41, 160; on creativity, 3, 93, 103, 105–7, 137;

233

Cobb, John *(cont'd)*
  Darwin and, 94; on death of God movement, 137; on determinacy, 113, 171; Dewey and, 160–61; on faith, 91, 93, 98, 137; on freedom, 136–37, 141; on God the creator, 168–69; on Holocaust, 140; on immanent creative transformation, 145–46; on Logos, 103, 196; on natural theology, 77, 108, 147–48; on need for unity, 136; panpsychism of, 66; pluralism of, 92, 184–87, 190–91; on possibilities, 159–60; postmodernism of, 147–49; relativism of, 148–49; Tracey on, 147–48; on transcendence / immi-nence, 146, 179, 186; Whitehead and, 86–90, 171
Cobb, John, works of: *Back to Darwin*, 94; *Christ in a Pluralistic Age*, 92, 108; *A Christian Natural Theology*, 108; *Founders of Constructive Postmodern Philosophy*, 148; *God and the World*, 108; *The Structure of Christian Existence*, 108
Colapietro, Vincent, 217n4
Communion (Eucharist), 125
community / individuality, 20, 162–63, 181
Confucianism, 112, 124, 184
consciousness, stream of, 58, 62, 206n6
constructivism, 14, 148, 193–94; Cobb and, 75; idealism and, 11, 12; neoprag-matism and, 56; Peirce and, 37–38; to pragmatic constructive realism, 71–73; realism and, 4–5, 11–20, 26–30, 194
contingency, 6, 167; Hartshorne on, 138–39; Hoffmeyer on, 172; Neville on, 114, 118, 120, 143, 166; Tillich on, 27, 80, 81, 82
Corrington, Robert, 46–47, 48, 62; on determinacy, 163; Dewey and, 160, 161; on evolutionary love, 53, 68; Neville and, 163–64; on nothingness, 70; on panpsychism, 162; pantheism of, 160, 163, 171–72, 177; PCR and, 72, 162; on sign systems, 161–62; Tillich and, 164
cosmological ultimates, 84, 120, 136, 146, 187
cosmology, 169, 189; cosmogony and, 150; ontology and, 79–80, 83–84, 133–34; of Whitehead, 82, 134, 160, 165
Cournot, Antoine Augustin, 138
creation ex nihilo, 114, 140–41, 149, 160, 168
creationism, 191
"creative interchange," 100–101
creative transformation, 106–9, 169, 173, 179, 185–86, 188; immanent, 145–46
creativity, 6; Cobb on, 3, 93, 103, 105–7, 137; Griffin on, 143; Hartshorne on, 138–39; James on, 7; Neville on, 115–16, 140, 150–51, 187, 210n4; Rosenthal on, 88, 163; Whitehead on, 142, 143. *See also* ontological creativity
Crusades, 180

Darwin, Charles, 16, 59, 94
Dawkins, Richard, 125, 128
Deacon, Terrence, 67
death of God movement, 86, 92, 137, 148
deconstructivism, 148. *See also* constructivism
deduction, 3, 64–65, 86
democracy, 190
Descartes, René, 2, 92; James and, 63; Leibniz and, 116–17, 182; Peirce and, 2, 34–38, 57
determinacy / indeterminacy, 113–16, 150–53, 177–81, 195; Cobb on, 113, 171; Corrington on, 163; Hoffmeyer on, 172; Neville on, 4, 145–46, 166–71
Deuser, Hermann, 169
Devitt, Michael, 13–14
Dewey, John, 61, 102; Cobb and, 160–61; empiricism of, 58; on evolutionary love, 53; instrumentalism of, 101; Putnam and, 56, 57
diamonds, 38
digital / analog codes, 173–74, 177
Dorrien, Gary, 91, 169

doubt, 195; belief and, 34–35; Cartesian, 2, 34–38, 57; "living," 35
Duhem, Pierre Maurice Marie, 200n18
Dummett, Michael, 13
Duns Scotus, John, 71
dynamic / immediate objects, 47, 161, 178

empiricism, 58
Eucharist, 125
evolution, 142, 164; biosemiotics and, 5–6, 156–59, 162, 172–73; creationism versus, 191; Darwin and, 16, 59, 94
evolutionary love, 6, 48–50, 53, 67–71
evolutionary paradigm, 16, 24, 37

faith, 27, 189; Barth on, 78; Cobb on, 91, 93, 98, 137; ontological, 128–29; Robinson on, 157–58
fallibilism, 194; Neville on, 112; Peirce on, 34, 53
Feuerbach, Ludwig, 5
Feyerabend, Paul, 5, 17–20
Fisch, Max, 46
Ford, Lewis, 148, 176
freedom, 116; Cobb on, 136–37, 141; Hartshorne on, 138–39; Neville on, 134–35, 138; paradox of, 190; "semiotic," 156, 162, 174, 177
Frei, Hans, 20, 26

Galileo Galilei, 19
Gandhi, Mahatma, 134
gene theory, 16
genomes, 162, 173–74, 177
God the created, 171–82, 195–97
God the creator, 111–31, 134, 151–52; concrete determinations of, 165–71; criticisms of, 140–43, 163; as ontological ultimate, 187
Golden Rule, 185
Griffin, David, x–xiii, 97, 142–43, 148
ground-of-being theology, 1, 105–7, 159, 194–95; Neville and, 137–38, 143; Peirce and, 146; pluralism and, 187–88; symbols and, 176
groundless grounds, 38, 196

Hartshorne, Charles, 51, 55, 205n6; James and, 206n6; Neville and, 138–39; Peirce and, 88
Hegel, G. W. F., 44, 49
Heidegger, Martin, 98
hermeneutics, 5, 54–55. *See also* meaning-making
Hick, John, 187
Hildebrand, David, 57
Hinduism, 20, 124, 186
Hitler, Adolf, 135
Hoffmeyer, Jesper, 156, 162, 172–74, 176, 215n30
Holocaust, 124, 140
Hume, David, 2, 92, 119

immanence. *See* transcendence / immanence
immediate / dynamic objects, 47, 161, 178
indeterminacy. *See* determinacy
induction, 3, 38–42, 51, 58, 64, 68, 157
instinct, 20, 24, 165
instrumentalism, 12; of Dewey, 59, 61, 101
Iraq War, 180

James, William, 7; empiricism of, 58; Hartshorne and, 206n6; Peirce and, 62–63; pluralism of, 163; Putnam on, 56; on truth, 13
Jesus Christ, 136–37, 186, 188; Barth on, 28, 29, 79; Cobb on, 77, 91, 95, 98–103, 108–9, 186, 191; Neville on, 123–25, 128; Robinson on, 157, 158; Tillich on, 28, 79; Whitehead on, 97, 108; Wieman on, 100–101
Job, Book of, 136, 138

Kant, Immanuel, 30, 92; James and, 63; Peirce and, 47, 64; Tillich and, 81
Koch, Traugott, 148
Ku Klux Klan, 57, 79, 216n78
Kuhn, Thomas, 4–5, 16, 191; Feyerabend and, 18, 19

Lakatos, Imre, 191–92
Lamarck, Jean Baptiste de, 68

language games, 14, 31, 55, 155
Leclerc, Ivor, 89–90
legisign, 158
Leibniz, Gottfried Wilhelm, 96, 116–17, 182
LGBTQ+ community, 79, 125, 180, 191, 211n43
Lindbeck, George, 20, 26–27
Logos, 103–6, 103, 137, 196
Lorentz equation, 42

Malraux, André, 93
manifestation beliefs (M-beliefs), 23, 26
McDowell, John, 14
meaning-making, 3, 121, 156–57, 173–77, 183–84; hermeneutics and, 5, 54–55
modernity, 92, 147–49
Moore, Edward, 69
Murphey, Murray, 68
musement, 47–48, 51
myths, 18, 80; Cobb on, 102; Sellers on, 54; Tillich on, 148

natura naturans ("nature naturing"), 160, 164, 172
natural theology, 77, 108, 147–48
Nazism, 79, 124–25, 135, 140, 211n42
neo-Nazis, 57, 79, 216n78
neoliberalism, 148
neopragmatism, 53–57, 71–73; James and, 63; Rorty and, 56, 62. *See also* pragmatism
Neville, Robert, 72, 184–85, 210n4; on altruism, 135; on Barth, 27; on broken symbols, 82, 84; Corrington and, 163–64; on creativity, 115–16, 140, 150–51, 187, 210n4; on fallibilism, 112; on free will, 134–35, 138; on God the creator, 111–31, 165–71; Griffin on, 142–43; on ground-of-being, 137–38, 143; on indeterminacy, 4, 145–46, 166–72; modernism of, 147–49; on ontological creativity, 134–36, 163–67, 170; on Peirce, 78, 87–88, 122, 142; pluralism of, 187; realism and, 75; relativism of, 148–49; on symbolic truth, 83–84; Tillich and, 27, 81, 174–75; on transcendence / imminence, 146, 148, 178; on transcendent indeterminacy, 145–46; United Methodist Church and, ix–x; Weiss and, 149–50; Whitehead and, 7, 86–90
Neville, Robert, works of: *Behind the Masks of God*, 112; *Boston Confucianism*, 112, 184; *Comparative Religious Ideas Project*, 112; *Creativity and God*, 133, 134; *God the Creator*, 111, 129–31, 134, 140–43, 151–52; *The Highroad around Modernism*, 148; *Philosophical Theology*, x, 116; *The Truth of Broken Symbols*, 122
Noë, Alva, 25–26
Nozick, Robert, 144, 145, 165

ontological creativity, 115–16, 133–36, 163–67, 170; determinacy and, 166–67; Rosenthal on, 171; worshipfulness and, 142–43
ontological method, 80–81
"ontological shock," 177
ontology, 130, 187; cosmology and, 79–80, 83–84, 133–34, 150; Covington's, 163–64; Neville's, 163–67, 210n4
Orange, Donna, 49–51, 146

panentheism, 48–50, 181, 195
panexperientialism, 204n41
panpsychism, 162, 194; of Peirce, 6, 48, 51–53, 64–67, 165, 178, 182
pantheism, 50, 51, 85; of Corrington, 160, 163, 171–72, 177; materialism of, 179
PCR. *See* pragmatic constructive realism
Peirce, Charles Sanders, x–xii, 5–7, 33–52, 87, 188–89; biosemiotics and, 155, 158, 165, 172; categories of, 3, 6, 39, 43–45, 78, 152, 193–94; on chaos, 142; classical pragmatists and, 57–64; constructivism and, 37–38; Corrington on, 164; Descartes and, 2, 34–38, 57; on dynamic / immediate objects, 47, 161, 178; evolutionary love and, 67–71; on fallibilism, 34, 53;

ground-of-being theology of, 146; on habits, 144–47; on historical process, 178–79; on inquiry, 35; James and, 62–63; Kant and, 47; on learning, 188–89; metaphysics of, 87–88; on musement, 47–48, 51; neopragmatists and, 53–57; panentheism of, 48–51; panpsychism of, 6, 48, 51–53, 64–67, 165, 178, 182; pluralism of, 188; pragmatic constructive realism and, 53–73; Putnam on, 56; realism of, 38, 44; Rorty on, 55–56; semiotics of, 41, 122, 152, 155, 158, 165; on skepticism, 34–35; Thagard and, 30; theological views of, 47–52, 70–71, 146, 164–65, 169, 181; Tillich and, 49–51; on truth criterion, 71; Whitehead and, 69; Wittgenstein and, 55
pheromones, 156
phlogiston, 15
Plato, 98, 190
plausibility, 127–28
Plotinus, 156–57
pluralism, 144, 184; of Cobb, 92, 184–87, 190–91; of Feyerabend, 19; of James, 163; of Neville, 187; of Nozick, 145; paradox of, 190; of PCR, 9–10, 187–88, 191–92; of Peirce, 188; of Whitehead, 189
Popper, Karl, 17, 18, 190–92
possibilities, 71, 102–6, 134–40, 159–65
postmodernism, 147–49, 193–94, 193–94
pragmatic constructive realism (PCR), xii–xiii, 3–4, 53–73, 133–53, 193–97; biosemiotics and, 156–59; constructivism and, 11–12, 71–73; God the creator in, 165–66; model of God and, 155–82, 195; pluralism of, 9–10, 187–88, 191–92; postmodern critiques of, 148–49; on transcendence / immanence, 146, 171
pragmatism: analytic, 54–55; classical, 54, 87; definitions of, 56; Menand on, 183; misuses of, 38; Peirce and, 33–52. *See also* neopragmatism
probability theory, 69

pseudogenes, 162
Putnam, Hilary, 56–57

qualia, 44
qualisign, 157–58
quantum mechanics, 16
Quine, Willard, 16

Raposa, Michael, 49–51, 165
realism, 2, 6, 193–94; constructivism and, 4–5, 11–20, 26–30, 194; of Dewey, 58; Neville and, 75; of Peirce, 38, 44; Scholastic, 71; scientific, 14–15; semantic, 13; structural, 15; of Tillich, 82
relativism, 19–20
retroduction, 41–42, 149
rhizoid, 173–74
Robinson, Andrew, 155–59, 176–77
Rorty, Richard, 55–56, 62, 63
Rosenthal, Sandra B., 6, 64, 87, 146; on community / individual, 162–63; on creativity, 88, 163; on ontological creativity, 171

Scholasticism, 71
scientific theories, 4–5, 14–19, 59, 149, 186, 191
scientism, 4, 148
self-transcendence, 109, 150, 157, 186
Sellars, Wilfrid, 54
"semantic realism," 13
semiosis, 158–59, 172, 176–77
"semiotic freedom," 156, 162, 174, 177
semiotics, 39–40, 72, 155–59, 183–84; of Corrington, 161–62; of Peirce, 41, 122, 152, 155, 158, 165. *See also* biosemiotics
Short, T. L., 69–70
Shults, LeRon, 129
signification. *See* meaning-making
sinsign, 158
Slater, Gary, 157
Southgate, Christopher, 155–59, 176–77
stream of experience, 58, 62, 206n6
swastika, 124–25, 211n42

symbols, 3, 6, 126, 167, 171, 187; broken, 82, 84, 120–27, 130, 151–52; of God, 9, 84, 130, 167, 174–77, 180–82, 195; Tillich on, 84, 175–77; transcendent, 127
syncretism, 112
synechism (continuity), 3, 48–51, 68

Thagard, Paul, 30
theism, 7–8, 91, 146–49; idealism and, 13; personal, 147–48; substance, 1, 7–8, 105, 107, 140; Trinitarian, 155–59
theonomy, 195
Tillich, Paul, 27–29, 195–96; Alston and, 81–82; Corrington and, 164; on "courage to be," 128–29, 173; Kant and, 81; Neville and, 27, 81, 174–75; on ontological approaches, 79–80; on "ontological shock," 177; Peirce and, 49–51; realism of, 82; on religious myths, 148; Robinson and, 157; on symbols, 84, 175–77; *Systematic Theology*, 130; beyond theism, 77; on theonomy, 195; on truth-seeking, 79
tolerance, 190–92
Tracy, David, 147–48
transcendence / immanence, 118–20, 137, 145, 195; Cobb on, 146, 179, 186; interpretation of, 177; Neville's concept of, 146, 148, 165–66, 179; PCR and, 146, 171
"transcendence" theory of truth, 41
Trinity, 29, 155–59

Trump, Donald, 180
truth, 4–5, 14, 61, 188; Barth on, 27–28; James on, 13; Neville on, 83–84; Peirce on, 39, 41, 71; Tillich on, 27–28, 79
tychism (chance), 3, 7, 36–37, 68

ultimates: cosmological, 84, 120, 136, 146, 187; ontological, 130, 187
underdetermination, 15, 16, 71, 192
United Methodist Church, ix–x, 180
universals, 55, 139

van Fraassen, Bas, 15
van Woudenberg, René, 25

Ward, Roger, 203n66
Weiss, Paul, 55, 111, 149–50
West, Cornel, 216n78
Whitehead, Alfred North, 1–2, 7, 49, 69, 95–97; Cobb and, 86–90, 171; cosmology of, 82, 134, 160, 165; on creativity, 142, 143; on "genetic" structure, 170; Griffin and, 142; on Logos, 103–4; need for unity and, 136; Neville and, 7, 89–90; pluralism of, 189; *Science and the Modern World*, 133; on transcendent God, 146
Wieman, Henry Nelson, 100–101
Wildman, Wesley, 23–25, 39
Wittgenstein, Ludwig, 14, 54, 55
worshipfulness, 136, 142

www.ingramcontent.com/pod-product-compliance
Lightning Source LLC
Chambersburg PA
CBHW030538230426
43665CB00010B/937